Dumbocracy in America

ALSO BY ROBERT BRUSTEIN

The Theatre of Revolt
Seasons of Discontent
The Plays and Prose of Strindberg (editor)
The Third Theatre
Revolution as Theatre
The Culture Watch
Critical Moments
Making Scenes: A Personal History of the Turbulent Years at Yale
Who Needs Theatre
Reimagining American Theatre

Adaptations of Drama:
    The Father (August Strindberg)
    The Seagull (Anton Chekhov)
    When We Dead Awaken (Henrik Ibsen)

DUMBOCRACY
in AMERICA

Studies in the Theatre of Guilt, 1987–1994

ROBERT BRUSTEIN

Elephant Paperbacks

IVAN R. DEE, PUBLISHER, CHICAGO

DUMBOCRACY IN AMERICA. Copyright © 1994 by Robert Brustein. This book was first published in 1994 by Ivan R. Dee.

First ELEPHANT PAPERBACK edition published 1995 by Ivan R. Dee, Inc., 1332 North Halsted Street, Chicago 60622. Manufactured in the United States of America and printed on acid-free paper.

Library of Congress Cataloging-in-Publication Data:
Brustein, Robert Sanford, 1927–
    Dumbocracy in America : studies in the theatre of guilt, 1987–1994
/ Robert Brustein.
        p. cm.
    Includes index.
        ISBN 1-56663-093-3
        1. Theater—United States—Reviews. 2. American drama—20th
century—History and criticism. 3. Theater and society—United
States.
PN2266.5.B78   1994
792.9'5'09730908—dc20   94-17515

For the May in my September

Contents

Acknowledgments

THESE articles and reviews were first published in *The New Republic*, except for "The Theatre of Guilt" (*American Theatre*), "Dumbocracy in America" (*Partisan Review*), "Havel Disturbs the Peace" (*New York Times Book Review*), and "Lionel Trilling" (*Yale Review*). "Harold Clurman and the Group" is based on a talk I gave at Hunter College.

I have been particularly lucky in my editors and proofreaders and wish to thank them for helping to improve my prose: Leon Wieseltier, Ann Hulbert, and Alexander Star at *The New Republic*, Remo Airaldi and Sean Abbott at ART, and Ivan R. Dee.

R. B.

Dumbocracy in America

Introduction

THE most controversial article in this collection of essays and reviews is the one that gives the book its subtitle. When "The Theatre of Guilt" first appeared in *American Theatre*, a magazine for the theatre profession, it was roundly denounced by a number of respondents. I was more puzzled by the unanimity of the reaction than hurt by its ferocity, since pieces of mine on similar subjects, most notably in *The New Republic*, had rarely provoked such consistent outrage. What surprised me was to find such uniform dismissal of an argument I thought at least would spur debate. It is true that theatre people, though often warmhearted, also tend to be sensitive to any questioning of their codes or procedures. Still, I was struck anew by the gulf between what is collectively affirmed in the arts (and the university) and what is assumed by most other elements of society, including many intellectuals.

The title essay, "Dumbocracy in America," was my subsequent effort to analyze this disparity, and so, I see upon reflection, were many of the articles and reviews that predate the offending *American Theatre* article. That guilt, blame, hurt feelings, and all the paraphernalia of victimology have become the motives for artistic creation has been a source of great interest and concern to me. I share a number of political convictions with my theatre colleagues, particularly a belief in equal opportunity for all Americans and a resistance to any constraints on creative expression. But just as it was possible in the past to struggle for more equitable distribution of wealth without becoming a Stalinist, so it should be possible today to resist censorship and support social justice without adopting the rigid dogmas of political correctness. Alas, that posture has become increasingly difficult. Artists and intellectuals are respected largely for how orthodox they are on various social issues, while artistic and academic institutions are esteemed not for advancing culture or preserving thought so much as for contributing to community services or advancing political causes.

3

But if this book has a single theme, it is that culture cannot do the work of politics. Both may follow parallel paths but nevertheless belong in separate compartments. While political thinking could certainly benefit from a little more creative imagination, it is my belief that creative activity is almost invariably diminished when it conforms to ideology. The measure of a nation in history is not the wars it wins, or the laws it passes, or even the programs it enacts, but rather what Arthur Schlesinger, Jr., has called "its character and achievement as a civilization." This primarily means the character and achievements of its artists, few of whom ever found distinction as political thinkers. Chekhov believed it was his purpose to pose the problems, not to offer solutions, "to be a free artist and nothing more," and that strikes me as exactly right. I recognize that to prefer the idiosyncratic creations of an individual talent to the progressive ideals of a social movement may strike the reader as the rigid posture of a retrograde old crank. But it is a preference I first adopted at the feet of the great modern playwrights, starting with Ibsen, and have held—no doubt too insistently—since my first book, *The Theatre of Revolt*.

My absolutes, then as now, have been the independence of the dramatic artist and the integrity of dramatic art, which need to be continually guarded against any forces that might compromise or debase them. These forces sometimes include a few of my critical colleagues on the aisle, which explains why I have been rude enough at times to question their taste and dispute their authority, especially when their powers were being exercised without accountability. Instead of advancing the arts in our time, they have often left the artist feeling like a convicted felon without an appeals court, doomed by a judgment with no basis in law (I admit that my own critical opinions might strike some readers as equally dismissive).

My defense of the theatre artist must seem like a rather quixotic endeavor when the theatre seems to have lost its influence as a central force in the American consciousness. But I persist in the delusion that at its best, and even less than best, the stage can provide telling metaphors for the condition of our society, the quality of our ambitions, and the state of our souls. Unlike many people in the profession who regard theatre as if it were the whole world, I look on the whole world as if it were theatre (for all my dislike of didacticism, plays are of no interest to me unless they reflect some larger issue than personal relationships). This accounts for my incorrigible impulse to treat the theatrical occasion as a springboard for cultural generalizations.

So if this book is worth reading, it is not as a series of opinions about plays or players but as a cultural history of the late eighties and nineties. And this was a period of notable events, among them the death of Joe Papp, the rise and fall of his chosen successor, JoAnne Akalaitis, the swift emergence of *her* successor, George C. Wolfe, the growth of gay, black, and feminist theatre, and the burgeoning power of the *New York Times* critic Frank Rich, a key player in all these transitions. This was a time, too, when multiculturalism and cultural diversity began to dominate our thinking about the arts, with both good and bad results. And it was a time that featured some very interesting visits from abroad, which helped (I refer especially to productions by Ingmar Bergman and Ariane Mnouchkine) to change our thinking about the stage.

Dumbocracy in America is divided into three parts: Positions, a cluster of articles on theatre and society; Performances, a collection of play reviews in the context of the age; and Profiles, an assembly of pieces on the careers, achievements, and deaths of a few exceptional artists and thinkers. Although some are appearing here for the first time, virtually all of these articles and reviews were written for an occasion. Gathered together, I hope they offer insight into that greater occasion we provisionally call our civilization.

POSITIONS

The Theatre of Guilt

"I HAVE heard that guilty creatures sitting at a play / Have been struck so by the cunning of the scene that presently / They have proclaimed their malefactions." In this celebrated passage, Hamlet not only suggests the method he will use to expose the guilt of Claudius. He also lays the foundation for his poetics of the drama. For just as Shakespeare rewrote an old *Hamlet* play for tragic purposes, so his protagonist proceeds to adapt an old play called *The Murder of Gonzago* for moral purposes, adding "some dozen or sixteen lines" about his mother's adulterous marriage. Hamlet's revisions may be designed to chastise Gertrude, but his major moral objective in selecting the material is to expose the criminal conduct of his uncle—"the play's the thing wherein I'll catch the conscience of the King."

The belief that the critical function of drama is to arouse the remorse of "guilty creatures"—the use of the theatrical apparatus as a means of identifying and condemning offenses—was probably more congenial to the avenger Hamlet, who was an ethical Platonist, than to the more objective Aristotelian artist who conceived him. Nevertheless, this belief has been at the heart of Western theatre ever since the Middle Ages. It has also been at the heart of the Christian tradition that originated Western theatre in the form of mystery cycles and morality plays, though it cannot be explained away as a purely religious conviction. The Theatre of Guilt has, if anything, grown more powerful under secular liberalism. Indeed, it probably reached its culmination in modern realism which, from the nineteenth century to the present day, has built its drama on a foundation of accusation, recrimination, and atonement.

Like Hamlet, realist playwrights generally look for an illicit secret buried inside a character or an action, first to be exhumed, then expiated and punished. Since this is also the job of policemen and jurists, the Theatre of Guilt often reproduces the atmosphere of the precinct or the courtroom, complete with investigations, arraignments, indictments, and sentencing. Lacking access to the constabulary or the legal system for redressing wrongs, the hero must undertake the investigation and dispense justice by himself, just as Hamlet, after his initial procrastination, assumes the role of justicer and executes the guilty culprit-king. Hamlet's quasi patricide resembles that of the Greek matricide, Orestes, who killed his mother after Clytemnestra helped to murder his father, Agamemnon. But implicit in the last play of Aeschylus's *Oresteia* trilogy, *The Eumenides,* is the hope that society, through such newly created legal structures as the Court of the Areopagus, will relieve the tragic hero of his responsibilities for blood vengeance, putting an end to retributive remedies (and possibly tragic drama) for all time by establishing impartial formal agencies to resolve disputes.

Despite the presence of a sophisticated judicial system in modern times, not to mention the increasing use of litigation, Western realist drama has continued to center on guilt, expiation, and punishment through the intervention of a central dramatic character. The classic play in this genre, and the presumed model for so many later works of the kind, is Ibsen's *Ghosts.* Ibsen's protagonist, Mrs. Alving—like *her* prototype in Greek drama, Sophocles' Oedipus—becomes aware that something is poisoning the atmosphere of her ancestral house. The Alving inheritance is built on lies, and now her own son is afflicted with a disease he contracted from his profligate father. Bit by bit she exhumes the guilty secret—only to discover, again like Oedipus, that the culprit is herself. By failing to bring joy into her husband's life, by obeying dead outmoded conventions of morality, she started in motion inexorable engines that eventually destroy her entire family line.

Note, however, that in Ibsen, as in Sophocles, the same person plays the role of investigator and malefactor. It is as if Hercule Poirot, after being hired to solve a murder mystery, discovered after exhaustive investigation that he himself was the unwitting culprit. Or if Perry Mason learned that his client was indeed innocent because his defense attorney, the same Perry Mason, had unknowingly committed the crime. The fundamental sin both of Oedipus and Mrs. Alving is not pride—or in Oedipus's case even patricide and incest. It is ignorance. The play may be a thing to catch the conscience of a suspect, but the conscience belongs to the questing protagonist.

This pattern conforms to Yeats's definition of poetry as proceeding from our quarrel with ourselves—as opposed to rhetoric which proceeds from our quarrel with others. Many of Ibsen's plays, particularly his doctrinaire early prose dramas, are more rhetorical than poetical both in their language and in their indictments of the social world and the pompous Philistines who run it. But if Ibsen claimed to be "more of a poet and less a social philosopher than is commonly believed," this conviction was based on a belief, as he wrote in another context and realized in his best plays, that "to write poetry means to pass judgment on oneself." In short, the artist was not in a position to chastise others before exploring the darkness in his own soul.

This is hardly to say that Ibsen expected us to spend our lives in guilt and remorse. In *The Master Builder*, Hilda Wangel exhorts Solness to develop a "Viking spirit," to free himself from a sickly conscience by rising above traditional Christian concepts of good and evil, right and wrong. Strindberg also subscribed to the transvaluation of moral values announced by his favorite philosopher, Friedrich Nietzsche, as a method of escaping the limitations of Christian-Liberal-Socialist victimology and creating a superior breed of tragic hero, worthy of the Greek myths. So did Bernard Shaw, who believed that the Life Force was helping to breed the Superman, "omnipotent, omniscient, infallible, and withal completely, unilludedly self-conscious: in short, a God." Even Chekhov frequently urged his morally flaccid characters, most of whom identified themselves with Hamlet in their remorsefulness, nervousness, and vacillation, to refrain from self-flagellation and get some "iron" in their blood.

This perspective allows not only poetic but heroic dimensions for the theatre. The heroic protagonist is one who takes his fate in his own hands, who is capable of braving the furies in his own soul, who acts on the basis of self-knowledge and assumes responsibility for those actions: Ibsen's Brand, Solness, and Rubek; Strindberg's Jean, Father, and Stranger; Shaw's John Tanner, Caesar, and Saint Joan. But compare some of the later playwrights assumed to be writing in the same tradition, particularly in the United States. Their characters are usually victims rather than heroes. They cast blame on others without engaging themselves. They indict not the protagonists but their oppressors. More rhetoricians than poets, they assume that the prime function of theatre is to arouse the spectator's guilt.

In its American manifestations, in fact, the Theatre of Guilt has tended to be not just rhetorical but even shrill and self-righteous. Beginning in the thirties this country experienced a strain of radical political writing more akin to melodrama than tragedy in that the forces of good were invariably associated with poverty and the forces of evil with wealth. In these quasi-Marxist plays, the common objective was "a life which wouldn't be printed on dollar bills" (*Awake and Sing*). In the forties the availability of Nazism as the embodiment of absolute evil encouraged an extension of this melodramatic formula in the plays of Lillian Hellman, Robert Sherwood, and others, while William Saroyan, in *The Time of Your Life*, conceived a totally innocent world marred only by a single evil character named Blick whose murder redeems the entire human race.

After World War II, admittedly, American drama grew considerably more sophisticated under the influence of considerably more mature playwrights. But even our most poetic dramatist, Tennessee Williams, was unable to imagine a universe without victims at the center, usually the casualties of an unfeeling, brutal, sexually repressed society. As for Arthur Miller, he brought the Theatre of Guilt to some new level of intensity, combining the social-political concerns of the thirties with the deeper psychological motifs of his own time, in a series of plays that were often compared with Ibsen's. Although they do resemble such theatrical Ibsen polemics as *Pillars of Society* and *An Enemy of the People* (which Miller adapted), most of his writings—rather than being about liberation through self-discovery, as in the mature Ibsen—center on guilt and expiation, following a climactic confrontation that leads to catastrophe.

The confrontation usually involves the culprit's son, a high-school Hamlet catching the conscience of a business-class king. This development is most obvious in *All My Sons*, but it also informs Miller's best-known play—often called the finest tragedy of modern times—*Death of a Salesman*. At the heart of the play, sometimes blurring its social message, is the guilt of an errant husband. Coming to visit his father in Boston, Biff discovers that Willy has a woman in his room.

If Willy has been cheating on Mom, however, someone has been cheating on Willy. Willy may be guilty of adultery, but Howard, his boss, is guilty of callously sacking an aging employee who has outlived his usefulness. (Biff, who shares Willy's resentment at being thrown away "like an old shoe," is another Odetsian character scorning a life being printed on dollar bills.) Nor is Howard the only guilty culprit. Some other entity is involved—a large amorphous entity without a name. As Linda Loman tells us in a famous subjectless sentence, "Attention, attention must finally be paid to such a man." The passive voice is deliberate. Miller is unwilling, in 1948, to have his characters face the audience, as playwrights did in the thirties, and accuse paying customers of failing to provide enough sympathy or substance for the jobless and unemployed. Still, Linda Loman's exhortation is an implicit call to the conscience of society as represented by the wealthy middle-class audience.

In later plays, *The Crucible* for example, Miller continues his preoccupation with guilt in society and guilt in the family. John Proctor, like Willy Loman, has cheated on his wife and must be punished for it. But more important than the personal adultery of the guilty protagonist is the communal guilt of society. The witch-hunts pursued in Salem during the time of the Puritans are a metaphor for the persecution of Communists and Communist sympathizers initiated in Washington, D.C., during the time of McCarthy and the House Un-American Activities Committee. The play represents an effort, extremely courageous at the time in that it exposed Miller to congressional retaliation, to indict contemporary Red-baiters and shame a passive nation into recognizing its own compliance. Insofar as shame is public, it can lead to action far more effectively than guilt, which sinks you in impotence. Yet the playwright's more absorbing theme remains disabling culpability. In *Incident at Vichy*, a Miller character says, "I don't want your guilt, I want your responsibility." In truth, he really wants both.

David Rabe's early plays were also orthodox contributions to the Theatre of Guilt, indicting the middle-class audience for its complicity in the Vietnam War. Rabe first came to prominence as a disciple of Miller, a fundamentally social dramatist who, like Miller, identified the nexus of corruption in the heart of the family. Like Miller, he also made modest departures from realism in order to expose the crimes of the nation at large. Following the end of the Vietnam War, however, Rabe managed to escape the sterile cycle of guilt and atonement with works like *Hurly Burly* and *Those the River Keeps* that derive their strength from a firmer understanding of the self. In this he was joined by a significant number of dramatists—among them David Mamet, Sam Shepard, Ronald Ribman, George C. Wolfe, Craig Lucas, Paula Vogel, Jon Robin Baitz, Christopher Durang, Tony Kushner, and others—who, whether using realistic or satirical or expressionist devices, managed to complicate the melodrama of accuser and accused.

Some of these are among America's finest playwrights, but most of them write from the fringe. What continues to dominate mainstream American drama after the war is the Theatre of Guilt. To be sure, it undergoes a shift in focus if not in approach as our national issues change from economic inequality and aggression against other nations to such domestic problems as racism, sexism, homophobia, and indifference to the sick and disabled, especially those suffering from AIDS. But the tone, form, and format of these dramas remain substantially consistent with the tradition.

The sin of slavery has always been the primal curse on the house of America, just as the Irish problem has always been in England. As a result, African-American theatre has usually displayed an activist bent, particularly in the sixties plays of Ed Bullins and Leroi Jones (known today as Amiri Baraka). With the arrival in the eighties of the prolific August Wilson and his cycle of plays examining racism through the American decades, black activism is more subtly embodied within a naturalistic framework. But the intent is clear enough: to provide black and white audiences alike with a documented history of oppression, whether in the music industry (*Ma Rainey's Black Bottom*), or in baseball (*Fences*), or on chain gangs (*Joe Turner's Come and Gone*), or in slavery and its aftermath (*The Piano Lesson*), or in urban ghettos (*Two Trains Running*).

Wilson is often compared to O'Neill. He is like O'Neill largely in the scope of his ambitions. His debt to Arthur Miller is much more pronounced (*Fences* is virtually a rewrite of *All My Sons*). O'Neill was a tragic writer because of his capacity—crude in such early works as *Mourning Becomes Electra*, perfectly realized in late plays like *A Long Day's Journey into Night*—to probe the guilt and lacerate the conscience of a character very much like himself. By contrast, Wilson remains entirely fixed on the sins of the white oppressor in his mistreatment of black victims. He has yet to create a character who reaches any understanding of the self as a consequence of self-motivated actions.

This is equally true of Miller's Willy Loman, who commits suicide without ever learning the source of his anguish, and it is true of most of the characters in the Theatre of Guilt. They preserve their own innocence through being victimized by others, generally from the wealthy white male ruling class. Which aspect of this class is guilty depends on the political perspective of the author. Feminist theatre invariably sniffs out blame in the male society; gay theatre locates it among homophobes; racial theatre indicts the entire white world (David Henry Hwang's *M. Butterfly* does all three). And the rash of sickness and disability plays, beginning with Michael Cristofer's *The Shadow Box* (cancer), extending through *Children of a Lesser God* (hearing impairment), right up to *Marvin's Room* (leukemia, strokes, mental illness, and damaged vertebrae), not to mention the current anthology of AIDS-related dramas (*As Is; The Normal Heart; Eastern Standard; Falsettos; Lips Together, Teeth Apart; The Destiny of Me; The Raft of the Medusa**), treat illness not so much as a metaphor as an opportunity to score the indifference and insensitivity of the audiences who watch them.

Some years ago I described this genre as "plays you're not allowed to hate" because of their inspirational themes and morally elevated characters: "In the past, this used to be a political drama—people resisting a corrupt political system or fighting for the Loyalist cause during the Spanish Civil War. More recently, it has almost exclusively featured ethnic and sexual minority groups, thus increasing the quota of moral extortion. To fail to respond to plays about blacks or women or homosexuals, for example, is

*And, since this writing, countless others.

to stand accused of racism, sexism, homophobia, or getting up on the wrong side of the bed.... Meanwhile, the theatre becomes an agency for consciousness raising, with audiences being tutored and entertained for considerably less money than a modest contribution to an effective rehabilitation program."

My tone is flip not because I find the causes unsympathetic— far from it—but because I do not believe the theatre to be either a suitable or effective place for social reform and moral blackmail. Activist plays will always be with us, and the theatre is large enough to accommodate every variety of expression. But we must beware of confusing quality with good intentions or the expression of talent with the effusions of a warm heart. Although major artists can sometimes write powerfully from humanitarian motives, these are more often the incentives of second-rate plays and minor playwrights. Buying tickets to such works is usually like putting a small contribution in the collection plate at church and ignoring the homeless in the neighborhood. How many people are moved to real sacrifice by theatrical exhortations?

Theatre people have always had a soft spot for causes—rarely the cause of theatre. Smarting over recurrent charges that their work lacks social dimension, many American playwrights have begun to compensate through displays of conscience, preaching liberal sermons to already converted parishioners. Many American star-actors, ashamed of a profession that lacks respect in our culture, are more often seen at benefits than on a stage (award ceremonies often sound like benefits, with the winner making speeches on behalf of a pressing cause or oppressed group). We have moments of silence, days without art, addresses from the stage, demonstrations, petitions, and marches. What we don't often have in our mainstream drama is a distinguished dramatic art.

And one of the reasons, in my opinion, is that we are losing a sense of distinction between our function as theatre artists and our function as political witnesses. Those of us who want to help combat social evils can do so by participating in the political process, because, flawed though it is, the political process remains the only effective avenue to social reform. This means supporting people in a position to reform society, by voting, lobbying, proselytizing, agitating, contributing. But as theatre artists our obligation is to penetrate the puzzles of the human heart: to honor complexity, appreciate mystery, expose secrets, invade dreams. The function of dramatic art is to disclose not the effects but the *causes* responsible for our condition, not the symptoms but the *sources* of errant and aberrant human behavior. From such disclosures we regain the capacity to be tragic human beings instead of social victims, complicated creatures of will rather than simplified subjects of sociological inquiry. At its best the theatre helps us explore what Cocteau called *le gloire obscure*, the link between the criminal and the heroic, the enigmatic and the legendary. For the play's not "the thing" to arouse unproductive guilt in an ineffective spectator. It is an opportunity to expose the obscure elements, the hidden unpredictable qualities shared by *every* human soul.

[1992]

The Options of Multiculturalism

FEW will deny that the idea of "cultural diversity," however confused and jumbled its current applications, originated out of compassionate liberal feelings and progressive social values—chiefly, a desire to celebrate the many different racial, ethnic, and sexual strains and backgrounds that constitute the variegated quilt of American society. Anyone old enough to remember the fifties will have no difficulty recalling how uniform life seemed in those years when, to judge from such pop culture canvases as Nunnally Johnson movies and Ozzie and Harriet sitcoms (the theatrical equivalent being Wilder's *Our Town*), virtually everyone living in Eisenhower America seemed to belong to a prosperous white family named Jones living in a mythical Eden called Main Street. Dotted with steepled churches and corner drugstores, and populated by a bland assortment of teenagers who spent their leisure drinking ice cream sodas and dancing the jitterbug when they weren't walking a dog named Spot, this America was a land of milk (homogenized) and honey (vitamin-enriched), whose Rotarian inhabitants had a Pepsodent smile for everything except acne, the neighborhood bully, and the Communist Menace. Anyone not middle class, middle of the road, and pink of skin was likely to be invisible, while non-Caucasian cultural expression was usually relegated to out-of-the-way venues like Harlem night spots or Basin Street jazz clubs.

It is commonly assumed that the chief developments that later helped to revise this stubbornly false image, aside from Elvis Presley, Marlon Brando, and the Beats, were the civil rights movement, the Vietnam War, and the radical sixties. Each contributed a means of making the invisible visible, partly through political action, protest, and street theatre, and partly through clamorous demands for equal rights and cultural recognition. Before long, homogeneous America had turned into a host of competing, heterogeneous enclaves, each demanding its own share of media attention, admiration, awards, and foundation funding—a development soon to be subsumed under the blanket terms of "multiculturalism" and "cultural diversity."

To these causes I would like to add another: the collapse of communism at home and abroad. The growth of "multiculturalism" in America, unique though it may be, would seem to coincide with similar ethnic movements in Europe following *perestroika* and *glasnost*, notably the struggle for independence by the Baltic republics and other states in the Soviet Union, and the conflicts over autonomy among the Serbs, the Slovenes, the Croats, and the Muslims in Yugoslavia. In the East there has occurred a breakdown of a monolithic central government which has unleashed a long repressed sense of particular ethnic and cultural identity. In the West, of course, the story has been different; and yet the end of the cold war has provided the occasion for a turning inward, and a new insistence upon inner differences and domestic divisions. Historically this has usually followed the loss of a threatening outside enemy because, as political leaders have long known (and as Hitler demonstrated in his persecution of the Jews), there is nothing like an external object of fear and hatred to unify a country and give it common purpose.

When such a unifying icon is lost, however, it is never abandoned, only replaced; the Enemy Without becomes the Enemy Within. Now that the Right can no longer blame "Commies" and "Pinkos" for subverting our national morality, it has concluded (*vide* Jesse Helms and his squadrons of moral thought-police) that the body politic is being corrupted by artists and intellectuals, while the Left, whose enemy list was previously limited to McCarthyites, bigots, and extremists, has recently been adding those considered "insensitive" to racism, sexism, ageism, lookism, homophobia, to discrimination against minorities and the handicapped, and to the suffering of AIDS victims. These are all important issues, and it is true that our country has accelerating social problems to which many Americans remain indifferent. I'm simply suggesting that among the reasons for the current climate of racial and ethnic assertiveness is that, regardless of one's point of origin or political point of view, most people share a compulsion to identify and demonize the Other.

I mention this in the context of multiculturalism because for all its positive value as an idea, "cultural diversity" is sometimes choked by the same acrimonious vapors as wider nationalistic movements. What begins as an understandable hunger for recognition often develops into a less commendable thirst for power. The current attacks on Western civilization, for example, both in the university and in society at large, suggest how culture often gets confused with politics and identity with empowerment. Is it really necessary, in order to validate the existence of one group, to discredit that of another? Fundamental to multiculturalism is the idea that civilizations flourish by opening themselves to the impact of outside influences; yet many multicultural artists have been closing themselves to the West on the assumption that the West is closed to them.

That assumption is incorrect. Far from being "insular," Western civilization has always been a pushover for anything considered even remotely foreign. And I'm not just referring to the influence of the ancient Greeks on Renaissance and post-Renaissance Europe. Think of the impact of Chinese culture on eighteenth-century France and England, where *chinoiserie* was all the rage, or of French culture on the customs, fashions, and language of nineteenth-century Russian aristocrats. Or, to glance at individual artists, try to imagine Ezra Pound's poetry without the writings of Confucius and Lao-tse, the plays of Yeats and Brecht without the theatrical conventions of Noh drama, the paintings of Picasso or the novels of Conrad without the influence of Africa. George Gershwin's music is heavily dependent on black music, blues, and jazz, as are the rhythmic innovations of Aaron Copeland and Leonard Bernstein on the music of Latin America. Nor is this influence a one-way street. Japanese orchestral music relies heavily on the European repertory, while the Caribbean poet Derek Walcott's superb epic poem *Omeros*, set mainly on the island of Trinidad and featuring rich native characters, is actually a transcultural rendering of *The Iliad* and *The Odyssey*.

In every case the work of one civilization was invariably enriched after borrowing from another. Some ethnocentrists might charge that these were less borrowings than "appropriations," stolen without credit or acknowledgment. But if this was so in the past, it is hardly true today. Indeed, transcultural blending may be the most fully acknowledged artistic development of our time. It is certainly one of the most creative, especially in the theatre, where we have recently had some remarkable examples of such mixtures. Julie Taymor's *Juan Darien*, an Indonesian-style puppet show driven by Elliot Goldenthal's South American–style music, was based on Latin liturgical texts and a Uruguayan fable by Horacio Quiroga, while Lee Breuer's *The Gospel at Colonus* was a recreation of Sophocles' *Oedipus at Colonos* set in a Pentacostal black church, with rousing gospel hymns written by Bob Telson and sung by Clarence Fountain and the Five Blind Boys of Alabama. As for David Henry Hwang's *M. Butterfly*, this play combined the plot of *Madama Butterfly*, an Italian opera based on an American play, with the tale of a French diplomat undone by a Chinese spy performing in the Peking opera, all enacted on a modified Kabuki stage.

To my mind, however, *M. Butterfly* also displayed some of the dangers lurking within the achievements of multiculturalism, notably the compulsion to turn civilizations into battlefields. Hwang's theme is that the militaristic West is essentially homophobic while the pacific East is essentially feminine, and that the Western use of force against weaker Asian nations stems from a fear of sexual impotence: "The whole world is being run by men with pricks the size of pins." The problem with such large cultural generalizations is that they often substitute one form of stereotype for another (this one also fails to explain the aggressive policies of female leaders like Mrs. Thatcher, not to mention the atrocities committed by Asian countries like Cambodia and Red China). *M. Butterfly* suggests how a good idea can get distorted by tendentious ideology.

Within the context of "cultural diversity," therefore, there are many competing strains and currents, which I see forming into essentially two large categories. The first, recognizing that virtually all Americans, including "Anglos," are made up of mixed breeds and mixed bloods, is devoted to amalgamating the riches of many cultures into a blended artistic expression which reflects the variety of American life. The second, propelled by a tribal need to establish pride, prestige, and estimable "role models," is devoted to celebrating the style and achievement of a single culture to the exclusion of the others. The first category, inspired by Martin Luther King's dream of integration, believes in open opportunity according to merit rather than color—as reflected, for example, in the "nontraditional" casting of roles on the basis of talent rather than racial or ethnic background. The second, which is driven by such divisive energies as the black-power fires ignited after King's assassination by figures like Malcolm X, is committed to strict racial and ethnic orthodoxy, and the empowerment of disadvantaged people through the agency of culture. The first category tries to unify, the second to separate. Both operate under the banner of "multiculturalism."

As Diane Ravitch has observed, however, the second category is essentially a *rejection* of multiculturalism, and thus more accurately described as "uniculturalism" or "racial fundamentalism." The terms, as recent controversies in the arts suggest, get confused by conflicting aims and aspirations. In the first category, resident theatres, led by the New York Shakespeare Festival, have long observed nontraditional, or color-blind, casting policies in regard to plays, often to the dismay of critics. Not long ago, for example, Frank Rich of the *New York Times* criticized the casting of an African-American actor as Cloten in JoAnne Akalaitis's production of *Cymbeline*, noting that Cloten's mother and father were white, and further observing that Imogen would never have confused the headless trunk of a black man with the body of her white lover. Similarly, Samuel Beckett was incensed when the American Repertory Theatre cast black actors as Hamm and Nag in a version of *Endgame* (also directed by Akalaitis), an issue, combined with other objections, that almost led to a lawsuit. Still, the protests of critics and playwrights notwithstanding, audiences have long been accustomed to ignoring questions of color while watching plays, especially if they're familiar with the talents of a resident company. Suspension of disbelief, along with the power of actor transformation, constitutes the very essence of the theatrical event.

The flap over the casting of *Miss Saigon*, on the other hand, is an instance of second-category multiculturalism in the sense that Asian actors, with the endorsement of Actors Equity, were demanding not color-blindness but racial consciousness in regard to a Eurasian role. The argument was that, since Asian actors had few opportunities on Broadway, producers were obliged to cast even a mixed-breed character like the Engineer with someone of Asian descent. This reduced the issue of "cultural diversity" to a muddle, not only promoting racial typecasting instead of histrionic transformation but turning the theatre into an area of entitlement rather than a place for art. In this debate the concept of affirmative action completely eclipsed the idea of nontraditional casting, promoting a form of reverse discrimination that did little credit to any of the parties involved.

Basing his stand on similar principles, the African-American playwright August Wilson has been insisting that only black directors can do movie versions of his plays, beginning with *Fences*. He has also protested publicly (in an interview with the *Boston Globe*) against what he called George Gershwin's "bastardiz[ing] our music and our experience" in writing *Porgy and Bess* because black people had their own music. This is not multiculturalism; it is its very antithesis, racial exclusionism. Racial exclusionism assumes that one race cannot understand another, that all cultures are separate and distinct, that, in Brecht's words, "the generations look coldly into each other's eyes." It is this separatist dogma which declares that Wilson's plays are beyond white criticism, unless to call them masterpieces and award them prizes, and that anyone who believes the playwright's concentration on victimization makes his subject matter repetitive and limited (as I had the effrontery to suggest in a review) must be branded a racist, an elitist, or a fool. The effort to exclude and separate is often encapsulated in such catch phrases as the "black experience." But the fact is that, no matter how racially restricted are the surfaces of dramas like *Fences* and *The Piano Lesson*, they belong, like many postwar African-American plays, to the time-honored tradition of Western realism, closely akin to the blame-and-guilt plays of Arthur Miller.

Take *Fences*. Wilson's play is driven by his conviction that his hero, Troy Maxson, a gifted baseball player now reduced to "hauling white folks' garbage," is a victim of centuries of racial oppression. Just as he is forced to be a lifter rather than a driver because he is black, so the color of his skin has blocked him, like Satchel Paige, from entering the major leagues. To support this racial subject, however, Wilson concocts a conventional family drama, built on overworked baseball images, about the confrontation between an erring father and his indignant son, with a crisis identical to the climactic scenes in *All My Sons* and *Death of a Salesman*. Like Willy Loman, Troy Maxson has a long-suffering wife, a son with ambitions to be a football player, a crony with whom to share confidences, an infidelity that changes his life, and the obligatory backyard. The play even ends with a funeral—again like *Death of a Salesman*—giving the characters a chance to discuss the protagonist's futile dreams against the background of the nation's false values.

I cite these similarities not to criticize Wilson for lack of originality, but rather to show how, for all his assertions of black uniqueness, he uses familiar American themes of social victimization, accompanied by familiar American charges and recriminations. (George C. Wolfe has parodied such formulas in his satiric play *The Colored Museum*.) Yes, the language is enriched by black colloquialisms, and the play, like all Wilson's work, dramatizes the twentieth-century consequences of the original American sin of slavery. But there is certainly nothing here that cannot be understood—or even criticized—by white people, and there is certainly little to justify the claim of singularity or exclusionism. If anything, Wilson owes a lot more to white writers than to black.

And this leads to the reason why the exclusionary form of multiculturalism is so puzzling and disturbing. The great artists and thinkers of every culture have always looked for what is individual in humanity rather than what is general. Their works are likely to demonstrate how people tend to chafe under narrow classifications of any kind, be they political, social, racial, ethnic, or moral. The whole of Pirandello's works, for example, feature characters who long for some understanding of their fullness and complexity in the face of an external world more satisfied with simple formulas and categories. We value such art as an antidote to politics because, unlike political orthodoxy, it reminds us that what truly distinguishes human nature, perhaps its major unifying quality, is the element of surprise and unpredictability, the capacity to transcend externally imposed roles to achieve a richer individuality.

Yet the second category of multiculturalism seems to pride itself on being reductive and simplistic, which makes it as homogeneous in its way as the white culture of the fifties. It creates alternatives to cultural stereotypes, but these are sometimes equally self-limiting. The tribalist approach, to quote Ravitch again, "confuses race with culture, as though everyone with the same skin color had the same culture and history. It ignores the fact that within every major racial group there are many different cultural groups, and within every major racial group there exist serious ethnic and cultural tensions." To ignore these differences is to exchange one set of chains for another. It is to achieve self-definition through exile from the human family. Total absorption in a separate culture, like the adoption of separate tables, separate houses, separate clubs, separate studies, and separate schools, represents not multiculturalism but the return of segregation in voluntary form, the abandonment of hope for a national identity, the death of pluralism, the rejection of the great ideal of integration. It is true this concept may have been originally flawed insofar as the melting-pot ethos had the potential to eradicate cultural differences. Still, yesterday's melting pot was infinitely preferable to today's seething cauldron, and you don't give up on a good idea because of its flaws, especially when the alternative spells ethnocentric anarchy, tribal divisions, Balkanized enclaves. Martin Luther King used to say he was less interested in the future of black people than in the future of America. It was just that America's future was intimately bound up with the resolution of the black problem. It is hard to imagine such a majestic unifying statement being uttered today, when we have broken into dozens of isolated constituencies, each arguing for moral, social, and aesthetic supremacy. Still, a genuine form of cultural diversity continues to be pursued by many people in the arts. It must be pursued. Once our arts cease to follow that dream, we cease to be a nation.

[1991]

The War on the Arts, I

IN A closely reasoned essay in the Arts and Leisure section of the *New York Times*, Edward Rothstein recently expressed his concern over the policies of the National Endowment for the Arts and his fears for the future of this increasingly compromised government agency. Rothstein, who is chief music critic for the *Times* (and former music critic of *The New Republic*), argued that by succumbing to populist pressures and trying to represent every possible geographic, ethnic, racial, sexual, and aesthetic constituency, the Endowment was diluting its already pitifully thin resources. Noting the ongoing tension between "the elite character of the fine arts and the American traditions of egalitarianism," he called for a policy that was democratic in its inspiration but meritocratic in its tastes, at the same time acknowledging the unlikelihood of establishing such an "elitist" position in our fractured and fractious culture. His article climaxed with Alexis de Tocqueville's famous prophecy regarding the difficulty, if not the impossibility, of supporting a serious culture in a democratic society.

Rothstein lamented that, by following a pattern of representative (not fiscal) expansion that subordinates support for works of quality to majoritarian and sectarian concerns, the National Endowment is helping to implement Tocqueville's Delphic fears about American culture, and he is right. It is a scandal that such regressive policies should be fostered in an agency originally established for the *advancement* of the arts. Still, the Endowment didn't initiate those policies. For brief periods (most recently under the chairmanship of Frank Hodsell), it even tried to resist them. The NEA has simply surrendered to a variety of forces hostile to traditional ideas of culture, steamrolled into compliance by a massive anti-art juggernaut.

I use the military metaphors advisedly. Beginning during the Jimmy Carter years, and intensifying during the Reagan and Bush administrations, a covert undeclared war was launched and waged against the high arts, with considerably more effectiveness than the wars on poverty or drugs. This unequal action culminated in a major retreat—the surrender of most of the standards and values that make a serious culture possible. I do not mean to suggest that inspired artists no longer function in America, but rather that what was once a hospitable climate for their work has turned mean and indifferent. Native talent may be as abundant as ever, but never in recent years has it been so inadequately evaluated, published, produced, disseminated, and supported.

Although the ongoing war on the arts contains important economic components related to the recession, its thrust has been mainly political. Anti-art forces advance by means of a three-pronged incursion—from the right, left, and center of the political spectrum, all claiming endorsement from the majority. The assault from the right follows the battle plan of Jesse Helms and his minions of moral correctness. Conservative lawmakers, encouraged by the letter-writing brigades of the American Family Association, have concentrated on attacking and infiltrating the NEA. After the controversy over the Mapplethorpe and Serrano exhibits—and the subsequent cancellation of grants to Karen Finley, Tim Miller, and other controversial performance artists—the issue boiled down to whether the federal government should support any art offensive to taxpayers, with the rightist faction imposing content restrictions and many in the arts community shouting censorship.

The censorship charge was the most hotly disputed, even by those First Amendment champions, the press. Critics and journalists seemed unable to recognize that artists have as much right to free speech as they do, and that any threats to the privileges of one group ultimately threaten all. (National Public Radio reporter Cokie Roberts shocked the cultural community by suggesting it was time for the NEA to fold up its tent, not anticipating that, just a few months later, conservative legislators would try to block federal funds to Public Broadcasting because of its "liberal" programming). Even Rothstein was scornful of the "censorship" charge, arguing that the avant-garde, being just "another special interest group," couldn't claim its freedom of speech was being abolished "simply because the Government declined to finance a particular product."

One must concede that some of these artists were being purposely provocative and that some had a political agenda. It is nevertheless the obligation of government to secure and protect their political rights. This is the view of most constitutional scholars as well as of a Los Angeles federal judge who determined, in a class-action suit filed by Bella Lewitzky, that the National Endowment had violated the Constitution in requiring grant recipients to sign an antiobscenity pledge. The issue is not whether the government can refuse to fund "a particular product," but on what grounds the decision is made. Honorable people may question the quality of recipients, as Robert Hughes convincingly did in the case of Robert Mapplethorpe. But these panel-approved grants were overruled not because of artistic deficiencies but because of blasphemous or erotic—more accurately, homoerotic—content. As Jesse Helms said of Mapplethorpe, "He was an acknowledged homosexual. He's dead now, but the homosexual theme runs throughout his work."

Although Helms's primitive moralism was clearly in violation not only of free expression but the rights of sexual choice, the NEA caved in to right-wing pressure in the early days of its former chairman John Frohnmayer. Frohnmayer not only punished those institutions responsible for the Mapplethorpe and Seranno shows but canceled a grant for a New York art exhibit because he found the *brochure* too political (it was critical of legislators like Helms). Then an odd thing happened. As Frohnmayer matured in office, he was converted into a born-again civil libertarian, defending the rights of beleaguered artists so vigorously that President Bush, yielding to pressure from Pat Buchanan, fired him.

Frohnmayer's successor, Acting Chairwoman Ann-Imelda Radice, if anything, proved even more responsive to right-wing pressures on the arts, in spite of peer-panel revolts and protests from individual council members. Immediately after taking office she withheld grants from two college art galleries for featuring shows with erotic content. Still, despite her need to placate the Right, it is under Miss Radice that populist policies gained the greatest purchase at the Endowment. Not only did she announce that the agency would henceforth be more responsive to the will of the majority in handing out money, thus endowing the originally countermarket NEA with marketplace values, but she made it official policy to fund every species of ethnic and racial expression, regardless of its intrinsic value as art. Rothstein quotes a brochure in which the Endowment proudly boasts it has financially assisted "Hmong needlework, coastal sea-grass basketry, southeast Alaska native dance, American Indian basketry and woodcraft, Pacific Island canoe building and Appalachian banjo playing." It's a start, but why leave out Yoknapatawpha County bear hunting, Venice Beach snorkeling, Hillbilly belly scratching, and White House stonewalling?

It is here, under the rubric of regional, sexual, racial, and ethnic pride, that we enter the thorny thickets of "cultural diversity." For just as moral correctness provides ammunition against the arts for the militaristic Right, so the war machine on the Left is run by political correctness. In lockstep with the NEA's Expansion Arts programs, virtually every private funding agency—two or three notable foundations excepted—is now contributing the bulk of its grant money to multicultural expression, which is to say to new and incremental programs based on sociological rather than artistic criteria.

Now no sensible person denies that we live in a diverse society, that works of art can be created by people of every color and persuasion, that talented artists should be honored regardless of their origins, or that intercultural exchange can be a source of great artistic refreshment (see my essay "The Options of Multiculturalism"). Identifying and encouraging such talent is precisely what Martin Luther King meant when he said that people should be judged by the content of their character rather than the color of their skin. But he was talking about equality of opportunity, not equality of representation. And that is a particularly important distinction in the arts, which are responsive to what is rare and unique in human nature rather than what is demographic and statistical. Multicultural grantsmanship sometimes helps to increase the number of deserving minority artists in artistic institutions, which is a highly welcome move. It can also be a form of social engineering transferred to theatre, music, fine arts, and dance as a mean of enforcing changes through active intervention in the programming process. If Beethoven, Balanchine, or Brecht doesn't appeal to minority audiences, then find something that will.

In short, the arts, in the language of a recent granting agency report, are expected to have "a profound impact on American society and the changes that are shaping it"—at a time when institutions are struggling simply to survive. What motivates this coercive philanthropy? As H. L. Mencken wrote, "Every third American devotes himself to improving and lifting up his fellow citizens, usually by force; the messianic delusion is our national disease." Trying to compensate for the failures of society in an area least qualified to be an avenue of social change, the multicultural ideologists threaten to sacrifice hard-won achievements for the sake of evangelical gestures.

Alas, they sometimes end up subsidizing separatism instead. As I have repeatedly said, certain forms of "cultural diversity" are rapidly proving as exclusionary as any system that preceded it. This is true of radical feminism, and especially of the Afrocentric movement with its revisionist Egyptian mythology, paranoid anti-Semitism, and passion for self-segregation. Questions are being raised as to whether white people can understand works created by blacks, whether men can understand women's literature. Doubts are expressed over whether the art of Dead White European Males should interest women, whether the classics of Western culture can address the "experience" of black people. ("Why should they?" was the cogent reply of Irving Howe. "One reason for reading the classics is that they widen and deepen our experience, pulling us out of the all-too-visible limits that any single self is likely to have.") It has even been suggested that only black women possess the proper credentials to review plays or novels by black women. If you pursue this argument to its logical conclusion, the only person truly qualified to appreciate an author's work is the author herself.

The final assault on the arts comes from the center, and is reflected in the way middlebrow culture is currently being enshrined in the pantheon of artistic achievement (at least two recent books, and a cover story in *The New Republic*, have been devoted to exaggerating its importance). Now, no sensible person resents the existence of middlebrow expression, or would begrudge its many readers and spectators the pleasures of relaxing entertainment. Such work tends to confirm people in what they already know, but not everyone needs to experience the some-times monastic rigors of serious art. On the other hand, those who proselytize for the middle always need to denigrate the high, like the bully on the beach terrorizing the ninety-eight-pound weakling. One way to kick sand in the face of the guy with the glasses is to call him a snob (cf. Tad Friend in "The Case for Middlebrow": "highbrow is . . . a way of asserting cultural superi-ority over the less learned"). It's not enough for middlebrow stuff to top the best-seller lists or dominate award ceremonies. It also has to be inducted into the canon of preferred art. A special committee's proposed list (later revised) of books required of Harvard English majors included a lot of novels by popular and politically correct authors between 1920 and the present (includ-ing Zora Neale Hurston, Lillian Hellman, Kate Chopin, Adri-enne Rich, and Toni Morrison), but no Fitzgerald or Heming-way, no Styron or Bellow, no Roth, Malamud, Mailer, Pynchon, Gaddis, Heller, or Updike. The only protest (aside from my own) came from a colleague complaining about the omission of the Nigerian Wole Soyinka.

This downgrading of our major talents is an especially sadden-ing development after the seventy-year efflorescence of high art in America, following the "revolt from the village" against Babbitry and Boobocracy in the twenties. It was a movement distinguished by hospitable small publishers, little magazines, avant-garde thea-tres, adventurous galleries, and listener-supported radio, where new tastes were developed and new talent identified by such respected critics as Edmund Wilson, Lionel Trilling, Clement Greenberg, Eric Bentley, B. H. Haggin, Irving Howe, and Alfred Kazin. Now critical judgments are largely left to the mass media which arbitrates, thumbs up and down, literary and cultural approval. (The consumer's role is rather like that of Doctor Chebutykin in Chekhov's *The Three Sisters*, who gets all his information from newspapers.) Intellectuals, many of whom left the little magazines to work in journalism, are often pressured to lower their standards in order to appeal to wider audiences, while the professoriate, having dried out its brains with arid critical theory, lacks the nerve to resist preposterous assaults on the "Eurocentric" tradition. (Interestingly, historians have proved much less intimidated than literary academics.) The intellectual class is discovering with dismay that educational standards are being determined by TV and movies. Children learn about the Kennedy assassination from paranoid inventions like Oliver Stone's *JFK* and about American history from *Dances with Wolves*. As arts education disappears entirely from schools, rap and rock music are honored as mediums of serious social commentary. The trashing of the educational system is joined by the trashing of culture.

The debates of the fifties, between what Dwight Macdonald called "high cult" and "mid cult," would therefore be impossible today. The once proud and confident highbrow has fled the field, the target of a hail of arrows shaped as epithets. For the war on the arts is not only political but semantic. It proceeds by debasing language and redefining terms, in the manner of Orwell's "Newspeak." Vilification replaces reasoned discourse, and the clash of ignorant armies drowns out debate. Most cunning of all is the way the word "elitist" has been manipulated to mean aristocratic or exclusionary when its etymology refers to leadership. Without an elite in the arts, we have no leaders, which is to say we have no vision, which is to say we have no arts.

The irony of all this is that, despite the way the arts have been systematically bullied and abused in recent years, despite the claims of Right, Left, and Center to popular endorsement, a clear majority of Americans still believes in the importance of artistic expression. A recent Louis Harris poll suggests that most would be willing to pay an additional fifteen dollars of their own taxes (over their current sixty-eight cents) to support federal arts funding; 75 percent are opposed to government dictating what artists can create.

Sixty-eight percent of Americans say they would miss the arts if they were no longer available in their community, and that is perhaps the most poignant statistic of all. For the channels that support serious advanced expression are quickly drying up. The big cultural dinosaurs will probably survive, and some theatres and dance companies may hang on if they fill their schedules with enough crowd-pleasing holiday shows like *A Christmas Carol* and

The Nutcracker. But for all the reasons I've cited, high art in America is a dying animal, and dying along with it are our hopes for a still significant American civilization.

[1992]

The War on the Arts, II

AMERICANS are no doubt impatient with our endless debates about "obscenity," "blasphemy," and the National Endowment for the Arts. But the Republican Convention in August was a frightening demonstration that what at first seemed an intramural squabble over agency funding for artists has now become the basis for a broad-based plan to divide the entire nation along factional lines: "There is a religious war going on in this country for the soul of America," Patrick Buchanan stormed on the first night of the convention. "It is a cultural war as critical to the kind of nation we shall be as the cold war itself."

Buchanan's militaristic imagery is familiar enough in right-wing Republican lexicons, but his reference to the cold war confirms an earlier suspicion that the once marginal American artist has replaced the all-purpose Communist subversive as the primary virus of fundamentalist-conservative diagnostics, the disease carrier infecting the Democratic party and contaminating the nation. That this artist is often an activist homosexual—sometimes (as in the PBS *Tongues Untied*) an African-American activist homosexual—endows the pestilence with feverish sexual, racial, religious, ethical, and political symptoms. The "family values" platform (fortified by Buchanan's ominous proposal to "take back our cities" by "force") is obviously intended to demonize anyone who deviates from white middle-class middlebrow heterosexual husband-dominated prolife churchgoing habits. And what better candidate for this nefarious modern Satan than the gay or lesbian artist?

Military metaphors also permeate *Culture Wars*, an anthology of materials about the recent controversies in the arts culled by the critic and artist Richard Bolton. Bolton—himself the subject of a (dismissed) obscenity complaint for a Boston exhibition on "Censorship, Sexuality, and the Body Politic"—has sifted among thousands of essays, articles, and documents to select 101 pieces that lay out the whole sorry fracas in excruciating detail and from every point of view. In addition to including illustrations of the materials that originally stimulated the controversy (most notably Andres Serrano's "Piss Christ" and Robert Mapplethorpe's "X Portfolio"), he has contributed a balanced, well-reasoned, and comprehensive introduction.

To peruse all this stuff again is to gain an interesting historical perspective on the arc of the controversy—from Donald Wildmon's first alarum to his letter-writing American Family Association attacking Serrano for the "disrespect and desecration of Christ in our country," through the fulminations of Alphonse D'Amato, Jesse Helms, Pat Buchanan, Pat Robertson, Henry Hyde, William Dannemeyer, Dana Rohrabacher, and others (often in identical language) against "dirty pictures" paid for with "taxpayer's money," to the collapse of the Corcoran Gallery in the face of the Mapplethorpe protest and the waffling of NEA chairman John Frohnmayer over later controversies, and ending with Helms's 1991 letter to Jerry Falwell asking for help in battling "the homosexual 'community,' the feminists, the civil libertarians, the pro-abortionists, the flag burners... [and] their dangerous anti-family and anti-American agendas." The Bible-thumping, xenophobic, lunatic America depicted here would have baffled the imagination of Sinclair Lewis and clogged the pen of H. L. Mencken.

Clearly, Serrano and Mapplethorpe were ideally suited to inflame the religious and sexual sensibilities of the Right—the one for immersing an image of Jesus in "bodily fluids" (reverence itself, Serrano replied, compared with the "billion dollar Christ-for-profit industry out there"), the other for shooting photos of fists, cylinders, and bullwhips shoved up the rectum and fingers stuck into the penal canal (Mapplethorpe never replied, having since died of AIDS). Soon after, those inflammable Puritan sensibilities were ignited again by a group of performance artists when Karen Finley covered her body with chocolate, Tim Miller proudly exhibited his erect organ, and Annie Sprinkle (who was never funded by NEA) invited the audience onstage to examine her vagina through a speculum. Perhaps the most inflammatory event of all—which resulted in Frohnmayer temporarily overruling a grant to the Artist's Space—was David Wojnarowicz's catalog essay for the "Witness: Against our Vanishing" exhibit where, "in the privacy of my own skull," he imagined himself "[dousing] Helms with a bucket of gasoline and [setting] his putrid ass on fire or [throwing] rep. William Dannemeyer off the empire state building." The columnist Richard Grenier was equally benevolent about Mapplethorpe: "I think I'd sprinkle him with kerosene and burn him up... not just as self-expression but as *performance art.*" Arts wars obviously bring out the incendiary in both camps.

Regardless of the extreme nature of some of these statements and activities, the initial response of the artistic community— myself included in a piece Bolton reprints from the *New York Times*—was to defend the artist's First Amendment rights of free expression. I still believe it was the correct response. Kathleen Sullivan and Floyd Abrams have eloquently argued the civil libertarian position that to enjoin one persons's speech, however hateful, is to threaten us all, and to impose content restrictions on artists or to ask them to sign "obscenity oaths" was an unconstitutional act of prior restraint (in Sullivan's words, "The First Amendment applies whether the government is wielding its checkbook or its badge"). These opinions were later confirmed in the courts, and the restrictions were removed upon recommendation of the Independent Commission.

The Right continued to argue that sponsorship is not the same as censorship and that the Congress had the obligation to prevent "taxpayer dollars" from being wasted on artistic works the majority found offensive. But one of the more valuable inclusions in this anthology is the text of the original legislation of the National Foundation on the Arts and Humanities Act of 1965, signed into law by President Johnson, which held that "while no government can call a great artist or scholar into existence, it is necessary and appropriate for the federal government to help create and sustain *not only a climate encouraging freedom of thought, imagination, and inquiry, but also the material conditions facilitating the release of this creative talent*" (italics mine).

Like the Constitution itself, this originating document was both wise and prescient about the potential tyranny of the majority. And it clearly established the federal government's support for artistic freedom both from censorship pressures and from marketplace pressures (often the same thing). It was also careful to provide a buffer between congressional appropriations and the grant-making process in the form of peer panels. Some of the less rabid conservatives ("neocons" like Hilton Kramer and Samuel Lipman as contrasted with "paleocons" like Buchanan and Helms) argued that the panels—besotted with "multiculturalist" and "cutting edge" art—were no longer qualified to make sensible judgments. But regardless of its limitations, no one has yet been able to propose a better system for evaluating artists and arts institutions than the panel system—and for all the media noise, only about twenty grants were actually questioned out of almost a hundred thousand passed without controversy.

Important as it was for protecting the rights of artists, however, the censorship argument deflected our attention from the fact that only the most extreme voices were being heard on both sides. If Jesse Helms and his paleocon cohorts were characterizing art as essentially blasphemous and immoral, many of their opponents on the left were doing everything in their power to confirm that judgment. As the art critic Eleanor Heartney rather acidly put it, "Having at long last found a cause around which to rally, the art world is enjoying a rare consensus about its own importance as a last bastion of free expression in an increasingly censorious society."

Our self-congratulation was earned at the cost of politicizing the issue entirely. In defending ourselves against powerful right-wing prejudices toward blacks, feminists, radicals, and particularly gays and lesbians, the arts community has been forced to speak the language not of culture but of advocacy. The spread of AIDS, for example, has created a storm of angry provocation on the part of many homosexual artists, outraged at the society for its inadequate concern, outraged at the universe for the disease itself. As the art critic John Russell put it: "These are not people who go quietly and obediently. When they die, they die in rage. Foul in mouth and sometimes foul in body, they speak of hatred and choking. Who are we to reproach them for 'questionable taste.'" Allan Sekula adds, while criticizing the gay-bashing of Hilton Kramer and Samuel Lipman, "Robert Mapplethorpe and gays in general are being stigmatized for taking seriously one of the utopian promises of the capitalist consumer culture: the promise of liberated desire."

It was the effort to bring this promise out of the private closet and into the public gallery that first enraged the conservative opposition, which began to charge the NEA with teaching people how to sodomize each other ("Now you don't seriously think," asked Michael Kinsley of Pat Robertson, "someone's going to go this exhibit, turn to his buddy and say, 'Hey, so that's how it's done. Let's go try it ourselves,'" to which Robertson answered, "It's very possible").

Absurd as this sounds, what muddies the whole NEA issue is the tendency of extremists on both sides to confuse cutting-edge art with provocative sexual behavior. It's not just Buchanan accusing the gay arts community of trying "to provoke a Middle America too busy and distracted to be provoked; and to be honored and subsidized by a society they appear to loathe"; or Hilton Kramer saying that the "cutting edge" is represented by that which "is most extreme and disruptive"; or conservative artists like Frederick Hart speaking of "the cynical aggrandizement of art and artist at the expense of sacred public sentiments." It is a theme that also permeates the defensive, often hysterical statements of many of the artists themselves. Over and over in these pages, witnesses console their enemies by saying that the first obligation of vanguard art is to appall and scandalize. The result is a dialogue between two benighted factions with virtually no one arguing that offending the audience is a subsidiary effect rather than a primary purpose of advanced art, that shock is a possible result rather than the intended goal of new perceptions. Anything new is destined to disturb the nervous system. But in writing Molly Bloom's soliloquy in *Ulysses*, Joyce was hardly trying to bring a blush to the cheek of a young person. His objective was to investigate the consciousness of a sensual woman on the verge of sleep. In the act of exposing uncensored thoughts he exposed himself to censorship.

Similarly, Stravinsky did not intend to drive Boston matrons out of Symphony Hall by composing *Le Sacre du Printemps*, any more than Ibsen or Duchamp wanted to bring obloquy on themselves by writing *Ghosts* or painting *Nude Descending a Staircase*. In each instance the artist upset his contemporaries with works that now seem perfectly innocuous, simply by extending the boundaries of what is known. (Representative Ted Weiss is alone in understanding this sequence properly: "[Artists] speak the unspeakable, *even if* it manifests itself in horrifying, untidy, or esoteric matters.") The important thing is to make distinctions, and that is where those who generalize about the avant-garde are failing a crucial intellectual responsibility. Freezing us into militant postures, the arts wars have created an endless dance of provokers and provoked. Three years in the trenches have blunted our awareness that art has ground-breaking functions beyond the desire to violate the sensibilities of the straight society.

What I'm saying is that there has to be some avenue between the Scylla of art as a chapbook of moral decency and the Charybdis of art as an instrument of shock and sensationalism. We need a method of protecting the rights of activist artists, and keeping the religious right at bay, without surrendering to the idea that art has no purpose other than to offend. And we need more discussion about the wrongheaded opinion held across the political spectrum (and endorsed in Richard Bolton's introduction) that the highest potential of art is as an agency of social change.

Of course I'm not suggesting that culture be scoured of sexual or political content or that artists like Mapplethorpe be defended with purely formalist arguments. The folly of this was demonstrated in the Cincinnati trial where one art critic described Mapplethorpe's self-portrait with a bullwhip up his ass as an "almost classical" composition while admiring the "opposing diagonals" in his photo of a black man urinating down a white man's throat. Unlike Serrano's work, which is a serious effort, I believe, to address religious questions, Mapplethorpe's "X Portfolio" is a flamboyant exhibitionist's defiance of sexual convention, a dying man's rage against the dying of light. No one should have been surprised when people rose up in horror. It was precisely what the artist intended.

Whatever the value of Mapplethorpe's art, however, its qualities have now been wholly lost in controversy and factionalism. As Elizabeth Hess suggested in *Art on Trial*, the Cincinnati trial over Mapplethorpe was less an effort to determine artistic value than a clash between incensed political sects. ("Which is worse?" she asked. "Getting lynched by rightwingers in Cincinnati, or getting lynched by members of the art world?") Unless we are willing to accept factionalism as the future of American art—the stimulus of congressional investigations, trials and lawsuits, testimony and acrimony—it is imperative to remind ourselves of the original impulse behind vanguard or cutting-edge expression, and to remember that the avant-garde excesses of Dada and surrealism were only a very small part of it.

As is well known, modern history is replete with examples of banned and censored artworks, or artworks that caused riots: Manet's *Olympia*, Bulgakov's *Molière*, Pasternak's *Dr. Zhivago*, Synge's *Playboy of the Western World*, O'Casey's *The Plough and the Stars*, and so on. But it is important to remember that once the controversy died down, people were able to look beyond the things that originally shocked them to new and penetrating insights. How many of us began reading Joyce's *Ulysses* or Lawrence's *Lady Chatterley's Lover* or Miller's *Tropic of Cancer* for their famous erotic passages only to be drawn into worlds we had never expected or imagined? The same thing, I suspect, will be true of Tony Kushner's *Angels in America*—a raging "obscene" play about AIDS that is likely to offend some but which clearly transcends its subject to become a compassionate study of postwar America. Controversy makes stars of artists for all the wrong reasons, distracting our attention from debates that should be more aesthetic than political. As the photography critic Andy Grundberg writes, in the best essay in *Culture Wars*: "The prevailing critical response has been to circle the wagons. Instead of arguing about aesthetics, critics spend their time defending the notion that artists can do and say whatever they please. . . . In an era when 'political correctness' has become a criterion for judging art, this response is doubly dangerous. For one thing, it plays into the hands of those who equate the outer edges of art with a radical political agenda." In short, if modern art is to survive, we must find some way to protect the civil rights of artists without sacrificing our commitment to artistic standards—a task that will not be accomplished until the arts wars are brought to an end.

[1992]

Greenwich Village Follies

IN *Greenwich Village 1963*, Sally Banes, former performance art critic for the *Village Voice*, now associate professor of dance and theatre history and "chair" of the dance department at the University of Wisconsin, Madison, offers to establish 1963 as a climacteric year for American avant-garde art. The author's name resembles that of Sally Bowles, the expatriate heroine of Isherwood's *Berlin Stories* (a ubiquitous ingenue also featured on stage in *I Am a Camera* and *Cabaret*), and this is not the only likeness. The two women display a similar wide-eyed American innocence toward the outlandish cultures they survey.

In a term she borrows from Foucault, Banes calls the Village in the sixties a "heterotopia"—festive, playful, performative, leftist, exotic, and, above all, erotic. As you may deduce from the book's subtitle—"Avant-Garde Performance and the Effervescent Body" —she is particularly exercised by the corporeal, if not aerated, nature of her subject. My dictionary defines *effervescent* as "gently bubbling and hissing from the giving off of gas." I can't say whether this better describes her thesis or her style, but if someone ever does a play version of her book, it might be called *I Am a Jacuzzi.*

It is Professor Banes's conviction that the seeds of the sexual revolution, the counterculture, the peace movement, gay pride, postmodernism, "community, democracy, of work and play, of the body, of women's roles, and so forth" were sown in 1963, and that it all happened near Macdougal Street, under the approving gaze of *Village Voice* writers (Jill Johnston and Jonas Mekas are her most frequently cited authorities). Provincial as this notion may sound, there is undoubtedly a connection between experimental theatre, music, dance, art, and film in the sixties and certain developments in today's culture, though not everyone would find this a cause for rejoicing. It has often been argued that this movement, which she insists on calling "anti-Establishment," now occupies a central place inside the art world and the academy. Indeed, many believe we are living in a global Greenwich Village with the avant-garde representing the new American mainstream. Banes, for example, who also considers herself "anti-Establishment," not only occupies the "chair" of an academic department but sits on cushions (i.e., fellowships) from Guggenheim, Mellon, the American Council of Learned Societies, and Wesleyan.

Greenwich Village 1963, in short, is tailor-made to stoke the wrath of Hilton Kramer and all those other neocons who blame the sixties for everything they find deplorable in contemporary American culture, from Mapplethorpe's "X Portfolio" and Serrano's "Piss Christ" to Annie Sprinkle's labia displays and Karen Finley's chocolate rubs. And it must be conceded that, as described in this book, much of the artistic activity of the era looks pretty silly, a subject better treated by satirists than by publicists. Unfortunately, Banes permits neither humor nor levity to permeate her paeans and dithyrambs. Regrettably omitted from her discussion are the great sixties comics (Lenny Bruce, Nichols and May, Dick Gregory, Woody Allen, the Establishment and Second City companies), arguably among the most creative personalities of the time. While the period produced a number of capable and original artists, she never proves the case that they occupy an indisputable place in American cultural history. Most have value for her mainly as members of a movement, figures in a generation, faces in a decade, or (to embellish an image from Harold Rosenberg's "herd of independent minds") cattle in a hip corral. Banes tries to disarm such criticism with the familiar defense that the Village movement was a challenge to the "elite" tradition of modernism and its annoying aesthetic standards. The sixties avant-garde rejected the divisions "that Establishment culture had created—between mind and body, artist and audience, high art and low art, art and science, art and life." Indifferent to training, technique, and tradition, the movement was intensely hostile to all preexisting forms of professionalism, including critical judgments of value.

This was further suggested in the way the Greenwich Village avant-garde labored to invalidate the credentials of skilled craftsmen, not to mention gifted artists (it was particularly scornful of abstract expressionists). Everyone was capable of creating works of art. Everyone could be world famous for fifteen minutes. Professor Banes takes as her exemplary model a movement that has gone in and out of the public's brief attention span over the years (it resurfaced recently at the Whitney) known as Fluxus and founded by a graphic artist named George Maciunas. Paying early tribute to the "effervescent body," Maciunas based his aesthetic on flux (defined as "a fluid discharge from the bowels or other part"). In this Maciunas resembled no one so much as Stanley Kubrick's General Jack D. Ripper, another hoarder of precious bodily essences. Maciunas, however, had a most unRipper-like affection for Stalin. He followed a Soviet model in devoting himself to mass production in the arts, railing against the "bourgeois sickness" of "Europanism [*sic*!]," exalting amateurism, and initiating a leveling process related to a utopian model of cooperative work and life: "Fluxus," he wrote, "invites...every human to come forward to work or to play"—also, presumably, to discharge bodily fluids freely from the bowels or other part (Fluxus artists were divided over whether piss, shit, or ripe cheese was the preferred medium).

Intoxicated as she is with Fluxus, Professor Banes also extols less risible manifestations from this period—the Judson Dance Company, the Judson Poets Theatre, the Living Theatre, the Open Theatre, the Bread and Puppet Theatre, La Mama, Caffe Cino, and the like, not to mention Andy Warhol's Factory, Jonas Mekas's Underground Film movement, Allan Kaprow's Happenings, and the avant-garde jazz of Miles Davis, Charlie Parker, and Dizzy Gillespie. The movement provided some lively and colorful events and developed performers of considerable power, particularly in choreography (Lucinda Child, Meredith Monk, Trish Brown, David Gordon). In Sam Shepard (whom she doesn't discuss, preferring early Lanford Wilson) it had a major playwright. And in Howard Moody, the "Christian atheist" of Judson Church who removed the pulpit and the cross from the chapel and turned it over to artists, the movement also found a warmhearted patron. But there is something almost quaint about the majority of creations from this time, and in her nondiscriminating way Professor Banes clearly feels more confident ruminating about their political, social, and sexual significance than analyzing them as works of art.

What chiefly earns her admiration are projects related to "the reinvention of community," beginning with the tightly knit artistic fraternity of the Village. The Village community implies a collective, but, true to its rejection of walls, boundaries, and limits, it repudiates such smaller units as family or class (along with what Jonas Mekas called the community of "lawmakers, police, and philistines"). Banes can see the irony in a theory of community that excludes indigenous Villagers like the local ethnic population, and there is no question that Bohemia has always featured its own special forms of condescension. (When I was a young Village actor in the late forties, it was customary to greet sightseeing tourists with loud razzing.)

Despite its reverse snobbery, however, *Greenwich Village 1963* is both an historical record and a subjective celebration of the growing democratization of the arts in America—a development, first noticed (with alarm) by Tocqueville in the early nineteenth century, which has now reached some crazy culmination. The avant-garde disposition toward democratic art led it then, as it does now, to canonize mass culture. Banes rejects the intellectual position, fostered by Clement Greenberg and Dwight Macdonald among others, that links mass culture with the brutalization of society and the debasement of taste, preferring the liberal sociological argument that popular expressions are an extension of egalitarianism, therefore peculiarly American. Andy Warhol, in particular, is praised for creating saleable icons out of mass culture images, while other pop artists are admired for applying and exploiting such essentially commercial techniques as silk screening and cartooning. It is still not altogether certain whether Warhol's fascination with consumer kitsch was inspired by sincerity or cynicism, but Banes's assertion that pop art was an act of "resistance and dissent, a historically conscious and deliberate slap in the face to the custodians of high culture," must be analyzed against the extraordinary commercial success of this phenomenon, perhaps the first time in history that "resistance and dissent" created instant millionaires and insults were rewarded with lucrative gallery contracts.

Still, Banes believes a radical egalitarianism to be the motivating impulse of virtually the entire avant-garde in this period, stimulating not only a desire for greater dissemination and accessibility but a leveling fever that invited audience participation and authorized the ordinary as a crucial element of artistic content. Warhol's Brillo boxes and mass-produced Marilyn Monroe and Elvis Presley portraits, Joseph Cornell's found objects, the Happenings in which people ironed their clothes, shampooed their hair, and shaved their legs (or kissed, performed blow jobs, and slept for hours on end, as in Warhol films) were signals that anything was material for art, and anyone could produce it. "There is something very humble and happy," mused Jonas Mekas in praising Warhol's *Eat*, "about a man (or a movie) who is content with eating an apple." Or, as he gushed about Warhol's *Empire*, "If all people could sit and watch the Empire State Building for eight hours and meditate upon it, there would be no more wars, no hate, no terror—there would be happiness regained on earth."

Some people remained impervious to these hortatory utopian fantasies—at the first screening of one of Warhol's epic marathons, the audience started hemorrhaging out after the first quarter of an hour (no doubt rushing to embrace another fifteen-minute celebrity). But the belief that an inspired elect had somehow stumbled upon the secret of peace on earth, either through art, mind-altering drugs, collectivity, or advanced states of perception, was in the air long before Woodstock. At the root of this belief was a form of romantic anarcho-pacifism nowhere better exemplified than in the work of the Living Theatre under Judith Malina and Julian Beck.

1963 was a transitional year for the Becks, whose political commitment was previously rather subdued. Their early productions were determined more by theatre aesthetics than by radical politics, devoted less to communal events than to individual playwrights. The repertory featured plays by Paul Goodman, William Carlos Williams, Luigi Pirandello, and Jack Gelber (*The Connection* first brought the Living Theatre to national attention in 1959). And although the Becks occasionally genuflected toward reigning avant-garde fashions with semi-Happenings like Jackson Mac Low's *The Theatre of Chance* (the dialogue and action based on a throw of the dice), it wasn't until 1963 that the theatre fully embraced political activism. The event was Kenneth H. Brown's *The Brig*, a harrowing account of life in a Marine Corps stockade, rehearsed by Judith Malina in an extremely repressive manner. Malina believed that by throwing light on violence and confronting the "Structure," she could "penetrate its locks and open the doors of the jails." For Beck also, the ultimate purpose of the play was to "free all prisoners."

The Becks joined the ranks of those prisoners after the IRS closed down the Living Theatre for failing to pay taxes, and they were later arrested for staging an unauthorized performance of *The Brig*. Both served brief jail sentences—not for the alleged crime but for contempt of court when, despite repeated warnings, they repeatedly insulted a friendly judge. (I attended the trial as a friendly witness and watched Malina, attired in what she called her "Portia costume," conduct her own defense, interrogating her husband about her menstrual cycles.) Once having established themselves as martyrs, the Becks allowed their missionary zeal to outstrip their artistic purpose. Following some years in European exile, where they joined student revolts and helped occupy a theatre that hosted them, the Becks returned to this country in 1968 totally transformed in appearance and purpose. Their early Pirandellian experiments, designed to break down barriers between stage and auditorium, had by now developed into full-scale engagements between actors and audiences. At the first American performance of *Paradise Now* in New Haven, they led the spectators into the streets with the ostensible purpose of starting an anarchist revolution.

As Banes concedes, the Becks never actually described what life would be like when all prisoners were freed and all institutions destroyed. They simply believed that organized society obstructed the warm kindly currents of the human heart. "Natural man is...a good, beautiful, wholesome brute," Malina affirmed. "We want to say [men] can live together without [wars, prisons, and police]." These Rousseauistic notions are touching. But during "The Rite of Universal Intercourse" (the climactic scene in *Paradise Now*, when spectators joined the actors to express peace and harmony in a massive love-in), some good, beautiful, wholesome brute raped Judith Malina on the stage of the Brooklyn Academy of Music. Her reported response was: "I wouldn't have minded, if only he'd done it with love."

It's easy enough to mock the naive, self-righteous rhetoric of the sixties, when so many people, inspired by Freedom Marches and the Peace Movement, enraged by the senseless Vietnam War, had somehow come to believe they were a new breed of prelapsarian humanity. Not long after, however, certain factions of the New Left, notably the SDS and the Weathermen, would demonstrate that the "Structure" held no monopoly on violence and irrationality, and that perhaps Hobbes, Burke, and Freud had a point in proposing that institutions were protections against our darker human propensities. But if we should refrain from ridiculing the follies of the past, we shouldn't glorify them either. *Greenwich Village 1963* replays these events and endorses their rhetoric as if history had never happened.

Banes's single criticism of this glorious period is that it didn't anticipate the concerns of our own—the movement was not always what we now call politically correct. In her chapter "Dreaming Freedom" she regrets that however much the Village avant-garde spoke about community and defended civil rights, it never involved more than a small minority of blacks. Langston Hughes and James Baldwin had plays on Broadway, and such white dramatists as Genet (*The Blacks*), Fugard (*The Blood Knot*), and Duberman (*In White America*) were dealing with racial subjects off-Broadway. But aside from Adrienne Kennedy and Leroi Jones, whose *Dutchman* was a long-running success, blacks did not consider themselves members of the avant-garde, and even Jones left the Village (and changed his name) a short time after. There were no black Happenings, no black pop artists, no black Fluxus. Since socially marginalized African-Americans were more interested in entering the artistic mainstream, they considered the avant-garde to be "high art," no matter how communal and folk-oriented it considered itself.

The indifference of blacks toward the avant-garde did not prevent many Village artists from seeking inspiration from black culture. Banes correctly observes that the fascination with improvisation which pervades the theatre, dance, and other artistic activity of this time was stimulated by black music. The Open Theatre based some of its rehearsal techniques on "jamming," a series of associations arising from a theme, derived, as Joe Chaikin said, "from jazz, from the jam session." Both jazz riffs and verbal improvisation were central to Gelber's *The Connection*. And the various comedy groups of the time which Banes neglects to mention—Second City, the Premise, Nichols and May—all improvised skits out of suggestions from the audience.

There was, moreover, a good deal of mythologizing about what this author, though scorning the impulse behind it, identifies as the "essential positive primitivism" of blacks. While many black and white liberals of the sixties were eager to deny racial differences in their efforts to achieve full equality for African-Americans, the more radical artists (*vide* Norman Mailer's "The White Negro") were favorably comparing the natural, uninhibited physicality of blacks with what Banes calls "the etherealized bodies of Euro-American culture." Clearly the author is more sensitive to stereotypes about blacks than whites, and she is further confused by our ever-changing racial fashions. At the same time Banes concedes that the concept of "essential positive primitivism" was embraced by the black-power movement, she nonetheless finds it racially tainted when endorsed by whites. "I do not mean here to charge these avant-gardists...with racism; I only want to say that they were willy-nilly products of their era."

Well, so is Professor Banes, as she demonstrates in criticizing the Village movement for failing to be sufficiently sensitive to women: "Neither male nor female consciousness had yet been raised about the subtleties of female oppression." Just as white artists were prone to praise black bodies as "closer to nature," which she finds vaguely racist, so they were also eager to celebrate the glories of the female body, which she finds altogether sexist. "The gendered universe remains intact" in the work of such heterosexual artists as Lichtenstein, Oldenburg, and Rosenquist, simply because they made the mistake of painting attractive women. It is not explained how Lichtenstein could imitate the popular comic-strip style she so admires without drawing its familiar female icons. Sexual glamour is simply verboten: "In Pop Art and Happenings, in particular, the predominantly male artists often seemed to adopt uncritically—even at times to salute—the dominant culture's representations of women both as consumer and as sexual object to be consumed."

Despite her squeamishness about the consumption of beautiful sexual objects, Banes's book is really obsessed with sexuality, and reaches its climax, so to speak, with a chapter on "The Body as Power." There she glorifies anything that exposes what still might be considered private or personal about the physical life. Citing Claes Oldenburg's manifesto that roots art in the human anatomy ("I am for art you can sit on. I am for art you can pick your nose with or stub your toes on.... I am for the sweat of art that develops between crossed legs"), Banes goes on to eulogize the "effervescent body—with its emphasis on the material strata of digestion, excretion, procreation, and death... the amazing grace of fleshly reality." Examples follow definitions. Fluxus features pissing contests. Jim Dine's bathroom fixtures "deliberately soiled the rhetoric of the beautiful and sublime" by establishing the resemblance between "the plumbing—with its holes, bulges, and tubes—and the orifices and protuberances of the human body itself." Kaprow created a Happening that took place inside a womb. Stan Brakhage made a film about birthing ("The mother's body is no longer private, but literally open, sharing, begetting, and emerging... it contains and continues the family and the community").

But the "effervescent body" is not only a sexual and excretory organism. It is also a "gustatory body." Eating can be both a reproductive and erotic activity. Banes cites Ben Patterson's instructions for his *Licking Piece*:

cover shapely female with whipped cream
lick

. . .

topping of chopped nuts and cherries is optional

I'm surprised that she doesn't find Patterson's "shapely female" reference to be sexist (what disturbs me more is the absence of hot fudge). But the link between eating and other appetites is clear. From Andy Warhol's Campbell's soup cans to Oldenburg's BLT through Alex Hay's breakfast paintings and Robert Watts's chrome-plated lead hot dogs, food is treated as a metaphor for body parts, abundance, or articles of mass consumption. Banes concludes: "In early sixties artworks, the gustatory body is seen as permeable, sensuous, and collective. Feeding serves as a locus for the body festively and transgressively to be turned inside out and upside down."

Turning the body inside out and upside down brings us back to the prime function of the effervescent body, its sexual nature.

But whereas in bourgeois society sex is usually a private matter, the sixties avant-garde offered to make it "brashly public, often even a communal affair." Indeed, it usually took place in front of an 8 mm camera. Although censorship had loosened up considerably in this period, "The New Sexual Freedom Riders," as Mekas called his cohorts, were continually testing the boundaries of the obscene, many years before the National Endowment for the Arts decided to retaliate with content restrictions. Jack Smith's *Flaming Creatures*, described by Susan Sontag as "a paradise and hell of writhing, shameless, ingenious bodies," was a preliminary run for the group gropes in *Paradise Now*. Barbara Rubin's *Christmas on Earth* featured "a seemingly endless array of breasts and penises, vulvas, and exploring fingers" that were poked, prodded, and penetrated in a wide variety of heterosexual and homosexual partnering. And in Carolee Schneeman's film *Meat Joy*, men and women undressed each other, wrapped one another up in paper, rolled around on the floor, and cavorted with fish, chicken, and hot dogs in a series of "erotic rites [that] signify a sexuality of abundance and gratification."

For Banes, the significance of these works, especially those by women and gay men, is that they transgressed "the culture-bound question of gender divisions." Gay and female artists and choreographers were learning "to refuse gender coding" by treating the sexes identically. This could take the form of transvestism, as in Lanford Wilson's *The Madness of Lady Bright*, or reversing traditional roles, as in Barbara Rubin's *Christmas on Earth*, which featured a woman surrounded by a harem of men. Instead of having sex, in other words, people were now having gender together. And thus "the effervescent body so far outstripped even the confident body of the dominant culture that it actually helped produce a new culture, overflowing into an alternative space of cultural imagings made concrete. And the pressure of the effervescent body created a route into that space large enough for a mass counterculture to follow."

What Banes sees as the ultimate goal of these public sexual calisthenics is the polymorphous perversity celebrated in Norman O. Brown's *Life Against Death*. And it is altogether typical of today's intellectual fashions that a work purporting to be a study of an artistic movement should eventually deteriorate into a radical feminist brief for sexual and physical freedom. Although Banes insists that the Village avant-garde produced a "rich body of work of unprecedented diversity," she has only managed to chronicle its follies and highlight its evanescence. The avant-garde of any period is ultimately significant less for its artistic postures than for its artistic achievements. But the progress of the creative individual holds little interest for Banes, only the arrested development of the narcissistic personality. Although a number of gifted figures are mentioned in this book, not one is allowed to transcend a "position" to clarify our thinking or illuminate our sense of human existence.

What *Greenwich Village 1963* reveals, in short, is that the democratization of art means the deliquescence of culture and the liquification of thought. Hissing, bubbling, and fizzing to the end, Banes's "effervescent body" turns out to be merely a yearning for herd love, the erotic version of the community sing. Today, when the rights of personal and sexual privacy have been totally invaded by the media, when so many personal relationships are coming unstuck, and when self-love intrudes itself persistently in the guise of self-expression, it is tempting to see the origin of our current disorders in the avant-garde enthusiasms of the past. "Children of what was," the author concludes, "they became parents of what will be." True enough, but instead of absolution for the cultural excesses of these parent-children, we could better use a rigorous assessment of their artistic achievements. That assessment is still being awaited. For all its density and research, *Greenwich Village 1963* only leaves us with the sense that what Yeats called "the mad intellect of democracy" was, in this particular time and place, preparing to snap its last remaining synapse.

If Sally Banes is the publicist of this mind-blowing process, Allan Kaprow is one of its principal theoreticians. He is only a little more successful in repairing damaged brain passages. His essay series, *The Blurring of Art and Life*, is a more condensed effort to proselytize for the democratization of art, using many of the same examples from the period. Best known as the inventor of "Happenings," Kaprow, who is now a professor emeritus of visual arts at the University of California, San Diego, also has a rather extensive academic background, including graduate work in philosophy. He studied art history under Meyer Shapiro and claims Marcel Duchamp (also the philosopher John Dewey) among his seminal influences. Unlike Sally Banes, he is not an enemy of Action painting. Indeed, he expresses an almost filial affection for Jackson Pollock, whom he discusses with considerable insight. And although he has dedicated his life to replacing the abstract with the concrete, he considers Happenings to be a logical offshoot of Abstract Expressionism.

Kaprow defines Happenings, somewhat tautologically, as "events that simply happen." These chance events, much like the creative activities described by Banes, are improvised on the order of jazz, and though they may contain words, language is valued for its sounds rather than its meaning. A Happening is actually a form of antitheatre. Like much that Kaprow admires, it takes place outside such conventional cultural staging areas as playhouses, concert halls, or museums. Changing your shirt in a park, crossing a street only with people in red coats, listening to a dripping faucet—all these mundane events constitute what Kaprow calls "lifelike art" (as opposed to "artlike art"), a waggish antitraditional form of play intended to break down all remaining barriers between what is passively experienced and what is actively fashioned. Kaprow is painfully conscious that, if lifelike art resembles life more than art, then it is hard to define its intrinsic qualities. He is continually asking what makes work of this kind "art." His answers include self-knowledge, self-consciousness, and a rather Zen-like enlightenment, suggesting, somewhat poignantly, that despite his scorn for traditional mainstream art he still can't fully abandon the name of artist.

This despite his own admission that for the last thirty years his main artistic activity has consisted of things like brushing his teeth (albeit "attentively"). But for him even the most quotidian exercises can still retain aesthetic meaning. In his last essay, "The Meaning of Life" (1990), he writes, only half-humorously, that "cleaning a friend's kitchen floor with Q-tips and spit...could mean a) seeing life from another perspective; or b) testing your friendship; or c) making the simple seem complicated; or d) putting yourself (your spit) wholly into the job; or e) being free to cheat since no one will see you; or f) being on the track of something big; or g) getting some exercise." The essay ends with a recipe for making bagels ("You'll like them!"). Kaprow refrains from suggesting that the "meaning of life" can be found in the hole.

The Blurring of Art and Life might seem as ludicrous as *Greenwich Village 1963* were it not that the personality of the writer is so engaging and exuberant. Kaprow's desire for a truly nonexclusive democratic art is almost Whitmanesque. If describing a handshake or becoming conscious of breathing is artistic material, then everything is annexable to art and everyone is an artist. Kaprow carries this logic one step further by exhorting "artists of the world to drop out! You have nothing to lose but your professions." Art is always an imitation, which cannot improve on nature, and as a social instrument it is totally useless, having never changed a thing. Only when artists cease to be artists can they convert their talents into something purposeful, namely "play." Like a number of his contemporaries, Kaprow feels tracked, and trapped, by the culture. He finds it ironic that the desire to make a private art should be accompanied by so much attention from the media (Warhol, for example, had so many speaking engagements that he hired a stand-in to make university appearances). I suspect that Kaprow's theories are partly animated by a desire to repudiate celebrity, at once the artist's greatest temptation and greatest affliction. When celebrity comes to an end, then criticism will end with it, and critics will have to satisfy themselves with doing historical research in universities. Ultimately, then, behind all Kaprow's theorizing lies a willed effort to escape from the fatal artificial embraces of cultural journalists, art critics, and other agents of hype into a creative natural world of pleasure and community. It is a doomed effort, and often a labored one, but in Kaprow's writings, if not his Happenings, it represents a final appeal for artistic dignity in a money-made, celebrity-driven culture.

[1994]

An Embarrassment of Riches

(N.B. Since this article was written, Alex Witchel was removed from her post as a theatre columnist and Frank Rich abandoned drama criticism for a position on the op-ed page of the Times. *I am nevertheless including it in this collection because I still believe the issues I raised regarding their tenure on that newspaper to be unresolved.)*

EVEN before the disappearance of competing New York newspapers, the *New York Times* played an important role in the success or failure of Broadway plays. For the past twenty-five years the *Times* has played virtually the only role. And for eleven of those twenty-five years, this respected organ of the press has not only been adjudicating Broadway hits and flops but strongly influencing the aesthetic direction, artistic personnel, style, and content of American theatre—not only in New York but (now that resident theatres are trying out so many New York–bound plays) throughout much of the country. These eleven years have coincided with the reign of Frank Rich. And while it is not fair to hold one man accountable for the dwindling number and diminishing quality of plays and productions, there is almost universal agreement that a causal link exists between Rich's dramatic opinions and the crisis in the American theatre. Rich has defended himself against such charges by saying, with considerable disingenuousness, that producers, not critics, are responsible for closing plays. But his leverage has grown so potent that it is even being noticed by the mass media: a section of "60 Minutes" was devoted last year to Rich's reputation as the "Butcher of Broadway" (only a handful of his victims were sufficiently unintimidated to speak for the record, though scores more were willing to testify off camera). How did one man achieve such power? And what, if anything, can be done to mitigate the disproportionate influence of the *New York Times* on the American stage?

The answers to the first question are complicated and diverse.

First of all, the *Times*, largely because of the respect long enjoyed by its most celebrated drama critic, Brooks Atkinson, has always been a major player in the Broadway sweepstakes. Tacitly acknowledging that role, *Times* editors in the late sixties began to feature a second reviewer in their Sunday Arts and Leisure section, first Walter Kerr, then Benedict Nightingale, and now David Richards. But despite the qualifications of those Sunday critics (and Kerr and Nightingale were generally considered more knowledgeable and thoughtful than most of Rich's predecessors), the daily reviewers continued to wield decisive control over the New York stage. Even the highly respected Walter Kerr, a hugely influential figure as a daily reviewer, was virtually disempowered when he voluntarily moved to the Sunday Arts and Leisure. New York theatregoers, battered by rising ticket prices and accustomed to overnight opinions, had been conditioned to follow the advice of whomever occupied the first-string critic's chair.

In the case of Rich, the issue is not the quality of his writing. He is, in fact, an elegant stylist with a lively, witty, urbane mind. Indeed, his literary competence has arguably been responsible for exacerbating the problem, since it has helped to consolidate his position both with his editors and with a number of his readers. It is true that Rich's lacerating style more often resembles the machete-wielding of John Simon than the gentle advisory caresses of Brooks Atkinson, but he is not the first to make the wounding of defenseless theatre people a source of gladiatorial entertainment. Actually, Rich, a mild-mannered man in public, seems to have grown more cordial in his writing after samples of his bile were offered on "60 Minutes," and he is generous enough about establishing new stars and potential playwrighting talent. Whatever his mood, in my opinion, Rich's taste is essentially safe, middle of the road, and consumer oriented (he was nurtured, as he admits, on Broadway musicals). I don't much like his limited aesthetic or his ignorance of process or his disregard for unconventional theatre or his indifference to the classics or his infatuation with glamour. But critical disagreements are not the main issue. Everybody has the right to opinions and Rich, at least, commendably refuses to fudge on his. No, none of Rich's failings suggests a fatal weakness. The problem is not with his style or his tone or his taste but rather with his influence, with the fact that his is the *only* ruling opinion. I have often thought of Rich as a competent critic in the wrong place. Without the clout of the *Times*—as the critic, say, of *The Nation* or *The New Republic*—he might have been a perfectly harmless and even admired presence. Like anybody in the powerful chair he now occupies, he is clearly something of a menace.

Unlike books and movies, the theatre cannot survive its criticism, though Rich's influence does not always extend to big critic-proof shows. Andrew Lloyd Webber's musicals manage to flourish without his approval, and so do such audience-pleasers as *The Secret Garden* and *The Will Rogers Follies*. But the straight plays on Broadway and particularly in such off-Broadway (and pre-Broadway) venues as the Manhattan Theatre Club, Playwrights Horizons, Lincoln Center, Circle Repertory Theatre, and others are almost entirely subject to his tastes. In *The Seagull*, Treplev calls the stage of his time "conventional and predictable. ...When they offer me the same thing over and over in a thousand variations, then I take to my heels and run." He might have been talking about the Rich-influenced New York theatre. *Eastern Standard*; *Marvin's Room*; *Lips Together, Teeth Apart*; and *Falsettos*, among the more recent Rich-approved hits, all have their virtues to a greater or lesser degree. But they are also uniform enough in their middle-class furrow-browed angst, in their guilty perspective on contemporary victimology, and in their concentration on mental and physical afflictions, to make one think they were stamped from the same cookie-cutter. The fact that these are the approved plays of the nineties, while a significant number of more radical, controversial, and penetrating plays have failed to survive Rich's rancor, suggests that what passes today for serious theatre has been wholly shaped by his tastes.

While it is true that some theatre people, like David Hare, only complain when Rich dislikes their plays (they are happy enough with his praise), many major playwrights and important auteur-directors either have no place to work in New York any more or feel unwelcome there (an alarming number have even left the theatre). JoAnne Akalaitis, who inherited Joe Papp's mantle, has become such a source of unhappiness at the *New York Times* that her days at the Public may very well be numbered.* Not only are

*Akalaitis was fired a year later.

her productions regularly panned by Rich, but she is regularly assailed in the columns of Rich's wife, Alex Witchel, who now writes the gossipy "On Stage, and Off" column for the Friday paper. This one-two punch by a husband-and-wife team covering the same art form (a collaboration that has been called "an embarrassment of Riches") is a significant element in the growing abuse of power at the *New York Times*—and I'm referring not to nepotism but to the consolidation of opinion. Rich's favorites and friends are regularly featured in Witchel's accounts of their farewell dinners and TV appearances, while Akalaitis is mentioned in these columns only to spank her for canceled productions and declining subscription lists. If Rich scorns the presentations of a new resident company like the National Actors Theatre, Witchel follows up with an unfriendly story about how its director Tony Randall is withholding free tickets from seven hundred Tony voters (perhaps the only thing Randall is doing right). If Rich pans *The Will Rogers Follies*, Witchel notices how a "musical about a man who championed minorities had none in its cast." (Rich later confirms their intellectual compatibility with a note about how "a musical whose democratic hero champions the poor and downtrodden...opened without a single black performer in its large cast.")

When Rich savages *Nick and Nora*, putting that blighted musical out of its misery the very next day, weeks later he rubs in some salt with a six- or seven-thousand-word article in Arts and Leisure, complaining that the producers cheated the "consumer" by selling previews at full price, and worse, scolding them for not letting him in earlier to close down the box office. I'm not arguing for long runs of mediocre shows, but there is a difference between judging theatre and controlling it. It is not enough these days to kill a show at the *Times*. They have to kick the carcass too. Rich's *Nick and Nora* article, by the way, is typical of the intellectual level of the once more ambitious theatre section of Arts and Leisure. Once engaged with a broad range of theatre issues, it is now rife with backstage chatter about profits and losses, costs and overruns, when it is not running front-page articles (by Alex Witchel) about Joan Collins's wrinkled face and wrinkled career. Witchel's Friday columns, devoted to green-room gossip and professional feuds, are always bursting with statistics (perhaps reflecting her background as a management student at the Yale School of Drama). Nothing impedes her busy abacus— neither private agreements nor unreturned phone calls—so that you are continually being bombarded with irrelevant numbers: the size of Mike Nichols's royalty checks, the cost of moving a show to Broadway, the length of time it takes to recoup investments, in future no doubt the inseam measurements and arch-support size of the latest star.

I suppose the *Times* has always been interested in the business of theatre. This is the first time in memory when economics have totally obliterated artistic issues. It has also been traditional *Times* policy to print follow-up features on the playwrights, directors, and actors its critic praises. But I can't remember a time when features have also been written to endorse the critic's negative reviews. Witchel even uses "On Stage, and Off" to send ominous signals regarding shows that haven't yet opened. After *Falsettos* received what she, referring to her husband's review, called "raves" in Hartford and therefore guaranteed success in New York, the show proved unable (because of costs and scheduling) to recruit the Rich-sanctioned artistic personnel for its Broadway move. Intimidating rumbles circulated through Witchel's column, bespeaking future disapproval from the critic's seat.

I think it's clear enough that theatre opinion at the *Times* has now become a form of overkill, extending from the critic's notice to the features column to the pages of Arts and Leisure, and even to the *Times* radio station WQXR and the *International Herald-Tribune* (where Rich repeats his reviews). There are a number of other people reporting on the stage in this newspaper, but none commands a network of the size and power enjoyed by Frank Rich. One suspects the paper, despite disclaimers, exults in his power, and would not willingly surrender it. But this situation is, I believe, one of the factors helping systematically to destroy the New York theatre. The best solution is to dymystify the reviewer of the *New York Times*, and this can only be accomplished by adding a second daily voice, perhaps by moving Richards from the Sunday section, where he has no influence, to a side-by-side position with Frank Rich. A second daily opinion would instantly establish some accountability at the *Times*, reminding us that the theatre is subject to a variety of views, including the ones the reader or theatregoer holds himself. This procedure would be consistent, too, with that in other sections of the *Times*, where reviewers are appointed not as generalists but as specialists in the object under scrutiny (works by Stravinsky and U2, for example, like books by William Gaddis and Leon Uris, are assigned to differently qualified reviewers, and Vincent Canby shares his movie reviewing power with Janet Maslin—but the same theatre critic usually covers *Miss Saigon* and *Waiting for Godot*). Another solution, with which some resident theatres outside New York are now experimenting, is to end the debilitating symbiotic relationship between criticism and practice (and theatre is the only art which depends so heavily on the press for its survival). This means no more critics' quotes in ads or blowups of reviews in the lobby, which may encourage audiences to recognize that they are the best arbiters of their own taste. If the cowed New York theatre community could also stop relying so much on press quotes and newspaper advertising, Broadway and off-Broadway might begin to attract theatregoers with the independence to decide things for themselves. Whatever the solution, Frank Rich's stranglehold on American theatre must be broken. It is not healthy for artists, not healthy for audiences, not healthy for him.

[1992]

Postscript: Two years after this was published, Mr. Rich replied to it in the context of an 8,500-word article in the Times Magazine, *where he evaluated his own career as a drama critic. His references to me in "Exit the Critic" were almost entirely personal and speculative. Not only did he suggest that he fell from "my good graces" because he had praised August Wilson's* The Piano Lesson, *but he went on to charge me with racism, homophobia, nepotism, jealousy, hypocrisy, and an obsessive interest in his wife ("Often he would stare conspicuously at Alex before the lights went down at a performance we both attended"). Dismayed that Rich would respond to what I had intended as an evaluation of his influence on the theatre with an effort at character assassination, I wrote the following reply:*

Frank Rich may be politically correct, but he is not factually correct. There is not a syllable of truth in his characterization of my theatre or my views.

Because we don't often agree on the same plays, Rich charges that I am "uncomfortable with minority playwrights" and that gay writers are "another sore spot," adding that a "dwindled" number of contemporary dramatists work at the American Repertory Theatre. Well, in the last two seasons alone this "dwindled" number has included David Rabe, David Mamet, Han Ong, Ronald Ribman, Paula Vogel, Steve Martin, Suzan-Lori Parks, Eric Bogosian, Evan Handler, Peter Feibleman, Philip Glass, Stuart Greenman, and others, many of them gay and minority artists. Next year we plan a revised version of Derek Walcott's *Steel* (which we originated in workshop three years ago) as well as a piece commissioned from Anna Deavere Smith in her second ART visit. I resent even having to answer such charges. It is well known that ART is a wholly integrated company of actors devoted to plays of quality *regardless* (rather than *because*) of race, sex, or national origin. Indeed, our unwavering commitment to nontraditional casting was one of the reasons Samuel Beckett once threatened us with a lawsuit.

Rich also charges me with hypocrisy because I criticized his wife's position as a theatre columnist when I had cast my own wife in a play. As I wrote in "An Embarrassment of Riches," the issue was not nepotism but the consolidation and abuse of critical power. The ART has always employed a large number of spouses, both gay and straight. What concerned me about this relationship was how Rich and his wife were consistently promoting and attacking the same plays, artists, institutions, and theatre leaders. This was not judging the theatre so much as controlling it.

Space inhibits my correcting more such errors—there are at least seven—but apart from Rich's problem with the truth, the most important question still to be resolved is how a critic can misuse his position through the agency of an influential newspaper, most recently writing a self-exonerating account and "settling scores" with real or imagined enemies. I challenge Rich to debate these issues—rather than spin fantasies about my motives and character—in any public forum of his choosing. I will not be surprised when he declines.

PPS. To this date, Mr. Rich has not yet accepted my challenge.

[1994]

Dumbocracy in America

FEW will dispute that American cultural and university life has become subject to a whole new set of regulations—speech codes, revised canons, new departments, lowered standards, increased pressure for faculty and student diversity, excessive vigilance regarding the sensitivity of minorities—all in an atmosphere of intellectual constraint. The dispute centers on whether these are the best ways to advance the interests of the disadvantaged, and if so, whether it's worth jettisoning traditional artistic and intellectual values in order to accomplish this end. The conservative position is clear and unequivocal—a return to things as they were, regardless of the social and political consequences. Liberals are more divided over whether the current method of increasing the rights of minorities, a cause they approve, can achieve its goals without affronts to truth, history, art, reason, and civility.

Ironically, the popular phrase associated with this method— "political correctness"—has recently lost most of its currency, having been bombarded with ridicule from all sides of the political spectrum. Beginning with the conservative Dinesh D'Souza's *Illiberal Education*, a comprehensive look at the collapse of universities under pressure from radical demands, proceeding through Arthur Schlesinger, Jr.'s *The Disuniting of America*, deploring the fragmentation of the national identity by racial and ethnic entities, through Nat Hentoff's *Free Speech for Me—but Not for Thee*, recounting the liberal intolerance expressed toward this impeccably liberal author for opposing abortion, Robert Hughes's *The Culture of Complaint,* describing the fraying of American culture under assaults from right and left, and Jonathan Rauch's *Kindly Inquisitors*, cataloguing restraints on free thought through academic monitoring, "political correctness" has been subject to remorseless scrutiny in a variety of books and articles, with little intelligible response other than to deny the nomenclature. But how can anyone defend an expression that sounds so prim, narrow, and inquisitorial?

These broadsides may have succeeded in destroying political correctness as a phrase, but not as a sentiment. It has resurfaced, more powerful than ever, under the rubrics of "cultural diversity" and "multiculturalism" or, to use the prevailing White House slogan, "representing the true face of America." Whatever you call it, PC has crypto-Maoist roots and in extreme form is dedicated to a program not unlike that of the unlamented cultural revolution by the People's Republic of China—replacing an "elite" system with a "populist" agenda through egalitarian leveling. Chairman Mao's little red books now take the form of little black books by a variety of authors—including dictionaries of euphemisms advising us how to identify various members of minority groups without hurting their feelings (pale penis people, namely white males living or dead, are not assumed to have feelings). Such glossaries may seem ludicrous, but their impact on uninhibited expression can be menacing. Even more threatening is the related effort to proscribe offensive ideas, censor improper books and syllabi, and cleanse the culture of independent thought. In the movie *Invasion of the Body Snatchers*, people possessed by alien forces identify all those still left human by bugging their eyes, pointing their fingers, and issuing horrible guttural sounds from their throats. This strikes me as a good description of the way those dissenting from political correctness are now being treated in the arts and humanities.

This crypto-Maoist process is a heritage of the sixties. Many, if not most, of today's PC leaders were active members of the New Left twenty-five years ago. The radical students who once occupied university buildings over the Vietnam War and the "harassment" of the Black Panthers are now officially occupying university offices as professors, administrators, deans, and even presidents. Having helped to promote increased enrollment by minority students, a desirable goal, they are now responding to the inevitable consequence: increased demands for new departments, beginning with black and women's studies, and then extending to virtually every "oppressed" minority in the land. Meanwhile, today's students assume the old roles of the newly tenured radicals, using sixties methods to achieve their ends—protests, sit-ins, occupations, shouting down speakers, shutting down universities. At the University of Pennsylvania, for example, a group of black students expropriated an entire run of a student newspaper to protest a "racist" article, while at the University of California, Berkeley, Chicano students went on a hunger strike until officials granted their demand for a department of Chicano studies.

Some of these new departments have proved extremely useful additions, opening up whole new areas of research. Others have been created less to increase knowledge than to increase power and presence. This exposes the most serious consequence of PC in the university which is the growing politicization of academic life, usually at the cost of scholarship and learning. On the pretext that everything is political and always was, courses are created for no other purpose than to redress past injustice and validate minority claims. It is not surprising that hitherto ignored people should desire more information about their history and culture, not only in order to inform themselves but to educate others. Yet the need to increase self-esteem has developed malignant side effects, leading, for example, to conditions of self-segregation where hard-won advances in civil rights have been vitiated by separate classrooms, exclusive dormitories, and sequestered dining facilities.

In this politicized atmosphere, some members of the PC professoriat will not hesitate to use fabricated or skewed research in order to consolidate feelings of racial or gender superiority (the "sun people–ice people" theory and the current myths about the intellectual influence of "black" Egypt on Periclean Athens are only two examples). Just as historical fact is manipulated for racial purposes, so the issue of free speech becomes selective. PC professors and students can protest such speakers as Colin Powell for his position on gays in the military and in the same breath cite the privileges of free expression to defend the campus presence of notorious anti-Semites like Leonard Jeffries. (Some fellow-traveling academics—notably Stanley Fish of Duke— have even begun questioning the First Amendment when it doesn't promote social equality or conform to PC thinking.)

As demoralizing as the insults to truth, history, and civil liberties are PC restrictions in the field of knowledge. The multiplication of special studies and special departments has made it possible for minority students not just to be better informed about their culture but to go through college without learning about anything else. What Christopher Lasch called "the culture of narcissism" has now found its politically approved form. Students learn by looking in a mirror and studying themselves. And what they see has got to be "positive images"—no example of non-Caucasian brutality, or instance of female misbehavior, is allowed to upset the historical melodrama of minority victims and white male oppressors. It goes without saying that the university exists not to confirm what you desire to believe or believe already, but to extend the reach of your mind into areas of ignorance. Yet gays want to learn about the virtues of being gay, blacks study their own role models, and women search for instances of gender discrimination throughout the history and literature of the West (replacing the witch-hunts of the seventeenth century with twentieth-century warlock hunts).

PC's narcissistic agenda begins early, particularly in the schools. In a number of states, most notably New York, the basic subjects required for advancement in society are being replaced by a "Rainbow" curriculum more preoccupied with inspiring self-esteem and promoting tolerance than with teaching reading or writing. The time is nigh when eight-year-olds will have more knowledge about Native American totem rituals than about the multiplication tables, and will be better instructed in how to use a condom than how to apply the rules of grammar. In a recent newspaper cartoon, two little girls are walking down the street. One of them says, "My friend has two mommies," and the other replies, "How much is two?" The skills with which young people advance are being smothered in a wash of feel-good civics lessons, as if achievement were produced by self-esteem and not the other way around.

In culture the problem is, if anything, more acute. If there was a time when intellectuals could fight for social justice and high art simultaneously, when it was possible to study both Trotsky and Joyce (or, like Shaw in the British Museum, both Marx and Wagner), that time is no more. Today we are being asked to choose, in the belief that "elite" culture (the dismissive phrase for the entire Western tradition) is simply another instance of white male oppression. "Multiculturalism"—in its true sense the fertilization of one culture by another—has become a process for promoting exclusive "life-styles" and endorsing struggles for artistic supremacy.

Culture wars are nothing new. What is novel about "multiculturalism" is the effort of its practitioners and publicists to demolish what little remains of high culture in this country. Just as rock and hip-hop stations on FM radio often drown out the weaker signals of NPR's classical programming, so the multiculturalists, using a variety of political means and aesthetic arguments, try to drown out the weaker signals of high art. Although this is represented as another form of equal opportunity, popular or mass culture has never wanted for audiences or acclaim in America—or money for that matter (popular recording artists are now among the highest paid in the land). The branding of serious art as "elitist" is simply another power ploy to promote supremacy, by hoisting popular culture into the lofty niche formerly reserved for more complicated, profound, and discriminating work.

This is being done in a variety of ways, but primarily by trying to demolish our traditional standards and values. Just as all objective academic research is now labeled "political," a secret means of exalting Western civilization over that of the Third World, so the very idea of "quality" is assumed to be racist, a conspiratorial method of excluding popular and folk artists from serious consideration. In the multicultural aesthetic all values are relative—only high art is subject to absolute judgment, as a pernicious form of "Eurocentrism."

The Clinton administration reveals "the true face of America" by orchestrating an inaugural entertainment inspired by Hollywood (even Kathleen Battle was obliged to sing a popular song), commissioning an inaugural poem by a writer of modest talents, obviously chosen because she was an African-American woman, and otherwise behaving less like an appointments agency examining qualifications than a casting agency looking for types ("Get me a black female lawyer for the part of assistant attorney general!"). The "true face of America," apparently, has features primarily determined by color and gender, and those who fail to observe these new requirements are stigmatized for racism or sexism, even when their works have popular appeal. In July of this year an assistant dean at Harvard's School of Public Health wrote an op-ed piece in the *Boston Globe* attacking *Jurassic Park* because the survivors were blonde and the victims were dark. She had no comment about the color (or sex) of the all-female dinosaurs.

Many of the same quota systems and populist demands are being imposed on the serious arts by the cultural bureaucrats who control their fate. Whether in arts councils or private foundations, in the editorial offices of newspapers or from critics' desks, audiences are being scanned to determine the proportion of non-Caucasian faces, while art exhibitions, repertory theatres, opera and dance companies, symphony orchestras, and smaller musical groups (not to mention their boards) are continually evaluated according to racial, sexual, and other background considerations. In the past, such inquiries into the origins of any employee were usually considered evidence of discrimination, if not invasion of privacy. Today, through the reverse discrimination called "cultural diversity," this procedure is being used as a basis for most grant applications.

Funding blackmail is, in fact, the means by which political correctness, masquerading as multiculturalism, has proceeded to harass the world of serious art. In the past, public and private foundations, as well as individuals, usually gave their money to not-for-profit artistic institutions for general operating support. Today it is a rare foundation indeed that doesn't reserve the lion's share of its revenue for incremental multicultural projects. Artistic support, in short, is posited not on quality (most funders admit that excellence is an obsolete standard) but on evidence of affirmative action. *Hudson Review* and *Paris Review* both lost their federal subsidies recently because they failed to attract enough minority writers.

Whereas in the past artistic institutions were considered autonomous, today artistic directors are being forced to share their decisions with foundation program directors, panel groups, and service organizations. Edward Rothstein, music critic for the *Times*, recently wrote about a report from the American Symphony Orchestra League which decreed that orchestras "should reflect more closely the cultural mix, needs, and interests of their communities." They were ordered to overhaul themselves from the repertory to the board room, and hire consultants to begin "diversity sensitivity training." Otherwise funding sources would be urged to reserve their grants for "the inclusion of certain kinds of repertoire," meaning popular, folk, and racial-ethnic expressions. As Rothstein concludes: "This is not artistic leadership; the league is actually threatening its constituency: We know what is best for orchestras, and if you orchestras don't listen, our views will be imposed; your financing depends on your compliance.... This report is a disgrace."

Indeed, it is a disgrace, but it is not an isolated disgrace. In their humanitarian effort to increase the number of minorities in companies, audiences, board rooms, and repertoires, the minions of political correctness have succeeded in imposing personnel restrictions on not-for-profit arts groups very similar to the content restrictions being sanctioned by Jesse Helms and his moral myrmidons. Both have totalitarian implications. Those who refuse to conform to the required aesthetic cleansing are not sent to labor camps, as in Stalinist Russia, but rather to an economic Gulag where they are starved of resources. But the result is similar, and so is the disgusting Orwellian technique known as "sensitivity training," where people are asked to confess to unconscious racism and brainwashed of any thought diverging from current ideological conformity. It is a pitiful development indeed when some of the very same agencies responsible for the great resurgence of high art in this country between the sixties and the nineties are now preparing the way for its extinction.

Are these politically correct methods improving the lot of minorities? Yes, I suppose they are to some extent. While the dropout rate among black college students remains inordinately high, the numbers of African-Americans entering the middle class through law, business, education, and medicine has increased dramatically. Black, female, and Latino artists have also been multiplying exponentially, and while many insist their work can only be judged by black, female, and Latino critics (more evidence of narcissism), some are impressive by any standards. One hopes, as their number and standing increase, that minority artists will come to be regarded as belonging to a fraternity of creative people rather than to any special class, gender, race, or group.

A similar hope is that the more superfluous of the new

university departments will eventually wither away when their social work is done—as Marx foresaw the withering away of the state after the fulfillment of the revolution. But even this hope is daunted by the fact that Marx's utopian prophecy was never fulfilled. All that withered away was the Soviet Union, leaving a swarm of Balkanized nations menacing each other over bristling borders.

This resembles our present condition under political correctness—a series of hostile self-absorbed enclaves in a disunited America. I first wrote about this in 1978, describing the Balkanization of theatre audiences, and things have gotten much worse in the intervening years. Few Americans share or pursue a common good. Although our treatment of minorities, though far from perfect, is as good or better than that of any nation in the world, there is more protest and complaint here than in any nation in the world. You cannot clear your throat without hurting people's feelings or cough without wounding their self-esteem. (Were Jane Austen writing today, she would call her book *Sense and Sensitivity*.) This accounts for the spread of vigilant organizations, not just monitoring hateful actions but vetting speech for evidence of anti-Semitism, sexism, racism, ageism, lookism, or homophobia. Are our skins so paper-thin that words and names have power to inflict such lasting damage? Yes, judging from campus speech restrictions and episodes like the notorious "water buffalo" incident at the University of Pennsylvania. Nietzsche's advice is still relevant today: "Life is hard to bear, but do not affect to be so sensitive."

One of the worst side effects of political correctness is the way it chokes the aesthetic atmosphere. Simply put, it's boring. The politically correct are almost invariably humor-impaired, finding racist or sexual insults even in the most innocuous jokes. The phrases they use to describe these imagined slights eventually have a numbing effect on everybody's senses but are so contagious they become a substitute for thinking. Left-wing scholars and journalists, quick enough to charge other people with racial stereotyping, riddle their own prose with PC stereotypes and clichés. Language is used as a form of incantation by people who respond to any original idea as a dangerous form of deviance.

In one important sense, political correctness is even proving to be counterproductive. When words like "racism" or "sexism" or "homophobia" are thrown around so promiscuously, they cease to have any meaning. If you are continually accusing well-meaning people of prejudice, you may cease to recognize the genuine article when you stumble on it. How many have noticed, while the media are preoccupied with earthquakes like the hurt feelings of black coeds or the incidence of date rape, that the skinhead population of the country is growing at an alarming rate? The noisy majority in the arts and the universities may be successfully pushing guilt buttons, but the much larger silent majority in the factories and on the farms is either suffering compassion fatigue or preparing a violent backlash. (The white supremacist plot for a race war in Los Angeles may be a harbinger.) That is why liberals, who support the ends of social justice, must expose the stupid means promoted by the politically correct before conservatives and reactionaries abolish ends and means together.

I confess I have no easy solutions or ready suggestions to stem the tide of this movement. At the moment it is powerfully entrenched in the present generation and the next. Anyone who works with young people knows how indoctrinated most of them are in the ABCs of political correctness, how guilty they are about their white skins and middle-class privileges. For PC spreads its tentacles not only into culture and education but into television, radio, journalism, child rearing, even the Academy Awards. A Hollywood actor can't even open an envelope anymore without mentioning the plight of the homeless or deploring the situation in Tibet.

In the preface to *The Liberal Imagination*, Lionel Trilling quoted Goethe's remark that liberals have no ideas, they only have sentiments. Obviously little has changed in the intervening years. What has changed is the virtual monopoly on ideas by the conservative camp. Trilling had cautioned liberals to take as their motto, "Lord, enlighten thou my enemies," seeing intelligent opposition as the only way to develop a sensible body of liberal thought. He did not foresee a time when the opposition would dominate thinking while liberals sat impotent, mired in sentiment or paralyzed with guilt.

The growing library of books on PC suggests that liberals may at last be awakening from their long slumber. It is incumbent on us now to spur the liberal imagination further before the darker forces in our society initiate a reaction that none of us wants. An important way to start is by recognizing that equality of opportunity is not the same as equality of achievement. The democratization of art and culture for political purposes will only make us more benighted than we are, and dumbocracy in America is presently at its height. We must support and facilitate the entry of minority groups into the mainstream, but not by tolerating comforting lies and debased standards. It is neither racist nor sexist to believe that some people are more beautiful than others, some more intelligent, some more brave, and some more talented. It is only racist and sexist if we believe those qualities exist *because* of (rather than *regardless* of) race, sex, class, or religion. Both the politically correct and their reactionary opponents share that position, the one by denying the past, the other by denying the future. Chekhov once wrote, "Great writers and thinkers must occupy themselves with politics only in order to put up a defense against politics." Lest the mindless form of politics called political correctness roll over us like a juggernaut, obliterating all serious art and original thought, we had better find that protective line of defense, and find it soon.

[1993]

PERFORMANCES

Cold Hearts
(Les Liaisons Dangereuses)

Les Liaisons Dangereuses was written in the last decades of the eighteenth century by a French career officer, Pierre-Ambroise-François Choderlos de Laclos, who, bored at his post in the Bay of Biscay, had determined to dazzle his contemporaries with a scandalous novel. Like the better-natured, more erotic eighteenth-century English pornographic romp *Fanny Hill*, *Les Liaisons Dangereuses* was an explosive charge in the age of extreme social hypocrisy, when human relations, especially between the sexes, were usually treated as occasions for romantic sensibility and good breeding. English literature of the time was dominated by sentimental tragedies (Lillo), sentimental comedies (Steele), and sentimental novels (Richardson), while in France the *comedie larmoyante* and *drame bourgeois*, in the hands of such writers as Diderot, Beaumarchais, and Voltaire, were washing the populace with unguents of delicate feeling and democratic sentiment. In such an atmosphere a remorseless tale of aristocratic intrigue, where erotic relations were less a source of pleasure or romance than an instrument of dominance, cruelty, and power, was destined to become a work of high subversion, similar to the invasions of Lenny Bruce onto the heavily guarded moral ramparts of Eisenhower's America.

Christopher Hampton's adaptation of this novel, performed in a Royal Shakespeare Company production at the Music Box, manages to preserve the coldhearted machinations of the characters while introducing a moral and historical perspective that seems at once clever and oversaturated with hindsight. Technically Hampton has achieved a considerable degree of success in transforming a Richardson-like epistolary novel (*Les Liaisons Dangereuses* has the form of a series of letters exchanged between the two protagonists) into a dramatic action without violating the plot, the theme, or the invidious nature of the characters. His one misstep, I believe, is to bring the moral paraphernalia and social indignation of a later age to bear on events of the past. Choderlos de Laclos's two central figures suffer violent ends—Valmont is killed in a duel and Merteuil is disfigured by the pox—but this is less a form of retribution than the inexorable working out of their fates. At the end of Hampton's play the tumbrils are rolling, the guillotine is preparing to fall, a whole aristocratic class will be exterminated for the symbolical peccadilloes of Valmont and Merteuil.

Bored and heartless eroticism among the upper classes may have been one of the causes of the French Revolution, but it is wrong, I think, to take the behavior of these two aristocrats as typical since their success in seduction is largely due to the innocence of their equally well-born victims. This is like suggesting a social-political convulsion could result from Don Juan's debauching of womanhood, when it is his moral indifference that makes him so very unique among his own class. La Marquise de Merteuil and Le Vicomte de Valmont are also unique creatures and for much the same reason—their imperviousness to conventional moral law. They operate in the social waters of this story like great white sharks among a school of groupers, and you do not predicate the extermination of an entire world of fish on the behavior of a single predatory species.

Apart from the final moments of the play, however, Hampton manages to control his moralizing and allow his characters the full expression of their fascinating amorality. The metaphor that frames the action is that of a game—the action begins and ends with ladies playing piquet. For Merteuil and Valmont, former lovers now devoted to helping each other achieve new conquests, sex is equivalent to a game of cards. They are the card sharps, and seductions are their hidden trumps. Valmont is intrigued by two new challenges to his seductive powers: one a fifteen-year-old convent girl named Cecile Volanges, the other a married woman famed for her virtue, La Presidente de Tourvel. Cecile offers no particular difficulty. She is in love with Le Chevalier Danceny and, under the pretext of helping to unite the young lovers, Valmont obtains the key to her room and half seduces, half forces himself on the unwitting girl. Before long she has become an adept—rather like the female innocents of English Restoration drama who, however guarded they are from the ways of the world, soon prove more lusty and insatiate in their appetites than the wildest courtesans.

La Presidente de Tourvel presents a considerably greater challenge, and Valmont's approach to her displays the finesse of a master craftsman. Like Molière's Don Juan, he first pretends to piety and, when that doesn't work, admits he's a dissolute rake reformed by her virtue. What really wins her, however, is his shrewd refusal to take advantage of her momentary weakness when, in a remarkable scene of emotional ambivalence, wavering between guilt and passion, she finally admits her love. Not long after, he has achieved his goal and is boasting about the "unprecedented" event to Merteuil. It is at this point that these two scorpions, so perfectly mated in their cold venomousness, turn on each other with stingers raised. Merteuil can accept Valmont's promiscuity as part of the game. What she cannot endure is genuine love, and Valmont, for the first time in his life, has fallen passionately in love—with Tourvel. Arguing that he is about to become a laughingstock, Merteuil insists that he break off this "unsuitable" relationship. Valmont agrees, treating Tourvel with unspeakable cruelty ("My love had great difficulty outlasting your virtue"), only to destroy Merteuil's relationship with Cecile's swain, Danceny, in revenge. The hatred of the two antagonists turns vicious and, manipulated by Merteuil, Danceny kills Valmont in a duel ("In this affair," gasps the dying Vicomte, "we are both her creatures"). Tourvel retreats to a convent and dies in delirium and convulsions. Cecile is destined for a convent too; and Merteuil, "halfway through the eighties" and looking forward to "whatever the nineties may bring," suggests that the only thing left is "to continue with the game."

Love and death have always been the staples of European literature, but not until Strindberg, and to a lesser extent Wagner, had the fatal consequences of erotic entanglements been so profoundly explored as in this singular work by Choderlos de Laclos (well, perhaps we should also salute his contemporary, the Marquis de Sade). Lacking models of a similar kind in the English tradition, Hampton has borrowed his style from the one body of literature that continually equates sex not with romance but with cruelty and power while valuing exterior reputation over inner integrity, namely Restoration comedy. His Valmont and Merteuil resemble a more ruthless Mirabel and Millamant; Valmont's servant is a cockney; and the dialogue, while lacking epigrammatic form, is a compound of wit parrying and elegant sangfroid: "You've given me great pleasure," remarks Valmont to Tourvel, "but I just can't bring myself to regret leaving you. It's the way of the world." Moreover, the play (and in this it resembles Restoration comedy even more) is almost totally lacking in any real sensual moments—with the possible exception of Cecile's deflowering, and even this is signified by a single surprised gasp. *Les Liaisons Dangereuses* represents not so much sex in the head as sex in the pancreas, composed as it is of generous secretions of acid and bile.

Still, the evening is continually engrossing, and Howard Davies's production has the sharpness of an incision. Bob Crowley has designed a world of the boudoir decorated with smokey lattices and unmade beds and open drawers spilling silks, linens, laces. The interiors are in light pastels, the costumes all white as if in contrast to the tainted bodies they cover. Alan Rickman, as Valmont, grungily bearded with a three-day Arafat growth, moves with a languor that bespeaks supreme boredom. Lacking the energy even to raise his voice—it's a marvel he can be heard at all—he sustains a performance of leonine grace and danger with an effortlessness that almost seems at times to lack dramatic tension. Lindsay Duncan as Merteuil—a woman "meant to dominate your sex and avenge my own"—is frigidly beautiful, like a glacier, and equally unlikely to melt. She is stirred only by the passion of revenge, heated only by cunning, provoked only by the hope of conquest. But I was the most impressed with Suzanne Burden as La Presidente de Tourvel, for it is she who has the opportunity to move beyond brittle technical resources into emotional deeps. Depicting Tourvel as a woman torn between uncontrollable passion for Valmont and loathing for her own feelings, Miss Burden performs the seduction scene with a wrenching reality. I have rarely seen the traditional conflict between Love and Honor more convincingly portrayed.

I must also express my admiration for the other principals in the cast: Kristin Milward, Beka Edney, Jean Anderson, Lucy Aston, Hilton McRae. Together with the playwright, the director, and the designers, they help to bring an extraordinary, though not widely known, work of literature to the attention of a popular audience. Heaven knows how this audience will receive it, since *Les Liasions Dangereuses* is not a work that speaks very warmly of humankind, and it reemerges in a corresponding age of romantic lies and democratic pieties. Even with Hampton's moralistic ending, however, the play is a bracing antidote to romanticism and sentimentality, exposing the inner labyrinths of erotic transactions, the spiritual sores that lie beneath the powdered surface of sexual relations.

[1987]

Birds and Beasts of the West
(Serious Money)

CARYL CHURCHILL writes hard-boiled, unpredictable, untidy plays, and with *Serious Money*, now playing at the Public Theatre, she is at the top of her disheveled form. I was first exposed to the left hook of this unusual English dramatist when her early work *Owners* opened at a London Fringe theatre in 1972. It was a play about rackrenting in the East End, a terse treatment of social injustice in a style of episodic realism—ironic, cold, and detached enough to disguise a subterranean fury. The arresting thing about *Owners* was not its relatively conventional form so much as its disinterested radical posture. A product of a fiercely independent mind, it offered a negative Marxist critique unblemished by positive Marxist ideology. Since that time, in such plays as *Cloud Nine*, *Fen*, and *Top Girls*, Miss Churchill has been experimenting with more fantastical techniques, but her remorseless inquest into the English social system continues unabated. *Serious Money* may be the most incisive autopsy she has yet attempted.

It is also an extremely difficult, sometimes even repellent play. *Serious Money* is a prodigiously researched examination of the workings of the world's money markets, where virtually all recognizable human feeling is subordinated to a passion for acquisition. American drama is often faulted for lacking public dimension. What's missing from *Serious Money* is any sign of private emotion except for covetousness. This, I gather, is precisely Miss Churchill's point. In the world of money, all vestiges of softer virtues—love, loyalty, friendship, family feeling, the aesthetic sense—must be ruthlessly eliminated as obstacles in the path of profit; venality is the foundation stone of political and financial empire. In *Serious Money*, Pluto and Hobbes are reincarnated in the shape of Ivan Boesky (his spirit also haunts the movie *Wall Street*) whose tribute to greed as the basis for the health and wealth of nations is the theme of the play.

The result is a dramatis personae of ruthless robots whose behavior seems as automated as the computer systems they use to conduct their corporate raids, mergers, takeovers, deals, and arbitrages. The setting for *Serious Money* might be a Pac-Man game: squeaking mouths devouring other mouths before getting gobbled up in turn. These hungry mouths are filled not only with corporate corpses but with venal epigrams: "You don't make money out of land, you make money out of money." "Being in debt is the best way to be rich." "Anyone who can buy oranges for ten and sell at eleven in a souk or bazaar has the same human nature and can go equally far." One character would like to own "a big cube of sea, right down to the bottom, all the fish, weeds, the lot, there'd be takers for that." Another prefers a square meter of space "and a section of God at the top." Corporations are in business not to produce goods but to produce money, and governments (also money-making machines) exist to facilitate the process through deregulation.

The play begins with a scene from Thomas Shadwell's Restoration comedy *The Volunteers, or The Stockjobbers* involving the disposition of stocks and patents in the City of London, as if to prove that the System through the ages hasn't changed a bit. Miss Churchill then proceeds to compose a cacophonous aural-visual opera, simultaneously conducted in three different dealing rooms, the performers being jobbers and brokers screaming numbers at each other. (Audaciously, she has written most of the work in rhymed couplets and overlapping dialogue which accentuate the noisy bedlam.) Gradually a kind of plot emerges out of the Babel of buying and selling. A corporate raider named Corman is preparing to take over an old-fashioned firm called Albion (England?) which commands the loyalty of its employees and the support of the local community. Jake Todd, an industrial spy, has died under suspicious circumstances, and Scilla, his stock-dealing sister, appears determined to discover the cause of his death.

But Scilla, cheerfully admitting she is "greedy and completely amoral," is really more interested in placing herself on the ladder of financial transaction. And though Jake may actually be a suicide, she manages through bullying and blackmail to attain a profitable position of power. Miss Churchill is a feminist, but one of her theatrical virtues (also displayed in *Top Girls*) is a capacity to create female characters as covetous and corruptible as her males (she is equally democratic toward black American dealers and African plutocrats). Perhaps the most cunning figure in the play is a Peruvian businesswoman named Jacinta Condor who, when not speculating on the London metal exchange, is selling cocaine and paying off the Contras. And perhaps the most chilling scene concerns Jacinta's unsuccessful effort to make a date with a young American banker, when both are too busy arranging deals to find an hour for lunch or dinner.

The takeover of Albion is complicated by white knights and competitive bids and a government investigation, so Corman drops his interest in the firm in return for a knighthood. As "Lord" Corman he must improve his public image. A PR consultant advises him to think of culture: "You need the National / Theatre for power, opera for decadence, / String quartets bearing your name for sensitivity and elegance, / And a fringe show with bad language for a thrill." Corman becomes chairman of the board of the National Theatre. The cause of Jake's death is never determined. Jacinta starts dealing in China. Scilla becomes a rising star on Wall Street. Other characters become ambassadors or run for president of the United States or end up in jail. And the play ends with a rousing finale called "Five More Glorious Years," a tribute to the triumph of greed under Margaret Thatcher.

It is, as someone says, a dangerous system which could crash at any minute, but it is a source of incredible, if misguided, vitality, and it drives the play. None of Miss Churchill's rapacious birds and beasts of prey has a recognizably human moment, but then neither do the cormorants of Ben Jonson's *Volpone* or Henri

Becque's *The Vultures* or Bertolt Brecht's *Saint Joan of the Stock-yards*, the satiric tradition to which *Serious Money* belongs. Like her mordant predecessors, Caryl Churchill seems to have a sneaking admiration for the foibles of cheats and charlatans. Underneath her ferocious irony lies an understanding that the worst excesses of capitalism can be exciting and engrossing, which is why the most intelligent, dynamic people today are attracted to business. But she is also conscious of how debilitating such practices can be to the brain and spirit—of how "when the trading stops, you don't know what to do with your mind."

Max Stafford-Clark's all-English production is serviceable, if not altogether satisfying. The setting is not sufficiently abstract to accommodate the almost cinematic scenic structure, and the doubling, trebling, and (in the case of Alan Corduner) even quadrupling of roles compounds the confusion of what is already a difficult-to-distinguish cast of characters. (In a company of sixteen, for some reason, eight actors play the twenty principal parts.) The production numbers have a percussive punchiness, though they occasionally look like a varsity show, and the director usually navigates effectively through the verbose maze of the rhymed verse. But the absence of a human dimension in the writing prevents the acting from becoming truly distinguished, and the plot is too complicated to be absorbed in a single sitting. As a result, *Serious Money* is not a truly successful work of theatre. But it is something considerably more important—a scathing social anatomy of the greedy scavengers feeding on the rotting economic flesh of the West.

[1987]

Twenty-first Century Hamlet
(Hamlet)

INGMAR BERGMAN and the Royal Dramatic Theatre of Sweden (known as the Dramaten) have just left these shores for Japan and the Soviet Union, after appearing at the Brooklyn Academy of Music for little more than a week with their celebrated production of *Hamlet*. Probably because it was performed without simultaneous translation, this Swedish *Hamlet* was generally shunned by American theatregoers. What a pity! It is one of the most extraordinary theatre events of our time. Bergman has rethought every character, every relationship, every scene, every moment, in exquisite detail. The result is not simply a new approach to the central role that reflects the current style of a generation—the actor-oriented pattern of English Hamlets (Olivier, Burton, Warner, and so forth)—but rather a comprehensive original reading of the entire work that prophesies the nightmares of the future. Bergman's *Hamlet* radically alters our understanding of Shakespeare's play without altering its shape, thus vindicating and somehow even purifying the basic tenets of classical reinterpretation.

Paradoxically this achievement is partly earned by acting the play in Swedish. Those familiar with *Hamlet* would have found the foreign language no obstacle to understanding (Shakespeare provides an excellent English translation). Indeed, hearing the play performed in another tongue proves an oddly liberating experience. Instead of resonating to the sound of familiar verse passages, which tend to distract you from the line of action, you are permitted to absorb the soul of the tragedy as expressed through its racing plot, psychological relationships, social arrangements, and metaphysical overtones. Shakespeare intended his poetry as a medium, not as a fetish. By demystifying the verse, this production makes the play a theatrical rather than a lyrical experience, restoring its intellectual and emotional surprise.

The element of surprise is present from the beginning, when the curtain rises on an empty stage to a tacky piano rendering of the Merry Widow waltz. Bergman's setting (designed, along with the costumes, by Göran Wassberg) consists of a thin red circle on the stage floor bisected by a thin red line, a curved bank of arc lights suspended by cables, and a double row of horizontal lights upstage. What sets each scene, aside from a few pieces of furniture, is the arrangement of lighting equipment—along with the arrangement of equipage. In the first court scene, and in scenes to follow, a chorus of ten masked figures in crimson gowns and gray perukes assumes various sculptural patterns at the back of the stage (sometimes in the same position as the patterned arc of lights), like a chorus of judges presiding over the criminal action.

Morally there is much to judge in this excessively sensual and debauched court. Claudius makes his appearance rolling across the floor with Gertrude, then taking her from behind in full view of his red-robed courtiers. After reading Fortinbras's message demanding restoration of Norway's lost lands, Claudius wipes his ass with it ("So much for him"). In the prayer scene he is cavorting with a besotted hag who later turns out to be the aging Player Queen, her lipstick-smeared face fixed in a grotesquely stupefied smirk from the strong drink Claudius has poured down her throat (underneath her red wig is a mane of white hair). As played by Börje Ahlstedt, this Claudius is truly a bloat king, his ample belly glistening with sweat, his appetites blatant and voracious.

Hamlet's entrance is accompanied by a scraping noise—he is dragging a bentwood chair on stage—and he continues to scrape at us throughout the play. In black suit, black boatneck sweater, and dark sunglasses, this Hamlet looks like a Grotowski disciple from the Left Bank. He glares at the audience from his chair, a surly, sullen, sulky brat—Hamlet as spoilsport. Peter Stormare enacts a nervous, agitated, entirely unpleasant young man, with no tenderness for anything but the Ghost and the Player King (both played by the same paternal actor) and for Horatio, who excites his strongest feelings. He is brutal with Ophelia, mauling and almost raping her in the play scene. And he kills Polonius (a bureaucratic diplomat with an omnipresent briefcase) by stabbing him through the left eye behind the arras, delivering the *coup de grace* with full knowledge of his victim's identity.

Ophelia is witness to this scene, as she witnesses almost every brutal event in this brutalized court. But this is no consumptive, sensitive suffering plant. As played by Pernilla Östergren (the promiscuous maid of *Fanny and Alexander*), she is a somewhat chunky lass, feisty and argumentative, and, until her father's death, possessed of a strong will. Gertrude gussies her up for Hamlet by rouging her lips and fitting her out with red high heels, pulling down the strap of her slip as an afterthought. Östergren plays her mad scene—in Bergman's hands a powerful study of degenerative female psychosis—in a heavy brocaded gown and marching boots, carrying the bloody handkerchief Polonius used to stanch the wound to his eye. She also carries a dangerous pair of shears, with which she cuts off large tufts of hair, and, instead of offering flowers to Gertrude and Claudius, she hands out iron nails. A central character throughout, she even appears at the rainy funeral that follows her own death. The chorus of courtiers, now wearing black morning coats and black beribboned top hats, makes a dancing exit carrying black umbrellas. Instead of the usual chiaroscuro, a harsh light illuminates the entire stage area, including water pipes and exit signs. And Ophelia materializes at the back, in bare feet, blue slip, and flowered crown—now a ghost haunting her own burial service.

Every scene astonishes, every character is fresh. The Gravedigger is the top banana of a vaudeville show, equipped with bowler hat and bulbous nose, his song accompanied by two musicians on sax and trombone. Rosencrantz and Guildenstern are Tweedledee and Tweedledum—distinguished only by Rosencrantz's dueling scar—dressed in identical orange suits and wielding identical canes. Gertrude is a lustful matron with dyed red hair, Horatio is a golden-headed wag, Osric the successor to Polonius as a windy court diplomat. As for the Ghost, he is a confused ineffectual old dear, gliding along the floor in an oversized white robe.

There are, by the way, virtually no soliloquies in this production. Hamlet's "To be or not to be" is addressed to the Player King (a sympathetic surrogate father); Claudius's "My offense is rank" is a soggy confession uttered near the supine body of his passed-out concubine; Horatio reads Hamlet's letter before the entire court. No secrets are possible in this public world, since everyone is either too feverish or too desperate to fear disclosure.

The final scene turns this public world into a global village and, in a stunning *coup de théâtre*, launches the play into a new dimension. Having watched the armies of Fortinbras contending for a tiny patch of land, Hamlet has tardily resolved to take his revenge on the man who took his father's life and wife and crown (he scrawls "BLOD" in chalk graffiti on the stage right wing leg). Hamlet's growing maturity is marked by signs of physical deterioration (Stormare is pale and sallow in the last moments of the play), but also by his ability to develop a genuine human connection—with Horatio. Yet even this relationship cannot help him circumvent catastrophe. In a marvelously staged duel scene, after he is scratched on the arm with a poisoned rapier and exchanges weapons, he stabs Laertes through the neck. He is too weak now to kill Claudius, and the King contemptuously pushes his thrust away. The Ghost enters and clutches Claudius around the waist long enough for Hamlet to run him through.

Then comes the scene that focuses and resolves Bergman's concept, with the entrance of Fortinbras following Hamlet's death. The action thus far has occurred in an unknown European capital during an indeterminate period. Now we are in familiar territory. Outfitted like a Central American military leader in beret and jackboots, and accompanied by soldiers wearing black riot helmets and brandishing semiautomatics, Fortinbras marches on stage to the earsplitting sound of rock music emanating from a ghetto blaster. Surveying the carnage, he orders the soldiers to pitch the bodies of Claudius, Gertrude, and Laertes into a pit, then signals for Horatio to be led off and shot. "Four captains" of this totalitarian brigade bear Hamlet's body "to the stage"—the stage on which the players performed before the King. Fortinbras's last lines are a media speech orated in front of klieg lights, a hand-held video camera, and a microphone. "Go bid the soldiers shoot" is followed by shatteringly loud bursts of machine-gun fire.

It is a scene of fierce intensity that reverberates from your toenails to the tips of your hair, and it helps to redefine the meaning of catharsis for our time. This *Hamlet* is true to the age in evoking a lot more terror than pity, but the purgation is the same—shocks, tremors, thrills, and welling emotion. Through terror, Bergman uses Shakespeare's play to dramatize the Second Coming (Shakespeare himself predicted slouching beasts in characters like Iago and Edmund, and plays like *King Lear*), but piercing the barbarous gloom is the gentle softening light of Ophelia. The production is not rich in memorable performances—Stormare is hardly a definitive Hamlet. Yet by focusing attention on the arc of the action rather than on virtuoso acting, it demonstrates something perhaps more important—how a unified company working under the most deliberate rehearsal conditions can fulfill the inspired vision of a brilliant director.

We are told that Bergman's *Hamlet* was rejected by the First International New York Festival of the Arts because it failed to qualify as a "twentieth century" production. That is accurate in a way the festival never intended. For Bergman's *Hamlet* is the first production of the twenty-first century—a daring probe into the tone, mood, and theatrical techniques of the future. Let us hope it is not an accurate forecast of our political future as well.

[1988]

Dressup Plays
(The Substance of Fire; Our Country's Good)

A FRIEND of mine has a name for the work of young playwrights who address adult themes and subjects by simulating the styles of more established writers (Edward Albee's *Tiny Alice* is the prime example). He calls them "dressup" plays, by analogy with the way children like to dress up in their parents' clothes—little boys wearing Daddy's keychain, little girls teetering in Mommy's high heels. The "dressup" play is a step from the "diaper" play, Benedict Nightingale's label for the romance that theatrical neophytes like to spin out of their childhood traumas. But as a generic rubric it is equally condescending and more than a little dismissive. I borrow the phrase with apologies as a useful way of describing the perfectly respectable efforts of budding playwrights marking time while trying to accumulate enough experience to write about.

Although conceived with considerably more integrity than Richard Greenberg's *Eastern Standard*—a dressup play which furbishes a jejune plot with grownup accessories—*The Substance of Fire* by Jon Robin Baitz might be considered a plausible example of the genre. Baitz is a gifted writer, and his subject—the relations between a Jewish literary intellectual and his family—is hardly territory that has been exhausted on the stage. Baitz, furthermore, approaches this relatively original material with considerable compassion and intelligence. The dressing up is largely in the formal execution, which seems to me somewhat derivative, altogether grounded, incompletely imagined. In the solid production it is receiving at Playwrights Horizons, *The Substance of Fire*, like the author's previous *The Film Society*, signals the arrival of a potentially strong talent with unimpeachably decent convictions. What's presently missing is the visionary force, the imaginative fuel that would propel his work beyond the social earnestness associated with mainstream domestic drama.

The Substance of Fire has value largely as a study of intelligence in decay. Isaac Geldhart, a refugee from Nazi Germany, runs a quality publishing house on the brink of bankruptcy. Nobody at present is showing much interest in two-volume tomes about *The Destruction of the Sephardim During the Spanish Inquisition* or reprints of B. Traven and L. Pirandello. The firm hasn't published a popular book in seven years, and Isaac's projected six-volume series on Nazi medical experiments is hardly likely to dominate the best-seller lists. The occasion for the first act is a crisis meeting of the firm's directors who are also Isaac's children: Martin who teaches landscape architecture at Vassar, Sarah who does TV commercials, Aaron who has an MBA. The issue that divides them is the publication of a potentially successful manuscript which Isaac absolutely loathes.

What distinguishes this sequence is literate book chat and reflections on the modern publishing industry. While his children criticize his extravagances—he has paid a fortune for a postcard painted by Hitler—and his apocalyptic obsessions ("It's all death camps and napalm and atrocities with you"), Isaac regards himself as an out-of-step defender of serious literature, now defunct in a Philistine world. He is losing money, he thinks, because people have changed: "There used to be some silence to life—now there's none." Simon and Schuster is being run by an oil cartel, not people of sensibility. An author like Tama Janowitz writes not a book but a dress—"for an anorexic model."

Isaac's nostalgia, however, is fading into neoconservatism—he is contemptuous not only of trash but of Stravinsky and Diaghilev—while his relations with his children can be charitably described as indifferent. Aaron is just an "accountant." Sarah he scorns for her "Neighborhood Playhouse psychology." And he coldly rejects the affectionate advances of his "gardener" son,

Martin, to the point of refusing to join him for lunch. Unwilling to deal with his financial difficulties in a realistic way, he disdains any compromise or accommodation with "some shit-ass democratic committee" telling him what to do. The act culminates in a power struggle and a stalemate which will dissolve the firm, with Sarah concluding, "You just don't know how to love."

If the play had ended there it would have constituted a well-shaded character study of a familiar New York intellectual type, grown increasingly cranky in a changing environment—many neocon prototypes spring to mind. But Baitz proves unable to face the consequences of his own invention. The second act—it takes place three and a half years later in Isaac's dilapidated apartment—is mainly an encounter between Isaac and a psychiatric social worker whom Martin has engaged to evaluate his mental competence ("It would help if you could remember the days of the week." "Why?"). Although the play continues to focus on the deterioration of this misanthropic misfit—Isaac, in an extended depression, has been unable to pay his bills—it ends with a plunge into soapsuds. Isaac dissolves in tears after telling about the extermination of his family in the Holocaust and the medical problems of his children (Martin had cancer as a child). Having burned his Hitler postcard in symbolic repudiation of his past, he makes a dinner date with the social worker, leaving his house for the first time in years.

Baitz is not the first American playwright compelled to soften a mostly unpleasant dramatic character. The redemptive conclusion of John Guare's otherwise fine *Six Degrees of Separation* was recently and drastically revised by the scam artist on whom the work was based. Instead of asking his victims for help and forgiveness, as in the play, he's currently under a restraining order for trying to extort money from the playwright through threats on his life. In the American theatre, either for progressive or commercial reasons (they're usually the same), consistency of character is often less compelling than moral rehabilitation. *The Substance of Fire* has good performances from Ron Rifkin as Isaac, his British-Yiddish inflections applied like a vocal yarmulke, and from Patrick Breen, loose and effortless as Martin, while the director, Dan Sullivan, along with designers John Lee Beatty (sets), Jess Goldstein (costumes), and Arden Fingerhut (lights), create an illusion of size on a small stage. As for the playwright, he undoubtedly has a fine future ahead of him once he gets a fit on his own clothes.

Our Country's Good by Timberlake Wertenbaker wears the clothes of Bertolt Brecht and Caryl Churchill. Based on Thomas Keneally's novel *The Playmaker*, an historical tale about a group of eighteenth-century English convicts in an Australian penal colony enacting Farquhar's comedy *The Recruiting Officer*, it's been turned into a moral tale about theatre's civilizing influence on unlettered unfortunates. In his Pyramus and Thisbe sequences, Shakespeare proved a lot more inspired, if a lot less inspirational, about the rehearsal procedures of unlettered rustics. And Brecht and Churchill are considerably more tough-minded about the character of the underclass, which is why *Our Country's Good* strikes me as a dressup play. *Our Country's Good* has won a lot of awards in London and will undoubtedly win a lot more here. That's probably the best way to describe it—as an award-winning play. I've read it twice and seen it twice, first in Hartford, more recently in the revised Hartford Stage Company production at the Nederlander in New York. The Broadway version is more finished, but it still left me squirming. This is one of those works that instead of growing on you, grows off.

I failed to find a single believable character in the play, no one able to arouse any new understanding. The officers are either benignly tolerant or malignly bigoted, the exception being a Provost Marshal who agonizes over his inhumanity to man, while the convicts (played by the same actors) are largely conceived as nature's noblemen and women unjustly treated by a repressive society. As for the plot, this is fattened with repetitive debates over the value of convicts staging a play, the difficulty of rehearsing roles under the threat of execution, the growing love of a male officer for a female convict, and the boring conscience pangs of the Provost Marshal.

The writing is literate and a good deal more serious than the production, which struck me as artificial. There is some spine in Miss Wertenbaker's prose; Mark Larnos's direction weakens it. Virtually every scene, no matter how grim, concludes with a directorial tag—a look, a smirk, a grimace, a twirl—so that the audience finds itself being manipulated into applause, even when the issue is a hanging. The lights are turned down during scene changes; the Brechtian style demands they be turned up. Even costumes changes occur in the dark, though much depends on our knowing the roles are interchangeable. And Christopher Barreca's fine design of a ship reduced to its skeletal ribs, instead of being used as an organic part art of the show, functions mainly as decoration.

As for the acting, only two or three performances rise above the level of reppy competence: Tracey Ellis brings a delicate minimalism to the part of Mary, the semivirgin beloved of the fresh-faced Lieutenant (sensitively performed by Peter Frechette) who rehearses the convicts. And Cherry Jones contributes strength and resolution to the role of an unrepentant, rotten-toothed renegade gradually brought under the humanizing sway of Thespis (for the record, I should mention that Ms. Jones acts with my company, which is also the reason I'm convinced that her occasional gallery playing must be directorially imposed).

One ends up feeling cheated of enjoying the full version of *The Recruiting Officer* rather than seeing rehearsal snippets, for Farquhar's play, unlike award-winning works of the contemporary theatre, is robust, colorful, and full of surprise. And that, I guess, is the fundamental limitation of the dressup play, that it doesn't surprise. The purpose of dramatic art, in my view, is to tell the truth in an imaginative way, and the truth is always unpredictable. Lopahin destroys a beautiful cherry orchard and dispossesses the Ranevsky family—but he is an entirely decent fellow, the only one in the district who does a full day's work. Mother Courage represents Greed battening on War, and she's ultimately responsible for the death of her three children—but she also embodies the courage to be in the face of persuasive arguments for extinction. These are characters imagined by dramatic artists. They show that the human soul will not be tailored to the rigid measurements of politics and morality. They are created by writers wearing their own clothes.

[1991]

In the Belly of "La Bête"
(La Bête; Assassins)

STUART OSTROW, producer of David Hirson's *La Bête* at the Eugene O'Neill, is gaining a reputation as the Don Quixote of Broadway, not for his defiance of the commercial system, but rather—and this is a paradox—for trying to restore some of its abandoned values. He is quixotic in his determination to produce plays only if he believes in them. And he stubbornly refuses to cycle his shows (as even Neil Simon does now) through the resident theatre circuit, preferring the traditional method of producing in out-of-town theatre districts before opening in New York. With *M. Butterfly* this strategy succeeded because the work was a mixture of middlebrow ointments, an attractive concoction to those seeking light mental massage. With the more demanding *La Bête*, however, he has run into a hailstorm of hostile reviews and is fighting a losing battle to keep the play open.

It is amusing to think that a comedy of manners written in the manner of Molière—or rather of Richard Wilbur's translations of Molière—could be assumed to have a chance of surviving on Broadway without benefit of a star (Ron Silver departed the show in Boston). For one thing, it is composed in rhymed iambic couplets. For another, it is a highly literate *jeu d'esprit* about a seventeenth-century acting company residing (like Molière's early troupe and including some of its more famous members) at the estate of the Prince de Conti in Pezenas, France. This is hardly the stuff of Broadway dreams, though the play will probably become a staple in future schedules of nonprofit theatre companies. Its appeal is limited largely to educated audiences with some background in dramatic literature, who, I sense, will prove enthusiastic, if not fanatical, about its virtues.

A member of that species myself, I am moderately attracted to *La Bête*, though it strikes me as a bit of a stunt. I feel much more excited about its author. Anyone capable of impersonating so well the wit and style of another dramatist has the essential gift of *mimesis* and is capable of applying it not just to literature but to life. Hirson is a young American of thirty-three with a background in scholarship (studying at Yale and Oxford); his only other creative work is an adaptation of a Scarlatti comic opera. He seems to be steeped in the seventeenth and eighteenth centuries rather as Maxwell Anderson was steeped in the Elizabethan period, but the result is a headier brew and a more authentic evocation of an age. Anderson was less poet than poetaster, creating a clubfooted blank verse which approached sublimity only in the lyrics of "September Song." Hirson has an acerbic tongue and a superb ear, possibly trained by readings in Alexander Pope (*La Bête* also bears a resemblance to the *Dunciad*). Though not dissimilar from Prokofiev's ambitions in his *Classical* Symphony, it is essentially the work of a virtuoso interpreter rather than an original creative artist, undertaken with such energy and éclat that the author succeeds in devising a wholly convincing neoclassical artifact.

He has not succeeded in fashioning a convincing neoclassical plot or fully fleshed Molièrian characters. *La Bête* is a situation rather than an action about the intrusion into a dedicated theatre company—led by the actor-playwright Elomire (a conscious anagram)—of a self-regarding troubadour named Valère. Just as Elomire resembles not so much the good-natured Molière as the sour Alceste, so Valère reminds us of *Le Misanthrope*'s invincibly smug Oronte, and almost the entire first act is taken up with a twenty-five-minute monologue by this self-infatuated self-promoter as Elomire and his friend Bejart look on in disgust. Much of the second act consists of performing his ridiculous play, "The Parable of Two Boys from Cadiz," using actors from the company at Prince Conti's behest. Valère is wholly preoccupied with language—or rather with defiling language. He has invented a term called "verbobos" to describe his ugly neologisms, and he is eager to pass off his play as a comment on the way mediocrity is eclipsing excellence in France, unconscious that his own work is a prime example.

Enchanted by Valère, the Prince wants him in the company—over Elomire's strenuous objections. When Elomire makes the case that Valère's parable represents the very mediocrity the play is condemning, Conti rebukes him testily for daring to lecture a Prince. After he orders Elomire to accept Valère in his troupe,

Elomire decides to resign. The opportunistic actors, fearful of losing a comfortable refuge, abandon him. In an epilogue Elomire chooses penury and exile rather than compromise his artistic principles:

> Does any way less radical exist
> To keep ideals from being trivialized?
> The only way I know is to *resist;*
> Autonomy cannot be compromised.

The tone is a bit shrill, the expression a touch self-righteous, and Elomire the moral artist is nowhere near as engaging as Valère the makeout artist. (Molière had more complicated feelings about his own uncompromising idealist, Alceste, believing that such fanatics, while praiseworthy for their principles, have the capacity to destroy society.) I also wish the playwright had done more with another of his characters, Madeleine Bejart, who in actuality was Molière's mistress and the adoptive mother of his wife, Armande. Still, it is clear that Hirson is frying bigger fish than seventeenth-century poets and poetasters, that officially endorsed mediocrity is a theme he trusts we will recognize as familiar.

La Bête has been given an extremely finished production by that master of surfaces, Richard Jones. Abetted by the extraordinary sets and costumes of his close collaborator, Richard Hudson, Jones has tilted the play in a manner that positions the actors in a world of bizarre proportions. A series of drops on which are scribbled *Blah blah blah* prepare us for Valère's mutilation of the language, and the terrific white set, virtually empty except for gold scallop shell chairs and classical busts and Jennifer Tipton's blazing lighting, gives us a crazy sense of entrapment in forced perspective. The costumes are completely outrageous, both in shape and color—the Prince's ermined train so long it has to be carried behind him by four footmen. And the performances proceed at a manic pace that tests the speed and agility of the human tongue.

Among these performances there are splendid turns, particularly by Michael Cumpsty as a glowering Elomire, Johann Carlo as a tongue-tied Dorine, and Dylan Baker as Conti, a Prince with rotten teeth, alternately gracious and grating, effete and offensive. As Valère, Tom McGowan was entrusted with a hugely difficult starring role on very short notice; he should be cited for valor. An actor of sizable proportions expanded by a massive wig who preens around stage in leopard pantaloons, McGowan gives an entertaining performance, at times an irrepressible one—like a shameless drama student in a solo cabaret or a loquacious queen camping at a Greenwich Village party. If he seems at times to be inhabiting the part less than rending and shredding it—if there's something just a bit frightened hovering behind his eyes—that's understandable given the abruptness of the assignment. I enjoyed myself at this show. I hope its inevitably brief run and potential losses don't discourage Ostrow from taking further risks—and I hope one of them will be Hirson's next play. It's not often an American writer displays such a passion for language or the gifts with which to celebrate it. One must use these words hesitantly in a profession where success is measured by money, but regardless of its commercial fate *La Bête* represents the successful debut of an auspicious talent.

Assassins is the latest work of another auspicious talent, Stephen Sondheim, who wrote the music and lyrics to a book by John Weidman. In its present incarnation at Playwrights Horizons, it is a singularly bizarre performance. Sondheim has never been known for timidity in choosing material for musicals. *Sweeney Todd*, after all, was about a barber who sold off the dismembered parts of his murdered victims for consumption at dinner tables. With *Assassins*, however, he has chosen to memorialize tunefully the careers of that coterie of killers who aimed a variety of lethal weapons at the hides of American presidents, with John Wilkes Booth presiding as the tutelary spirit. People have reacted to his project rather like the stunned audience in Mel Brooks's *The Producers* after listening to "Springtime for Hitler" sung by a high-stepping Nazi chorus.

The difference is that Zero Mostel was purposely trying to achieve a flop; Sondheim's flop was thrust upon him. But what could he expect when he begins his show with a carny singer in a shooting gallery warbling "Hey, pal, come here and kill a president" and ends it with the sentiment that "Everybody's got the right to be different...Everybody's got the right to their dreams." One suspects that irony is intended. In fact, the disjunction between form (musical comedy) and content (murder) leaves the evening dripping with irony, not all of it planned. Sondheim's songs, for the most part, could be detached from their context and handed to disc jockeys, arousing the disquieting impression that these aberrant historical figures have been resurrected partly for the sake of selling platinum records. The assassins of *Assassins* are lurking in Tin Pan Alley.

Weidman's perfunctory book tracks the careers of John Wilkes Booth (who shot Lincoln), Charles Guiteau (who killed Garfield), Leon Czolgosz (who assassinated McKinley), Giuseppe Zangara (who tried to kill FDR), Samuel Byck (who planned to crash a plane into Nixon's White House), Lynette "Squeaky" Fromme and Sara Jane Moore (who both made attempts on Ford), and John Hinckley (who shot Reagan). The show concludes with Lee Harvey Oswald in the Texas Book Depository. *Assassins* contends that the common motive of all these people was a passion for notoriety, that Booth, for example, "killed a country because of bad reviews" ("Lincoln, who got mixed reviews, because of you now gets only raves"). Not political conviction, then, but celebrity is the spur, a view that even informs the scenes where Booth persuades Oswald to eschew suicide and make a name for himself instead ("You can close the New York Stock Exchange"). It is history seen through the eyes of show business. What is difficult to determine is how much of this is intended as mockery. Ironies begin to cohere only in the scenes featuring the incompetent failures. An imaginary encounter between Squeaky Fromme (Annie Golden) and Sara Moore (Debra Monk) is genuinely funny, replete with Manson stories and a shared love of Kentucky Fried Chicken, and so is the passion of Samuel Byck (Lee Wilkof in a Santa Claus suit) for Bernstein musicals. Still, the whole enterprise seems a little desperate, as does the staging of the normally confident Jerry Zaks. Scorsese's *Taxi Driver* provided much more insight into the motives of political assassins—and Altman's *Nashville* accompanied such insights with better music.

[1991]

Emerging British Directors
(The Liar; The Love of Three Oranges; The Good Person of Sichuan)

IT IS commonly assumed that theatre in our time is dominated by arrogant auteur directors—not without considerable grumbling from those who believe this development has usurped the traditional authority of playwrights and actors. But a great variety of different directors work in today's theatre, most of them relatively self-effacing. In a recent article, Oscar Brockett identifies at least four distinct directorial categories: 1) *Interpretive*, stemming from Stanislavsky, where the director remains faithful to the playwright's instructions (Elia Kazan, Alan Schneider, Jerry Zaks, Gregory Mosher); 2) *Translative*, stemming from Meyerhold, where the director may depart from the literal text to capture its spirit through metaphorical probes (Peter Stein, Ariane Mnouchkine, Giorgio Strehler, Andrei Serban, Ingmar Bergman); 3) *Found Object*, stemming from Brecht, where a play is reshaped according to the director's political, social, or aesthetic idiosyncracies (Lee Breuer and Mabou Mines, Elizabeth LaCompte and the Wooster Group); and 4) *Performance Art*, where the director is the author of the entire work (Robert Wilson, Martha Clarke, Tadashi Suzuki, Tadeusz Kantor).

Among these approaches it is the "interpretive" directorial mode that continues to dominate mainstream American theatre, which has always valued plot, character, and performance, while the current experimental procedures featuring visual ideas and thematic explorations still put conservative critics and audiences into spasms. Previously, with the notable exception of Peter Brook (at first a "translative" director, now one experimenting with "found objects" and "performance art"), the English theatre has been the traditional home of "interpretive" directors, whether staging classics or new plays. It is the subsidized stages of Europe and the Orient, not the West End or English repertory theatres, that have proved most hospitable to radical postmodernist techniques. Now this situation seems to be changing. As one who has often criticized English theatre—and its pervasive influence on ours—for stuffiness and conventionality, I am glad to admit that British directors are finally developing their own innovative styles.

You won't find any confirmation of this in Peter Hall's production of *The Merchant of Venice* at the 46th Street Theatre. Even critics who have praised his version concede that it fails to provide new insight into a play that shrieks for reinterpretation. Hall's is a picture-book production—decorated with illustrations and paintings from the Modern Reader's Shakespeare. The characters are costumed like engravings from nineteenth-century theatre, and the action is set in a spanking-clean Venetian piazza, sullied only by a single homeless beggar. The actors are identified alphabetically as the "Peter Hall Company," but like his recent "company" production of *Orpheus Descending*, this *Merchant* is clearly an occasion for a star performance. Too bad it doesn't have one. Dustin Hoffman has been cast in the part of Shylock, but he leaves no signature on the role. Few of the English performers bother to make anything but rhythmic sense of the verse—they act exclusively with their mouths and resonators—and Hoffman has curiously chosen to given an elocutionary performance too. But he lacks the vocal equipment. His youthful Shylock is without size, edge, power, or point of view. Luther Adler portrayed Shylock as a sorely tried victim, pushed to extremes by a vicious gentile society; Morris Carnovsky interpreted him as a venerable Talmudic scholar; Laurence Olivier conjured up a shrewd Victorian businessman. But Hoffman bleeds all color out of the part, turning Shylock into Willy Loman with a skull cap in a costume version of *Death of a Salesman* (*Death of a Merchant?*).

The only juice in this production is provided by spittle. Antonio and Gratiano spit on Shylock's head. Honing his knife in preparation for drawing his side of human beef, Shylock spits on his shoe. Leaning down to cut through his victim's breast, he expels a retaliatory gob into Antonio's face. Arguably, there's enough hawking, spraying, and spewing in this production to fill the Croton reservoir. But the only thing resembling a dramatic moment comes when Lorenzo expresses exasperation over Lancelot Gobbo. Geraldine James plays Portia like an angular, fidgety, bossy feminist; Leigh Lawson's Antonio has overtones of Jesus on the cross; Peter-Hugo Daly's Lancelot Gobbo is stock-company Dickens. In fact, the only thing that kept me sentient during this tiresome evening was admiring how English actors could add so many syllables to a simple word like "o-c-e-an."

Following this matinee performance, I flew to London for a weekend expecting more of the same and was pleasantly surprised by the three productions I saw there. At the Old Vic, Jonathan Miller—in his continuing effort to introduce the British public to unfamiliar plays from the continent—has directed *The Liar* (*Le Menteur*), an obscure comedy by Corneille. British versions of classical French drama are usually done like Restoration comedy or set in modern drawing rooms. Miller's *Liar* proved more faithful to the Gallic spirit. Played within an essentially white Magritte-like set by Peter J. Davison, which exposed the wooden and canvas construction of its canted doors and broken arches, *The Liar* was offered as a self-enclosed piece of stagecraft with presentational performances—particularly by Alex Jennings in the title role—that were unabashedly theatrical.

The play is a trifle in rhymed Alexandrines. Even Ranjit Bolt, the translator, calls it "gloriously unrepentantly superficial in the high baroque manner." The program note, entitled "Trivial Plays for Serious People," employs elaborate and rather unconvincing historical arguments to justify the play's frivolity. Molière would have taken a character like Dorante, the compulsive liar, and turned him into an obsessive *malade* with a spiraling effect on all around him. Corneille simply uses Dorante's lying as a device for postponing the romantic pairings at the end. Why exhume the piece then? Probably to display Miller's brilliant visual imagination and deft control of comic timing and characterization, or, more likely, to prepare for a production of Corneille's more weighty *L'Illusion Teatrale* to be directed by Richard Jones later in the season.

Richard Jones is one of those young English directors—others are two more Miller protégés, Steven Pimlott and Roger Michell, as well as the National's Deborah Warner and Nicholas Hytner—who have recently been exposing the British stage to imported theatre techniques. Jones has been deeply influenced by Meyerhold (an arcane name to an English theatre that just recently discovered Stanislavsky), and his two successes at Miller's Old

Vic (Feydeau's *A Flea in Her Ear* and an Ostrovsky adaptation called *Too Clever by Half*) were traditional farces subjected to expressionist exaggeration. I saw his production of Prokofiev's *Love of Three Oranges* at the English National Opera, and it confirmed the reputation of this imaginative institution as the center for the greatest directorial daring in the British theatre. This is the version that features the "scratch and sniff" cards designed to provide olfactory accompaniment to the citric quest of the opera. But although this gimmick attracted most of the publicity, it is the extreme playfulness of the show that makes it so appealing. With the Brothers Quay contributing the freakish outsized sets and Sue Blaine the farfetched costumes, this musical Gozzi adaptation seemed to be a cross between *The Wizard of Oz*, *Alice in Wonderland*, and *Monte Python*, with a bit of Christmas pantomime and Russian constructivism thrown in for good measure. One example of Jones's mischievous watercloset wit: the bogeyman Farfarello appears as a demonic farting machine, and the entire chorus confronts him wearing World War I gas masks.

Perhaps the strongest production I saw on this trip, however, was Deborah Warner's treatment of Brecht's *The Good Person of Sichuan* at the National Theatre. This play is better known as *The Good Woman of Setzuan* but, although "good person" is a more accurate rendering of Brecht's *gute mensch*, I suspect it was retitled partly for feminist reasons: Warner provides the work with powerful contemporary reverberations. Using the rarely produced "Santa Monica" version, which Brecht revised when living in California, the production has the selfish flier, Yang Sun, end up not as Shen Te's foreman but rather as an opium addict screaming for a fix, while Shen Te's profiteering includes adventures in the drug trade. Sue Blaine's design sets the action under what appears to be a demolished section of Waterloo Bridge (Brecht's "poor" are not identified as the "homeless," but the ruined environment is festooned with shattered bicycles which recall the recent massacre in Tiananmen Square).

A program note designates Sichuan as "half-Westernized." The production goes this more than half by thoroughly anglicizing every aspect of the action. The three gods appear first in bowlers, macs, and spats, Wang the water seller speaks with a Scottish burr, the barber Shu Fu is costumed in white clogs and a black suit, with a white carnation in his buttonhole, Yang Sun's mother is a British mum in a pink hat and shawl. The only Oriental to be seen on stage, in fact, is a little Chinese boy rooting around in a rubbish bin for food.

I felt a little momentary resentment over this further proof of how English theatre tends to absorb everything foreign into its own culture—and I was initially repelled by the way a "poor" play was being spread out all over the rich Olivier stage. By the second part, however, I was won over to Warner's concept by the strength of the acting and the consistency of the idea. Fiona Shaw's Shen Te embodies the subtle feminist implications of a production staffed largely with women by playing this warm-hearted prostitute as a physically unappealing human being—a bony, awkward schoolgirl in a unisex haircut and a print dress. Like the other women in the play, she doesn't display much softness or feminity; in fact, she's much more convincing as her alter ego, Shui Ta, the male "cousin" who saves the softhearted Shen Te from bankruptcy. Attired in a black suit, red tie, and white mask, Shaw plays Shui Ta like a gum-chewing Mafia hood with a pencil moustache and spiv accent, yet all the while managing to inform the role with a pervasive despair.

What's lacking in Warner's production is the naive simplicity of Brecht's parable which—like so many plays in his later period—was based on the conventions of oriental theatre. Yet there's a lot of fire in the evening; at times the director's social indignation even seems to surpass the playwright's. The production has not been very well received, possibly because the English public has never been very fond of Brecht. But with the aid of Michael Hoffmann's excellent translation and the uniformly strong acting of the entire cast, Deborah Warner here manages to consolidate her place in the forefront of the directors who are mercifully changing the face of English theatre.

[1990]

Public and Private History
(Henry IV)

THE two parts of *Henry IV* in Joseph Papp's Shakespeare Marathon consume six hours at the New York Public Theater. This puts the production on a scale with the Royal Shakespeare Company's *War of the Roses*, Peter Brooks's *Mahabharata*, Robert Wilson's *Einstein on the Beach*, the Paris and Hartford *Peer Gynt*—all those theatrical epics created on the assumption that modern audiences have iron backsides. Perhaps because my own bottom is less pneumatic than it used to be, I found this latest endurance test exhausting—not without rewards, but generally lacking in depth perception. JoAnne Akalaitis showed great inventiveness in her approach to a lesser play (*Cymbeline*), possibly because that mythological romance was more congenial to her extravagant imagination. She captures some of the historical sweep and grandeur of the *Henrys* but fumbles badly their comic exuberance.

This is unfortunate because *Henry IV* is not just a historical chronicle, like *Richard II* or *Henry VI*. It is also a sublime comedy, doubtless Shakespeare's greatest. The political and military efforts of Worcester, Northumberland, Glendower, Douglas, *et al.* to loosen Henry's already shaky hold on his crown have little interest for a modern audience—*Beyond the Fringe* ridiculed the stiffness of such historical confrontations ("Oh saucy Worcester") almost thirty years ago. There is still fascination in the relationship between Hal and his father, as well as in the rivalry between Hal and Hotspur. Yet what really distinguishes these plays are not the alarums and excursions of the nobles but rather the antic ribaldry of Falstaff and the evolution of the waggish Prince who rousts with him into the priggish King who sends him packing. These two roles have not been well cast at the Public, and they have been directed with all the charm and gaiety of a prison chaplain administering last rites.

It is a common assumption of scholars that Falstaff escaped from Shakespeare—as later Mother Courage was to escape from

Brecht. Designed to act the Vice in a Morality play that might have been called *The Rehabilitation of a Wayward Prince*, this obese, gluttonous, lying whoremaster was probably originally conceived as a bad angel who leads the hero from his true path. In Part I, Falstaff and Hotspur are intended to exemplify the poles of the military spirit (cowardice and sloth versus chivalry and courage). In Part II, Falstaff and the Chief Justice are meant to represent the poles of civic behavior (disorder and misrule versus order and justice). As for Hal, he bears a resemblance to the prodigal son of Morality plays, prone to riotous living, continuously tested and tempted, until his redemptive evolution into an ideal ruler—ready to try his newfound virtue on the fields of Agincourt.

If Shakespeare had merely realized his moral design, however, *Henry IV* would have been as rousing as *Everyman* or *The Castell of Perseverance*. But Falstaff was conceived in such a fever of inspiration that he ran away with the show. He is a Vice figure, all right, but his vices are so extravagant that they achieve Rabelaisian size, while his lies are not an end in themselves so much as a way of exercising an irrepressible imagination. Falstaff is a unique figure of comedy in being both satirist and scapegoat, jester and jest—"not only witty in myself," as he says, "but the cause that wit is in others."

This causal attribute starts with his appearance. He is a monstrous joke of nature—a nimble mind imprisoned in a "tub of guts." Discovered fast asleep, he is a creature of the night, a minion of the moon as well as a master of language, unequaled in his control of simile, metaphor, and improvisation. His indifference to law and order and the venerableness of institutions is at the same time dangerous and liberating—what Mark Van Doren described as "the kiss to common sense behind the back of respectability." Or as George Orwell put it, defining what he called the "Sancho Panza view of life," "He is your unofficial self, the voice of the belly protesting against the soul."

Louis Zorich, who plays the part at the Public, looks like Falstaff, with his bloated belly and white face hairs, and sounds like Falstaff, with his sonorous rolling voice. But he lacks Falstaff's vital energy. On first appearance he is spread across a bed snoring, with Hal at his feet, surrounded by a bunch of empty beer cans. This is promising, and the early tavern scenes carry a certain Breughelesque roughness, with characters fighting, farting, firking, and foining on stage, sometimes in threes. Still, there's no real joy in the horseplay and foreplay; and there's not much gusto or mischief in Zorich's Falstaff. He's middle class and middle range, domesticated and tame, like the impostor of the same name in *The Merry Wives of Windsor* (for which he would have been better cast). Shakespeare's joke is not that Falstaff lacks desire but that his desire has outlived performance. Zorich's Falstaff has outlived desire as well; he shows none of the melancholy of a young heart in a decaying body.

As for his accomplices, Peto and Bardolph, they are represented as a dwarf and a giant, while Pistol is a terrorist on a moped with a machete at his belt, brandishing grenades—less a cowardly braggart than a dangerous guerrilla, possibly left over from the director's version of *The Screens*. Mistress Quickly is a feminist scold, Doll Tearsheet a slatternly screech, Poins a Latino (Hal asks him, "Must I marry your *seester*?" and he answers *"Nunca, nada"*). As for Hal, played by Thomas Gibson, he is a rather callow youth—handsome but awkward, without the intellectual armor required to tilt with Falstaff (he's better in the scenes with his father). Gibson's Hal lacks what Kent sees in the face of Lear: authority. There's not a hint that he'll eventually grow up to be Laurence Olivier or Kenneth Branagh leading armies through France on Saint Crispin's Day.

The recruits in the induction scenes carry blunderbusses and carbines—one of them wears a tire around his neck suggesting a Kentucky necklace—which is typical of the way Akalaitis mixes styles and periods and ideas throughout the production. The effect is sometimes arresting, sometimes disorienting. One moment we're in Elizabethan England, the next in Bush's America. The robbery at Gadshill is staged like a silent-film farce; Quickly and Tearsheet are arrested by Victorian bobbies; York and the Lord Chief Justice are accompanied by jackbooted bodyguards armed with machine guns; a child is seen on stage at the beginning, turning the pages of a comic book (his corpse is later seen on the field at Shrewsbury); Falstaff, his Boy, Bardolph, and Peto are discovered smoking pot in an abandoned car seat. It's as if we've been placed in a time-space machine and whirled in several directions at once—maneuvers that are unobjectionable unless they're used to call attention to themselves, which is often the case here. They certainly call attention to the artificiality of the battle scenes, which are performed in conventional cut-and-thrust style against the background of war movies.

My quarrel with this production is that it's theatrical without being dramatic. George Tsypin's design, supplemented by John Boesche's projections and Jennifer Tipton's lighting, is a kind of flexible erector set that transforms into a variety of scenic modules. While it's versatile, the scenic surround rarely provides the show with a unified metaphor. (Tsypin's design for *Cymbeline* was considerably more organic.) But then Akalaitis's directorial ideas seem to lack any consistent purpose other than to surprise. Some scenes play very well: Hotspur's teasing banter with his wife, Lady Percy, and his ridicule of Glendower's supernatural powers; King Henry's morbid rage at discovering Hal with his crown. And although Part II seems underdirected, the production is rarely boring. Still, Akalaitis's work is oddly uninflected and uninterpreted; her contribution is mainly visual and stylistic, with perfunctory nods in the direction of pacifism or multiculturalism.

The acting, too, is pretty much a mixed bag. Jared Harris, who looks and sounds a lot like his father Richard, plays Hotspur with splenetic wit and manly vigor, while Larry Bryggman—hunched over like a depressed and guilty buzzard—has strong moments as the King. Lisa Gay Hamilton is a fine Lady Percy, enchanting when her husband is alive and affecting after his death. She displays unusual access to her emotions. I also admired Richard Russell Ramos, Rodney Scott Hudson, and Arnold Molina in lesser roles. But the most powerful performance of the evening comes from the composer Philip Glass, whose staccato, mournful jazz rhythms heighten the comedy and deepen the history, providing the dimensions often missed by the actors.

I saw this production of *Henry IV* soon after the conclusion of the Gulf War. There is much that is relevant to Operation Desert Storm in the way Shakespeare's characters prepare for battle and engage each other on the field. That potential makes the failed opportunities of this *Henry IV* all the more disappointing. I don't doubt that the war was very much on the minds of the company in rehearsal, but for all the visual contemporary references, only once did this production seem to be saying something to our time—when Falstaff, hearing of rebel army movements, remarks, "You may buy land now as cheap as stinking mackerel." Even as long ago as the early fifteenth century, war had the capacity to depress the real estate market.

[1991]

More Yuppie Realism
(Lips Together, Teeth Apart)

Lips Together, Teeth Apart is the most accomplished expression thus far of Yuppie Realism, an aesthetic now dominating non-musical American theatre with the encouragement and endorsement of certain influential New York critics. Literate and sophisticated, Yuppie Realism almost invariably focuses on upwardly mobile middle-class professionals, usually on vacation, in the act of exchanging witticisms while examining faulty relationships and compromised principles. Although Yuppie Realism will touch on serious subjects—primarily AIDS, homosexuality, and the mistreatment of women—it mirrors an essentially narcissistic society. Rarely, if ever, do plays of this type acknowledge that deficiencies of personal behavior have anything to do with any wider failures than political incorrectitude. Yuppie Realism, in short, is simply romantic wit comedy with a message, where the audience is allowed to pay for its entertainment with a dollop of liberal guilt.

Although also divided in tone, Terrence McNally's highly acclaimed play has considerably more consistency of purpose than Richard Greenberg's *Eastern Standard,* and although equally prone to cleverness, it succeeds in combining wisdom and wisecracks better than Wendy Wasserstein's *Heidi Chronicles.* McNally belongs to an older generation of playwrights than most other Yuppie Realists and therefore salts his work with more experience. His insider's knowledge of theatre (including opera) informs the jaundiced satiric perspective from which he regards his material. Formerly a disciple of Tennessee Williams, making radical raids on American sexual mores from the outer margins of society, he now seems, like other playwrights in this movement, to be writing in the vein of Philip Barry—wry, ironic, and lyrical comedies seasoned by middle-class rationality and urban angst.

The first time I tried to see *Lips Together, Teeth Apart* at the Manhattan Theatre Club, it was under water. A main had broken in the theatre, the stage was drenched, and the electrical system had been shorted. When I returned several months later to see the piece with everything in working order (though with two replacements in the cast), I was better able to appreciate the ironic appropriateness of the cancellation. Catastrophes associated with water constitute the central metaphor of the play. John Lee Beatty's realistic setting, a wooden deck located in front of three glass doors of a Fire Island vacation house, features a distant view of beach and ocean as well as a downstage swimming pool. The pool was previously used by a character now dead from AIDS, and the play climaxes in the death of an anonymous homosexual, seen on the beach, who commits suicide by drowning.

In a sense you could say all the characters are drowning, though the mortal condition of the two couples who comprise the dramatis personae is revealed only gradually through a haze of pranks and banter. When the action begins we hear a quartet from *Così fan tutte* resounding from the stereo next door, and the plot suggests the kind of sexual swapping that characterizes Mozart's opera. The parallel is not complete—one of the characters, Sam Truman, is the brother of John Haddock's wife, Chloe. But Haddock has had an affair with Sam's wife, Sally, about which Sam is vaguely aware.

This suggests a "relationship" play, and that's what it is, although McNally occasionally has bigger fish to fry—or drown. *Lips Together, Teeth Apart* is intended as a poem of desperation with all the characters on edge about something in their lives. Both couples are ill-matched. John characterizes his relationship with Chloe as "New England's longest-running fecund shotgun marriage," and Sally, inquiring about the meaning of "fecund," confesses that, after numerous failures to parturiate ("I can reproduce, I'm just unable to deliver them"), she is pregnant again, even though her husband is frightened of having children.

Chloe, a talkative guest of the Trumans, demonstrates the tyranny of unnecessary cares by bustling around the deck with a variety of canapés and courses which nobody wants to eat. And her husband, John, for his part, is afflicted with cancer of the esophagus, a fatal fact revealed early to the audience and to the other characters at the end of the play (he didn't want to ruin their weekend).

John's initial confession of illness is actually spoken to Sam who doesn't hear it. Sam stands frozen on stage with his hand in the air, a technique of revealing secret thoughts employed on occasion by the other three characters as well. It is a convention first employed by Eugene O'Neill in *Strange Interlude* (and properly satirized by Groucho Marx in *Animal Crackers*). It was awkward then; it is awkward now. But since McNally's ear for civilized discourse is considerably more precise than O'Neill's, it is a minor flaw in an otherwise expressive play. On the other hand, the unheard soliloquy—once a poetic method of taking the audience into your confidence—has since become a convention of soap opera. And like O'Neill's play, *Lips Together, Teeth Apart* at times skirts perilously close to sudsy dishwater—a kind of *Strange Interlude* for suburbanites, an infidelity play for the leisure classes.

Even though at times the characters seem to have little more at stake than not being able to make Black Russians without Kahlua (there is also much ado about the pain of removing a splinter), McNally provides a serious undercurrent that ripples beneath the waters of the beach house pool and eventually emerges through the surface chatter and arguments. John is vaguely racist ("11 percent of this country is black—it's amazing, I would have thought it was more like 50 percent"). He is, like Sam, also more than a little homophobic. Both the Trumans and the Haddocks are heterosexuals vacationing in a homosexual enclave of Fire Island (Sally inherited her gay brother's house after his death). This becomes the occasion for numerous suggestive jokes ("Suppose I wanted to whip my dick out" "This is Fire Island, Sam, I would strenuously advise against it") and acerbic observations (a male in a bikini looks like he's "flossing his ass"). But it also forms the basis for the covert theme of the play. Everyone suspects the pool is infected with AIDS, since Sally's brother swam in it with his black lover. At the climax, with their feet dangling in the pool, Sally drinks the water and kisses Sam, saying "Let's all get AIDS and die." This leads to her final confession, that she helped her brother commit suicide. She had been repelled by his homosexuality, by his touch and his smell; she wonders what she would think about having a homosexual child. But her divided attitude is dominated by feelings of love ("I'm glad I never saw my brother dancing with another man— now I never will").

Sally is a touching and complicated character when she is not being asked to function as a comic butt. The burden she bears is to misremember the titles of movies and the names of movie stars. July 4th fireworks remind her of *Catch Any Thief* with Cary Grant and Ava Gardner. At one point she manages to persuade all the skeptics that Irving Berlin's song is called "There's No Business Like the Show Business." But for all the gags about her klutzy memory, she is possessed of a genuinely morbid streak which makes her often seem near breakdown. An abstract painter, she is almost always abstracted. The anonymous swimmer who sheds his bathing suit and enters the sea ("Whoever you are, my small, beautiful, silent swimmer, come back safely") is a surrogate for her dead brother. She feels responsible for the swimmer's death too because she mentally urged him on ("He wanted to die and I helped him").

At the end, after all the obligatory confessions, the two couples watch a shooting star, just as previously they joined in a chorus of "America." Their unity is artificial, their reconciliations seem temporary. McNally has created a world in which everyone is merry and nobody is happy, even in the midst of recreational plenty. *Lips Together, Teeth Apart* tantalizes with possibility. There is matter here that could be extended into a public dimension. But for most of its length the play seems self-regarding, self-enclosed, as unanchored as the society it depicts.

John Tillinger's production is smooth, occasionally facile. The pacing has the rhythms of farce even in moments of pathos. We are never allowed to forget (to cite another McNally work) "it's only a play." This contrasts with the literalism with which Tillinger treats externals. Characters shampoo their hair under real running shower water; we detect the odor of real hamburgers cooking on the charcoal broiler; I could almost smell the pimentos on Chloe's freshly prepared canapés. Under Tillinger's direction, however, the acting is effortless and well controlled. Anthony Heald brings both delicacy and pain to the part of John Haddock, and cruelty too when he humiliates Sam in front of his wife. Nathan Lane, as the befuddled and wounded Sam, sounds like Groucho Marx imitating Shubert executive Gerald Schoenfeld. Roxanne Hart, subbing in a part originally played by Swoozie Kurtz, almost succeeds in closing the division between airhead and tragedienne that makes Sally seem so inconsistent, while Deborah Rush, subbing for Christine Baranski, is irresistible as the officious, garrulous Chloe ("I hope nobody minds if I shut up for a while"), a walking compendium of brand names and show biz references.

McNally's rather awkward title refers to the method Sally learned to cure herself of grinding her teeth. But it unwittingly defines a split in his play as well, between the relationship plot and the desultory social theme. Perhaps next time this gifted playwright will abandon Yuppie Realism and let us bite on something with our teeth closed too.

[1991]

Terror in the Bedroom
(Othello)

IT IS sometimes noted that *Othello* is the only major work of Shakespeare in which the engines of the plot are driven entirely by a stage prop. Uneasy over this emphasis on an embroidered handkerchief, commentators have been critical of the way Othello arraigns, indicts, sentences, and executes Desdemona solely on the basis of circumstantial evidence. It is true that Othello's judicial conduct is extremely perfunctory and abrupt, even by the standards of frontier justice. To murder your wife for adultery on the evidence of a single article of toiletry is tantamount to hanging an alleged thief because his necktie was found at the scene of the crime. Still, for us to question the instrumentality of the justice, or the wisdom of the "justicer" (as Othello calls himself), is to underestimate the powers of the true engineer of the plot, namely Iago, who is such a brilliant agitator of human behavior that his influence on Othello amounts to hypnotic suggestion.

For it is Iago's capacity to manipulate Othello's mind and character that really drives the action in such a remorseless manner. And "the pity of it" lies in the fact that the fate of the Moor is at the same time so predictable and so preventable. There is hardly a moment in this play when we cease to believe that Iago's treachery will be exposed, or when we lose faith that Othello's eyes will be opened and Desdemona vindicated. No matter how familiar we are with the plot, we never stop hoping that something will intervene to avert the tragedy. And Shakespeare feeds this hope. In Act IV, scene i, for example, during an encounter witnessed by Othello, Iago prompts Cassio to brag about his mistress. The unexpected entrance of Bianca should persuade Othello he's not speaking of Desdemona. Yet by claiming Cassio gave her handkerchief to his whore, Iago knows precisely how to tilt the exchange to madden the Moor. A master of skewed analysis, he is also a master of suggestive language. Through his graphic sexual imagery, he pushes Othello into a seizure, and it is Iago's reference to "goats and monkeys" that Othello remembers when he strikes Desdemona, in the process of welcoming Lodovico to Cyprus. Aside from being the wittiest man in the play, Iago has one of the most supple intellects and deceptive vocabularies in literature, combining the scorching vision of a Juvenalian critic ("It is my nature's plague to spy into abuses") with the imaginative gifts of a creative artist ("I have't; it is engendered"). It is he who writes Othello's play, controlling the ebb and the flow, the exposition, development, and culmination of his tragedy.

Iago is not the only playwright-intellectual in Shakespeare. The manner in which he manipulates Roderigo for financial advantage ("Put money in thy purse") is foreshadowed by Sir Toby's gulling of Sir Andrew Aguecheek. But his real kissing cousin is Edmund in *King Lear*, not only in the way each appeals to Nature to justify a lack of conscience but in their common capacity to exploit the overheard conversations of innocent people (Desdemona resembles Cordelia in the way she chooses a husband over a father). Still, when it comes to imaginative villainy, Iago is without peer. We watch him with the awe we owe the greatest minds, even those guided by a malignant daemon.

The eighteenth entrant in Joseph Papp's Shakespeare Marathon, a new production of *Othello*, recently played in Central Park with Christopher Walken in the role of Iago. He was a brilliant choice for a number of reasons, but the one thing he failed to show us was Iago's talent for dissimulation. For the sake of his credibility, "honest, honest Iago" must persuade everyone he is a bluff, no-nonsense soldier, from the same regiment as Kent or Hotspur. Iago admits "I am not what I am," but Walken is always exactly what he is, a mean-spirited, irritable nihilist, seething with a hate which originates in the groin and gnaws at his innards. (Walken's Iago is also obsessively neat, often smoothing out wrinkled carpets and rearranging discarded props.) One of the greatest naturalistic actors of our time, Walken plays so close to his colloquial self that he's almost invariably out of history in anything but contemporary roles (his brilliant Coriolanus, for example, had every attribute but nobility). On the other hand, the way Walken merges personality with character permits him to inhabit parts rather than perform them, and his relaxed, informal rendering of Shakespearean dialogue makes the language seem revolutionary, immediate, fresh, and new.

For me these qualities proved more than sufficient compensation for the absence of deception or guile in his Iago. Costumed like a character out of *Blade Runner* or *Road Warrior* (his punk red hair made him look like a malevolent Mad Max), wearing leather jacket, pants, and codpiece from a melange of periods, Walken virtually personified the naturalistic view of sex ("a lust of the blood and a permission of the will") that Shakespeare contrasts with Cassio's idealized courtly love. Walken also forced us to acknowledge that Iago's most intimate relationship is not with any of the play's characters. It is with the audience. From the moment this angelic-looking hood appeared on stage with Roderigo, weaving a web around his credulous victim, glazing his eyes, shrugging, loping, dancing, it was clear that Walken's whole focus was on the folks out front. Whenever he reached an aside or a soliloquy (the lights being lowered for a tableau), he put his arm around the shoulder of his frozen companion and addressed himself to us. Those moments were filled with such gall, such intimacy, such eroticism, that the audience didn't know whether to hiss him or kiss him. Innocent bystanders were being treated as co-conspirators, intriguers, abettors, complicit in his crimes. I can't remember a time when evil seemed so voluptuous and engaging.

Just as Othello is overmatched by Iago's cunning, so Raul Julia had difficulty competing with Walken's magnetism. Julia was an unusual choice for the Moor, not because he is a Latino playing a role now claimed by African-Americans, but because he is not quite mature enough to enact the ripe seasoned spirit of this aging general. Jane Greenwood, who did the excellent costumes for the show, dressed him sometimes like a sheik, sometimes like a conquistador, and, equipped with corsair moustaches and flowing black hair, he looked like a cross between Rudolph Valentino and Kevin Kline. This was a romantic rather than a heroic Othello, whose passions for Desdemona seemed to be inspired by jungle fever; each time they left the stage, Julia suggested they were going off to muss the sheets. (The same actor was equally sensual as Macbeth, spending so much effort embracing his wife that he hardly had the strength to knock off Duncan.)

Julia's lazy, hooded eyes, furthermore, give the impression of slyness and languor, qualities at odds with Othello's celebrated gullibility. T. S. Eliot suggests that Othello is cheering himself up in his big rhetorical moments. Julia pumped himself up. He reached for thunderous rage but didn't find the notes. What emerged were chants and intonations. Instead of feeling the part, he styled it, with exotic rhythms and foreign inflections. Without the pity of it and the terror, *Othello* remains a domestic drama. For all his genuine intelligence and dignified presence, Julia never managed to lift the play out of the boudoir.

Kathryn Meisle's Desdemona was more moving, despite touches of classic rep acting, and her bedroom scene was genuinely terrifying when she fled from Othello's murderous advances as from a rapist. But the actor who best captured the play's tragic quality was Mary Beth Hurt as Emilia. Hurt's easy, intimate acting made this strong-willed protofeminist ("Let husbands know their wives have sense like them") into an entirely contemporary woman, and her powerhouse explosions over Desdemona's body provided the deepest grief of the evening. I believe it was Samuel Johnson who said that Emilia wears her virtue loosely but doesn't cast it off. Hurt kept her moral clothes on while walking a balanced line between suggestiveness and brazenness.

Let me now praise the faceless hero of this *Othello*, the director Joe Dowling, who drew a consistently fine level of performance from his actors, particularly George Morfogen as a stately Brabantio, Michel R. Gill as a mercurial Cassio, and Tom Hewitt as an attractive Lodovico. Dowling must also be credited for a production that was well paced, clear, coherent, and often beautifully staged (the scene in the Duke's palace was arranged with the color and composition of a Rembrandt painting). Frank Conway's setting was a simple rectangular stone archway which, in Part I, framed an oval blue-carpeted platform suitable for prowling panthers. And Peter Golub's string and percussion music made ominous use of arpeggios and pizzicatas. Dowling managed to treat *Othello* both as a contemporary and a period piece. Bullhorns announced the arrival of the General, but the island of Cyprus was a compound of Caribbean exoticism and Mediterranean splendor, alive with festive activity. During the dancing and carousing, a huge head of the Cypriote Aphrodite presided over the festivities, only to be knocked on its side during the brawl between Cassio and Roderigo. It remained on stage for the rest of the play as if to remind us of the death of love.

And the death of a transcendent love between two mismatched yet oddly compatible people is what continues to give such power to this heartbreaking story. Iago names so many motives for destroying Othello that Coleridge called him a "motiveless malignity." Yet surely Iago's central motive is his hatred of other people's consummated affection, since he is incapable of love himself. Walken's disgust and loathing upon watching Othello and Desdemona embrace reinforced this motive in a manner that made my flesh crawl. It is one of many things in this flawed but riveting production that are imprinted indelibly on my mind.

[1991]

The Schelpic, Part II:
Escape from Saigon
(Miss Saigon)

FOLLOWING debate over the New York casting, saluted with a front-page photo in the *New York Times*, *Miss Saigon* has come from London to the Broadway Theatre. Thanks to a shrewd, stubborn producer, Cameron Mackintosh, spectators are stampeding to pay $100 a ticket to cover the musical's $10 million-dollar cost; the advance sale is said to be $36 million. No wonder the audience starts clapping before the curtain rises; they're endorsing their own expenditures. A somewhat more jaundiced critical battalion is no more able to slow the inexorable advance of this juggernaut than Saddam Hussein could stop the tanks and planes of General Schwarzkopf. *Miss Saigon* not only depicts the amorous adventures of American servicemen in Vietnam but features a fully rigged helicopter landing on stage in iconic homage to our ignominious flight from Saigon. Not since the chandelier floated down from the flies in *Phantom of the Opera* have music, mayhem, and machinery been merged in such riotous excess.

Although *Miss Saigon* exploits a less than heroic event in U.S. history—not to mention the anti-Western seduced-and-abandoned theme of *Madama Butterfly*—Americans don't come off ignobly. The Pinkerton conceived by Alain Boublil and Claude-Michel Schonberg has been changed from a callous naval officer into a warmhearted marine who does everything possible to save a helicopter seat for Butterfly, only to be frustrated by pushing crowds and military commands. Back safely in his American suburb and married to a woman of his own race, he suffers conscience pangs in the form of bad dreams. When he learns his lost Butterfly is living in Bangkok with the child he sired during their brief relationship, he returns to the Orient to find her, accompanied by his understanding blonde wife.

Butterfly—in the Boublil-Schonberg version she's more like a cocoon—is no longer a guileless Japanese geisha. She's now a guileless Vietnamese Lolita from the country, named Kim. Kim was abducted from her village to work in a whorehouse called Dreamland, whose proprietor—the Engineer—peddles her "virgin ass" to GIs. She falls for Chris, the first Yank she sleeps with, who regards her, in turn, as "the one good thing I've found out here." After one night in each other's arms, they vow to sing an eternal duet and soon after join in a musicalized Buddhist wedding ceremony, thus proving that any plots too silly to be spoken, or any events too implausible to be acted, can always be sung.

The marriage is interrupted by the appearance of Kim's intended, a Viet Cong named Thuy who curses her for breaking her father's word. In a subsequent scene—it takes place three years later, after Saigon has been rechristened Ho Chi Minh City (an event celebrated by a mammoth production number in front of a huge golden statue of Ho)—Kim is blindfolded and reviled as "the American whore." Thuy reappears. He's a high army officer now and still demanding his contractual rights. Kim shows him her little boy ("Now you see why I must tell you No"), and shoots him when Thuy draws a knife on the child. Although they'd both prefer a passport to the States, Kim and the Engineer escape to Thailand where he continues to peddle bar girls, Kim included, to American servicemen. Like Chris, Kim is suffering conscience pangs. She is plagued by the ghost of Thuy, his face daubed with #10 pancake, who sings "You will never be free, not as long as there's me." Nevertheless, she is resolutely determined to make her child a U.S. citizen even at the cost of her own life.

This is also the purpose of Children of Servicemen, a nonprofit organization led by Chris's marine buddy, John, who gives a stern musical lecture at the beginning of the second act on the obligations of GI parenthood. John's lecture is illustrated by filmed sequences which momentarily sober up the show biz binge with shots of suffering Vietnamese children. But have no fear. The shining nobility of musical theatre is soon restored. Knowledge of his paternity has magnified Chris's conscience pangs ("I shattered Kim; now Ellen too"), and so he goes to Bangkok to do the right thing.

The obligatory reunion never takes place. Instead of finding

Chris, Kim comes upon Ellen and implores her to take the child to the States ("There are days," muses Ellen, "when your life clouds over"). After another big production number in which the Engineer fantasizes about "The American Dream"—an enormous white car with flashing headlights which excites him so much he mounts it sexually—Chris finally finds his child. In an orgy of self-sacrifice, Kim shoots herself and the two lovers kiss bloodily amidst the crescendo of the music.

Everything is created and performed with all the smooth mechanical efficiency we have come to expect of the Schlepic, that profitable export which for the past ten years has been bestriding our musical stage like a colossus. Although it is occasionally distinguished by some soft, bluesy sax numbers, the uninterrupted music of Claude-Michel Schonberg never matches the rousing pitch he hit in *Les Miserables*. Like the glutinous strains of Andrew Lloyd Webber, the score often seems to have been squeezed through a pasta machine, while the rhyme schemes, in the monosyllabic lyrics of Richard Maltby and Alain Boublil, appear to have been composed on a computer. Nicholas Hytner, the director, has concocted a production that may have been influenced by Peter Sellars's approach to John Adams's opera *Nixon in China*, with its simulated Red Detachment of Women choreography complete with masks and automatic weapons, alternating with interludes borrowed from *South Pacific* and *Teahouse of the August Moon*. And although John Napier's production design, painted with panels of hoistable silk and David Hersey's pinpoint lighting, is exquisite to look at, the chief physical attractions of the evening are the helicopter and the automobile, both of which left me with the desire to board them and escape from Saigon myself.

As for the performances, these are hard to judge considering the thinness of the written characters. Jonathan Pryce, looking a bit like Stanley Laurel gone to seed, brings sleaze, smarminess, and physical agility (he seems to have more arms than an octopus) to the role of the Engineer. And Lea Salonga as Kim breaks through the impossible Stella Dallas nobility of her part with innate freshness and innocence. Kim's tiny child, Tam, as played by Brian R. Baldomero, draws the kind of focus, with his sweet vulnerability, that used to tempt W. C. Fields to murder child actors. And the chorus of bar girls—interchangeably used as Vietnamese and Thais—display enough thighs, bosoms, and behinds to satisfy the most discriminating readers of *Playboy*.

I think I might have enjoyed *Miss Saigon* a little more had it been a little less self-righteous. But I'm not a fan of sermons on guilt in musical form. *Miss Saigon* shares its misplaced hortatory tone with a large number of middlebrow dramatic works. Ever since Rodgers and Hammerstein first informed us, in *South Pacific*, that "You've Got to Be Taught" to be racially prejudiced, what was once a genre of unashamed theatrical escapism has been generously scattering liberal pieties into its profit-making entertainments. In *Miss Saigon*'s program, passing for dramaturgical material, is a photograph from *France-Soir*, taken in 1985 and reputed to have been the "original inspiration" for the musical. It shows a crying half-caste child being threatened and manhandled by a group of Vietnamese. The photo is touching, and Mr. Mackintosh is sufficiently moved by *Miss Saigon*'s inspirational plea for the relocation of GI orphans to contribute the cost of two tickets at each show to the cause. This is generous, even considering that the youngest of these Vietnamese children must be at least eighteen by now, and might be more grateful receiving royalties for their unauthorized participation in the filmed sequences. But it is a real question whether this glitzorama is an appropriate vehicle for stimulating charitable impulses—and whether people seeking a night on the town are going to respond to such exhortations with anything more practical than passing nods and sentimental sighs. I seem to remember audiences at *Nicholas Nickleby*, after the curtain came down on an impoverished waif in the hero's arms, gingerly wending their way past the homeless lying on the streets of New York.

I hesitate to throw doubt on the motives of the people associated with this show, but I am disturbed by the way theatre is increasingly trying to justify itself as a medium for solving the world's problems. Let us be clear about the limitations of the stage, even in its most serious manifestations. It cannot cure AIDS. It cannot resolve racial conflict. It cannot do away with toxic waste. It cannot end unemployment. It cannot stop wars. It cannot wash your car or mow your lawn or repair your driveway or improve your schools. In short, as Chekhov told us, the theatre is not empowered to solve problems, only to present them correctly. And the correct presentation of problems is the task of dramatic artists capable of understanding the immense and untidy complications of life, not of theatrical entrepreneurs recycling *Madama Butterfly* at a hundred bucks a throw.

[1991]

The Dreaming of the Bones
(The Shadow of a Gunman; Dancing at Lughnasa)

IRISH theatre, for reasons that presently remain elusive, seems to be having another renaissance, at least to judge by the number of productions visiting these shores. One-man shows based on literature by James Joyce and Brendan Behan are circulating on tour; Samuel Beckett has become the favorite subject of international conferences; Sean O'Casey's *The Shadow of a Gunman* is just completing a successful visit to a number of American cities, including Boston and New York; and Brian Friel's imported *Dancing at Lughnasa* is firmly settled on Broadway after unanimously positive notices from exuberant reviewers.

Seeing the O'Casey and Friel plays back to back reveals how much they have in common with each other and with the whole corpus of twentieth-century Irish writing. *The Shadow of a Gunman* takes place in a Dublin tenement during the early twenties and owes a lot to Zola and Ibsen. *Dancing at Lughnasa* is set in the thirties in rural County Donegal and combines Chekhovian techniques with nostalgic memory devices borrowed from Tennessee Williams's *The Glass Menagerie.* Yet, despite their international influences, both are concerned with obsessive Irish themes, notably the collision between romance and reality which results from the national disposition for mythicizing and dreaming. In his 1949 book *The Irish: A Character Study*, Sean O'Faolain identified this leitmotif as a prime characteristic of the Celtic nature—a conclusion Bernard Shaw had reached forty-five years earlier in *John Bull's Other Island*:

Oh, the dreaming, the dreaming, the torturing heartscalding, never-satisfying dreaming. . . . An Irishman's imagination never lets him alone, never convinces him, never satisfies him; but it makes him that he can't face reality nor deal with it nor handle it nor conquer it.

This appetite for fancy and imagination results in an incurable romanticism that tends to confound fact with fiction, and history with myth. It may also explain why the early church chose not to conquer the pagan gods that were thought to inhabit the island so much as to assimilate them (Saint Patrick, for example, was actually a Christian version of a primitive, many-sided deity named Dagda). Indeed, pagan myth and Christian scripture are not always distinguishable in the Irish mind. Joyce, in his *Portrait of the Artist as a Young Man,* wrote of how his friend Mat Davin's imagination was shaped by the "broken lights of Irish myth. He stood towards the myth . . . in the same attitude as towards the Roman Catholic religion, the attitude of a dull-witted serf." As for Yeats's concept of the Celtic Twilight, this was an effort both to celebrate these myths and convert them to poetic purposes. Many of his early poems, notably "The Unappeasable Host," describe the dualism of paganism and Christianity assumed to coexist uneasily in the spiritual universe of Ireland.

O'Casey, who was reared in an atmosphere of abject poverty, shared this sense of incredible incongruity from his early manhood. The land shaped for him by story and myth—a land of love, laughter, and pagan freedom—was nowhere to be found in the slums of Dublin. What he saw instead was despair, avarice, filth, drunkenness, and priestly oppression. In his first three plays—*The Shadow of a Gunman, Juno and the Paycock,* and *The Plough and the Stars*—it was his intention to represent, honestly and painstakingly, the Dublin of his experience—its squalor, violence, and pestilence. But Irish realism is almost an oxymoron, and while he never adopted myths or dreams as a panacea for poverty (except perhaps in *Cock-a-Doodle Dandy*), he was soon to substitute myths of his own making in a utopian vision of a future world under the flag of communism (*The Star Turns Red*).

By the time of his first play, *The Shadow of a Gunman,* O'Casey has not yet formulated an alternative political position. Instead it is the purpose of this "slum dramatist" (as he was called) to examine the awful repercussions of dreaming away reality. Donal Davoren, a would-be poet, is caught in the grip of other people's illusions, which he is reluctant to unmask. The romantic Minnie Powell thinks he is a gunman "on the run" for the IRA, and when a real gunman drops off a stash of bombs in Davoren's flat, she throws away her own life in an effort to protect him from the Black and Tans. Davoren is left with his shame and guilt, an imaginary hero, a shadow of a gunman, doomed to spend the rest of his life with the fatal consequences of his imposture: "Oh, Donal Davoren, shame is your portion now till the silver cord is loosened and the golden bowl be broken. Oh, Davoren, Donal Davoren, poet and poltroon, poltroon and poet."

Around this posturing hero O'Casey collects what were soon to become a familiar crowd of storytellers, drunks, and swaggerers, including Seumas Shields, his peddler-roommate, the Orangeman Adolphus Grigson and his wife, and the Dickensian malapropper Mrs. Gallogher. As will also soon become common in O'Casey, a woman proves to be the major victim of male heroics as well as the only truly courageous figure in the play. Minnie Powell is a hero worshiper whom Davoren is only too eager to impress, though she would like nothing better than to see him die for his country. But by offering to hide the bomb stash and getting shot through the "buzzom" as a result, it is she, not Davoren, who becomes a sacrifice to the cause of Irish freedom. For O'Casey it is not the male revolutionaries who carry the burden of suffering but the female civilians—Minnie Powell, Juno Boyle, Nora Clitheroe.

Appropriately enough, it is a woman—O'Casey's daughter, Shivaun O'Casey—who has directed the current revival at the Symphony Space with a company drawn from her theatre in Newry, Northern Ireland. She has staged it with true feeling both for the tenement comedy and gunmetal grimness of the work, disguising its occasional thinness of plot with characterizations of richness and depth. Niall Buggy is particularly effective as the belligerent Seumas Shields, hopping into his torn pants without removing his pajamas, and generalizing wildly about the Irish character. It is a performance which instantly puts him in a class with the legendary Irish comedians F J. McCormick, Jack Mc-

Gowran, and Barry McGovern. Michelle Fairley is enchanting as the idealistic Minnie Powell; Ian Fitzgibbon enacts an appropriately grandiloquent Davoren; and Pauline Flanagan creates a splendid Mrs. Grigson, puling and nattering like a demented sewing machine. Indeed, virtually the entire cast gives strong reinforcement to a playwright who, if not yet quite mature, gives promise of soon becoming a true chronicler of disappointed dreams.

Brian Friel's *Dancing at Lughnasa* (Plymouth Theatre) is a more fully developed play than *The Shadow of a Gunman*. But though it deals with some of the same themes—notably the tension between paganism and Christianity, between romance and reality—it lacks O'Casey's punch and passion. I have always found something a little restrained and commonplace about Friel's writing, and the rustic domesticity of *Dancing at Lughnasa* makes it no exception. For all its charm, the play has virtually no incident and the characters are tame. Friel owes as large a debt to Chekhov as O'Casey does to Ibsen (later Strindberg); yet he captures only the surface of Chekhov's apparent aimlessness, rarely the depths of crisis and upheaval. "People are having a meal at table, just having a meal," Chekhov wrote in describing his method, "but at the same time their happiness is being created, or their lives are being smashed up." Friel's five sisters each have some unhappiness in their spinster lives, generally relating to unrequited love (the absence of eligible men in this world is appalling). But the most they can summon in rebellion is an occasional tart word or, at the climactic moment of the play, to break into dance.

Dancing, generally to music of the thirties played on a radio called Marconi, is in fact Friel's central metaphor, and he connects it with the pagan rituals of the vestigial harvest deity Lugh. The appeal of paganism is further enhanced by the career of the sisters' uncle, Father Jack—a "leper priest" who, having spent many years in Ryanga, is under suspicion by the church for having converted to African tribal customs. If you're expecting some of the unspeakable things experienced by Kurtz in Conrad's *Heart of Darkness* ("the horror, the horror"), forget it. The most unusual experiences Jack can offer to titillate the sisters are goat and calf sacrifices, polygamy, face-painting, and ritual dancing.

One sister, Chris, after an affair with an itinerant Welshman, Gerry, has had a child by him (the child is Michael, the narrator, who also plays himself as a boy). The oldest, the puritanical Kate, is a teacher and an advocate of Christian morals. Agnes and the rather simpleminded Rose are seamstresses working at home. Maggie, perhaps the most tragic of the five because she is the most spirited, is condemned to permanent spinsterhood. Nobody gets what she wants, and Michael—like Tom Wingfield in *The Glass Menagerie*—escapes from the house and from these five wounded Lauras only to realize he is still bound by vivid dreams and anguished memories—dreams and memories of dancing.

Dancing at Lughnasa is a sweet and sometimes eloquent play, written with strong sympathies for all its characters. And while I found the acting of the men somewhat weak, particularly Gerard McSorley's ineffectual efforts to play the child Michael and Donal Donnelly's rather wimpish stab at the spoiled priest Father Jack (a shade of the great Irish characterizations), the women are splendid, with Dearbhla Molloy as the warm and waspish Maggie topping a strong sisterhood. Still, the themes of the play have already been better explored by more vigorous playwrights, and the idea of a Pan figure (the Welshman) unsettling the women like a fox in a henhouse was long ago exhausted by D. H. Lawrence and Tennessee Williams. In short, the play seems to me derivative, tepid, and a little banal—a puny evocation of a time when Irish writers dreamed mighty dreams.

[1991]

Melting the Concrete
(*Murmuring Judges; The Sea; The Resistible Rise of Arturo Ui; The Madness of George III*)

THE Royal National Theatre, that massive fortress that rose to dominate the South Bank of the Thames in 1976, has over the years turned into a curious anomaly. Jonathan Miller once dismissed Sir Denys Lasdun's highly visible building as a "concrete Colditz." Yet despite its admittedly forbidding official architecture, the National has a warm, inviting interior, including comfortable public spaces, bars, restaurants, performance areas, and bookshops. The theatre no longer supports a permanent acting company, as it did in the early Olivier years at the Old Vic. I managed to identify only one featured actor (Michael Bryant) appearing in more than one play. But although this kind of extravagance inflates the size of the budget and deflates the pleasures of ensemble work, the National still runs as many as six or seven shows at any one time in three adjoining theatres. Perhaps the hardest task for an institution calling itself "National" is to be sufficiently representative of the nation as a whole—its admixture of classes, races, cultures, and tastes. In our country this would be an impossible task. In England, whose character is still relatively homogeneous, the National continues to manage its mission with relative ease.

The National defines that mission as embracing a diverse repertoire, including classics, new plays, and neglected works from the whole of world drama. The five productions I visited during a recent trip were a fairly typical representation, except for the absence of Shakespeare (still the resident playwright of the RSC, a company presently performing at Stratford while the Barbican is shut for repairs). The National's new plays include Alan Bennett's *The Madness of George III* and David Hare's *Murmuring Judges*. The neglected work is Edward Bond's haunting *The Sea*. And the classics, both of them modern, are Brecht's *The Resistible Rise of Arturo Ui* and Garcia Lorca's *Blood Wedding*. Almost all of these productions are tolerable and one is quite marvelous. But the impression is polyglot. Like the New York Public Theater (the American institution it most resembles), the National is less a theatre than a theatre center, producing semi-autonomous shows in a number of different spaces. Like the Public, it gives an impression of variety and activity at the expense of a consistent style.

The most exhilarating production I saw on my trip was *The Madness of George III*, the most trying was a crude, poorly acted version of *Blood Wedding*, set in Cuba with a racially mixed cast (yes, English theatre also features its share of multiculturalism from time to time). Richard Eyre, the director of the National, is represented by his staging of the new Hare work, the second in a trilogy about England's social institutions (the first, called *Racing Demon*, was a satire on the clergy). Performed in the Olivier Theatre with its vast open stage, the production collapses a play whose legs were pretty wobbly to begin with. A cast of twenty-five actors plus multiple extras populate a number of locations, including the Inns of Court, the Old Bailey, the charge room of a police station, and a cavernous prison, while, for the purpose of a single scene lasting less than five minutes, a car drives up (in a rainstorm!) to deliver spectators to a Covent Garden performance of *The Magic Flute* (the opera house is represented by a huge inner proscenium surrounded by bewigged and liveried footmen). David Hare's assault on the injustice of a money-besotted legal system is largely drowned in the maelstrom of a money-drenched production.

Despite its title (a Scottish phrase for contempt of court), *Murmuring Judges* is not so much a play about scandalized jurists as about the barristers and police officials who perpetuate a callously indifferent system. Using a "Hill Street Blues" format too banal to detail here, the action follows the trial, imprisonment, and unsuccessful appeal on drug charges of an innocent Irishman framed by a corrupt detective. The only person concerned enough to help him is a beautiful black female lawyer, who is joined in the climax by a policewoman sufficiently conscience-stricken to inform on her colleague. Hare continues to see the social world as a caucus of corrupt men exposed by idealistic women, while his writing technique (like much of the performance) is in that broad declarative style which American actors call "indicating."

"Indicating" also mars the National's production of *Arturo Ui* at the Olivier, where Anthony Sher, following and echoing his performance as Richard III, plays Brecht's fuehrer-gangster in a manner both galvanic and boring. Scooting around the stage like a gorilla on stilts, he hurls himself into the part with abandon but never reaches much depth, a high diver arcing gracefully into a two-foot pool. His impersonation of Hitler is essentially cosmetic—he's better at imitating Al Pacino—while the rest of the cast spends most of its energy trying to manage Chicago accents. Di Trevis's production of Ranjit Bolt's translation is also largely "indicated," underscoring parallels between the play and the Nazi period through slides, film, and program notes, as if the audience were in a state of total amnesia about the rudimentary facts of Third Reich history.

The program notes for *The Sea*, at the Littleton, consist entirely of Bond's recent poetry, which is appropriate considering the poetic reverberant nature of the action. First performed in 1973 at the Royal Court (where it featured Ian Holm), the play has developed a rich underwater life over the years, as if encrusted with strange marine forms. This quality is fully realized in Sam Mendes's stark precisionist production, especially in Bob Crowley's stage design, a compound of windowed interiors and pebble-strewn exteriors, all dyed in hues of green that seem to immerse the characters and events in the chambers of the sea. It also features extraordinary lighting by Paul Pyant who, with minimum effects, creates one of the most harrowing storms I've ever seen on stage. The style of *The Sea* sometimes reminds one of the Yarmouth scenes in *David Copperfield*, sometimes of the undulant murmurous music of Virginia Woolf's *The Waves*, sometimes of *The Tempest*, and like those works its theme is death by drowning. But the play is also uniquely Bond. No one else could have conceived the scene in which a draper, driven to fury by the capricious behavior of a customer, slices his dangerous scissors into yards and yards of expensive material while inveighing against creatures from outer space. *The Sea* has a plot—the mortal conflict between an upper-class dowager (majestically played by Judi Dench) and the crazy, alien-obsessed draper (a brilliant performance by Ken Stott)—and it ends with one of Bond's customary appeals to action ("I told you this so you wouldn't despair, but you must change the world"). It's true richness, however, lies not in revolutionary politics but in mystical metaphors and bizarre shifts of mood. You absorb it subliminally like the roaring of distant waves.

Nothing in Alan Bennett's career as a wit and social satirist could have prepared us for the authority and maturity he displays in *The Madness of George III* (Lyttleton). The play signals the arrival of an important epic playwright. On the surface the work is an effort to redeem a much maligned historical figure from his traditional characterization as a tyrant, buffoon, and madman, mostly on the basis of recent medical evidence. George, it seems, was indeed not mad, as he alone believed, but suffering from porphyria, a disease characterized by *symptoms* of madness (and also by purple urine, hence its name). To settle for another clinical explanation of George's condition, however, is to fall into the same snare Bennett satirizes so brilliantly throughout the play, namely a belief that curing the malady is less important than naming it properly. One of George's doctors ascribes the king's disease to "flying gout" or "rheumatism in the head," another to his stool, another to his arrogant spirit—and each prescribes another ghastly method of treatment, whether purges, bleeding, blistering, straitjackets, or "a good spew and a good sweat." I doubt if the new nomenclature will result in any better treatment, much less a cure.

Bennett's satire on benighted medical practices reminds me of *The Doctor's Dilemma* (and of Shaw's Doctor Walpole, whose universal cure is to "stimulate the phagocytes"). But the uniqueness of his play lies in the way it manages to evoke an entire historical epoch. The action begins with four red-coated equerries walking backward down a set of golden stairs (an eloquent design by Mark Thompson), followed by magnificently dressed couriers entering upon the stage to Handel's brilliant *Royal Fireworks* music. Before long we are deep into the intrigues of Georgian politics, represented by the opposition of two Whig parties: those serving the king (led by the younger William Pitt), and those seeking to displace them (led by Charles Fox). The Fox party hopes to replace George with his son, the Prince of Wales, a fat ignoramus with a weakness for furniture (Michael Fitzgerald plays the part as if he had just stepped out of a Gillray caricature). In this seedy atmosphere of power politics, George's growing dementia becomes a sacrifice to human ambition as the various politicians propose their own doctors and remedies in an effort to ensure that the king will never recover.

George himself—in a stunning performance by Nigel Hawthorne—is depicted as a simple, uxorious man with a passion for farming, who disintegrates before our eyes from a robust and wily Hanoverian (who adds "What, what?" to every declaration) into a tormented slovenly Lear-like figure afflicted with colic, sweats, running sores, and pains in the legs ("my blood is full of cramps—lobsters cramp my bones—my limbs are laced with fire"). Eventually a physician suggested by the Lady Pembroke seems to alleviate his agony through a torture of his own devising (his primitive mental therapy consists of breaking down the king's spirit). But it is more likely that the disease just runs its course. At any rate, the king is eventually, if temporarily, restored to sanity, with the capacity to name his own children, though not to name the lost colonies (he still splutters over the word "America"). Told that he now seems more like himself, he replies, "I have always been myself—I have just learned how to *seem*. What, what?" The "what, what?" and the appearance of yellow urine signal the restoration of sanity, and, only mildly shaken by reports of "minor disturbances in Paris," he returns to the task of ruling his kingdom.

Actually, George's affliction returned to plague him for the last twenty years of his life, removing him from the throne and giving the corpulent regent a long-deferred opportunity to indulge his infatuation with (regency) furniture. But the final ascent of the court up those golden stairs to Handel's shimmering trumpets describes a circle of English history as well as anything to be found in modern theatre. The entire company is superb, and Nicholas Hytner's flawlessly orchestrated production brings the National Theatre to a splendid fulfillment of its theatrical mission.

[1992]

Opinions, Opinions
(Four Baboons Adoring the Sun; Death of the Maiden; 'Tis Pity She's a Whore)

I STARTED a bit of a *logomachia* recently by proposing that one way for the *Times* to relax its monolithic control over the New York stage was to move David Richards from the Sunday Arts and Leisure section, where his influence is minimal, to an equal position on the daily with the all-powerful Frank Rich. I wasn't, as some readers assumed, offering comment on the comparative abilities of neighboring *Times* critics. I was suggesting, rather, that audiences might become less sheeplike about following a daily reviewer's judgments if they could read two different notices on the same page. When a sick patient is told he has a fatal or lingering disease, he usually seeks a second opinion. Why should the fabulous invalid be condemned to permanent hospitalization by a single diagnosis?

If you vetted *Times* theatre notices over the last two weeks, you might have noticed that, aside from the similarity of their names, Rich and Richards have been sharing very little in common lately. Rich was entranced by Ariel Dorfman's writing in *Death and the Maiden* but appalled by Mike Nichols's production. Richards's reverse judgment panned the play while praising the acting and directing. Ecstatic about John Guare's *Four Baboons Adoring the Sun*, Rich implied that anyone who didn't find it moving was probably emotionally deficient. Richards, silent about his own problems, found emotional deficiencies in the work. Rich, consistent with his new benevolence, forsook his customary animus toward JoAnne Akalaitis to extol her production of *'Tis Pity She's a Whore*. Richards found it histrionically inept.

The issue is not who's right or wrong about the quality of productions. It's hardly unusual for reviewers to disagree, and even the best critical minds can make bad calls. We revere Bernard Shaw for his ideas, wit, and analytical power, though he was wrong regarding Wilde's *Importance of Being Earnest*, just as we read Kenneth Tynan for his remarkable capacity to describe the theatrical event, though he preferred theatrical events created by John Osborne over those by Samuel Beckett or Jean Genet. No, the issue is not a critic's batting average. Only posterity will decide on that, assuming posterity continues to have an interest in the matter. The issue, rather, is whether one individual on a single New York newspaper should be allowed to decide the fate of the whole theatrical enterprise.

What should concern us, in short, is the confounding of critical opinion with critical infallibility. Opinions are the most provisional, partial, and common equipment in a reviewer's toolbox— any layman can have them—so it is dismaying that the relationship between subjective judgment and absolute power should have grown so tight at the *Times*. Theatregoers reading the conflicting views of Rich and Richards cheek by jowl would be reminded that even the most informed opinions are subject to reasoned dispute. They might even be encouraged to develop their own opinions by going to see the play the critics disagreed about. The least we might expect is that the public would grow to understand that the theatre exists for other purposes than for critics to make judgments on it.

Having cleared my throat by questioning the importance of opinions, let me offer my own debatable evaluations of the productions disputed by Rich and Richards, hoping that my disagreements, however negative, will be an incentive rather than a deterrent to interest in the plays. I confess I didn't see a lot of virtue in Ariel Dorfman's *Death and the Maiden* (Brooks Atkinson Theatre). The work is about a woman—from a "country [probably Chile] that has given itself a democratic government after a long period of dictatorship"—who, with the help of her reluctant husband, turns the tables on the right-wing sadist she believes had raped and tortured her. I found the plot preposterous, resting on more coincidences in a day than most people experience in a lifetime, and the style struck me as conventional agitprop realism. It's as if *Extremities* had been rewritten for a benefit held by Amnesty International, or *The Boys from Brazil* were being refilmed for a meeting of Human Rights Watch. The heroine defines "the need of the country" as to "somehow put into words what has happened to us," but her own words are hardly a model of expository prose ("I want you inside me a lot," she says to her husband, who later reflects, "We can explore all the frontiers but we'll still have that unpredictable female soul"). Dorfman creates some Pirandellian suspense over whether the fellow sitting bound and gagged in this comfortable house is actually the Mengele-type doctor who liked to play Schubert while torturing his victims with electric shocks (she never saw his face), or just a poor schnook who gave her husband a lift in his car. It's sensible of him not to resolve this, but then very little is resolved in this play, other than the heroine's passion for vengeance.

The production style belongs less to Santiago than to Beverly Hills. Tony Walton has designed a triangulated suburban home with plaster columns which Mike Nichols has rented to three good Hollywood stars: Glenn Close, Richard Dreyfuss, and

Gene Hackman. The actors do what they can, considering Close
and Dreyfuss are miscast as husband and wife, and they're all
miscast as earnest South Americans. Actually, I found Nichols's
direction relatively subdued, compared with his usual habit of
pumping laughing gas into toothache plays. But then no one
either on stage or off seemed to regard this event as anything less
than an obligation.

Four Baboons Adoring the Sun (Vivian Beaumont) started, we're
told, as a sketch for an opera by Leonard Bernstein. It's still a
sketch and still pretty operatic. (Would that Bernstein had lived
to compose it, thus sparing us Stephen Edwards's lanolin underscoring.) I suspect that the spirited John Guare rushed it into
production too fast—three or four drafts shy of completion.
Guare's purpose in his recent work has been to force conventional people into unconventional situations, toward a crisis of
self-realization that might be summed up by Rilke: "You must
change your life." In theory it's a lofty idea, but the practice
sometimes wobbles off the edge of the diving board. What else
accounts for the moist ending of *Six Degrees of Separation*, where
an upper-class woman victimized by a black scam artist later
realizes that *he* is really the victim and chides herself for failing to
save him.

In *Four Baboons*, two lovers and the nine children they have
between them go on an archaeological dig in Sicily. Haunted by
ancient gods, these tourists fall prey to phantasmagoric experiences. Two of their children, barely into their teens, decide to
make love (against their parents' wishes)—and the boy, who
identifies with Icarus, climaxes their ecstasy by jumping off a
mountain to his death. The girl, having refused to join him,
guiltily regrets losing her "one chance to be a goddess." But the
real stunner comes when the boy's father also blames her ("Why
didn't you jump?"), and breaks up with her mother as a result
("Why do you have a child and I don't?"—actually, he still has
three). Questions "conventional" people rarely ask. But then they
haven't shared such unconventional experiences.

Perhaps the play would have seemed a little less absurd had it
received a less overheated production. But Peter Hall has used the
occasion to get his colored lights going again. On Tony Walton's
huge tribal circle, backed by a large turning globe and often

belching smoke, the stage shivers and shakes and separates (during an earthquake), while a scantily clad baritone satyr named Eros sings and kibitzes throughout, showing generous portions of his bare behind. Eros, representing pagan sexual freedom, turns the play into a Cliff's Notes version of D. H. Lawrence's *Sea and Sardinia*. The part is not well played, but neither are the other roles. It's hard enough to perform along with nine young children. But it's even harder when kitsch music and sound effects are continually competing with the dialogue. The evening's worst failing is to make some very good actors look uncomfortable. Stockard Channing tries to charm her way through an unwritten role, while James Naughton as the archaeologist lopes like a cowboy and croons like a baritone.

JoAnne Akalaitis's first production as the New York Public Theatre's artistic director displays her virtues in abundance—alas, the defects of those virtues too. Her version of John Ford's *'Tis Pity She's a Whore* is undeniably terrific to look at. Set in fascist Italy during the thirties, the production has a design by John Conklin that proves to be the best performance on stage—a compound of futurist and surrealist elements that ravish your eye while illustrating how easily art can become a slave to tyranny. As interpolated cries of "Duce" fill the air, and posters extolling God, Country, and Family materalize between the Roman arches of the stage, Conklin rolls on huge cutouts of a child's hands, anonymous nude women, tearful faces, inspired by De Chirico, Marinetti, Dali, and other artists of the time.

Akalaitis shows no squeamishness about exploring the sanguinary aspects of *'Tis Pity*—a repertory staple in Artaud's Theatre of Cruelty. Her finest moment, along with the blinding of Putana, is the culminating bloodbath when Giovanni, arriving with his sister's heart impaled upon his dagger, participates in another three or four deaths, including his own. The stage is literally awash in gore, the impact so full of horror that, for once in the history of this play, the audience refrained from laughing.

She is less successful in extracting the theme of the work, which is offered as an object lesson in the brutalization of women by macho males (including Giovanni—who writes a misogynistic obscenity in blood on the wall of Annabella's room). Women are certainly treated badly in *'Tis Pity*, but so is everyone. Ford wrote this incestuous version of *Romeo and Juliet* less to make a feminist point than to demonstrate (years in advance of Nietzsche and Dostoevsky) that when God is dead, anything is possible. The abnormal love of Giovanni and Annabella is about the only redeeming feature in a world of social, political, and religious corruption, and when he takes her life at the end, Giovanni is choosing the only course left to him, monstrous though it is.

Missing from this interpretation is not only Giovanni's intellect (the Friar describes him as "miracle of wit") but his motivating narcissism. He loves his sister largely because she's his twin—as one commentator says, they make love in a mirror and take identical vows. As played by Val Kilmer, however, he is simply an edgy, sulky, shambling boy, while Jeanne Triplehorn's Annabella, befitting her victim status, is too subdued. Neither of these characters evokes much pathos, when the greatness of the play lies in the way the playwright redeems their corruption from an even more corrupt time. Their last scene together has virtually no love, warmth, or reconciliation when it should be breaking your heart. Since these are actors well trained for the stage (and not just for close-ups in *The Doors* and *Basic Instinct*), one has to conclude that Akalaitis has misdirected them, especially when virtually all the other roles—with the intermittent exceptions of Erick Avari's Vasques and Jared Harris's Soranzo—are indifferently performed. No one on stage reveals an interior life, and the comic scenes are execrable. "This part has been scurvily played," says one of the characters about another in the play—he might have been indicting almost the entire cast.

Still, the event is well worth seeing just for the brilliance of its colors and the boldness of its approach. Akalaitis may be wrongheaded and reductive to make this great seventeenth-century classic conform to contemporary feminist views, but the force of her commitment and her remarkable imagination must compel respect. Much more thought, preparation, and sweat went into the making of this blood-soaked masterpiece than our hasty opinions can do justice to.

[1992]

What Do Women Playwrights Want?
(*Laurie Anderson; The Baltimore Waltz; The Death of the Last Black Man in the Whole Entire World*)

IN A celebrated essay Virginia Woolf speculated about an imaginary sister of Shakespeare who might have equaled or even surpassed her brother's creative genius had she not been doomed to obscurity by male assumptions about appropriate female roles. (Recently Gloria Steinem mused in a similar way about Mozart's imaginary sister.) For centuries, narrow sexual conventions worked to restrict female achievement in the arts, particularly the public arts, and most particularly the theatre, where only actresses were allowed to reach any eminence, just a cut above that of royal courtesans. Before the twentieth century, women playwrights were as scarce as women composers and conductors (or women preachers, to take Samuel Johnson's famous example), if you discount Hroswitha of Gandersheim, Aphra Behn, and a handful of even less memorable talents. It is true that prospects for women theatre artists—directors and designers included—brightened considerably from the 1920s to the 1950s—with the appearance in this country of Susan Glaspell, Sophie Treadwell, Hallie Flanagan Davis, and Lillian Hellman. But even Davis's Living Newspaper and Hellman's *Little Foxes* hardly prepared us for the spate of plays by women that have multiplied in the last decade. The theatre hasn't yet produced a female Shakespeare, or even a female Eugene O'Neill, though England's Caryl Churchill is surely as accomplished as anyone writing for the stage today. But in terms of numbers, if not in literary sophistication, American women playwrights now represent a significant movement that is surely unprecedented in history.

To that list can now be added the authors of three items under review this week, beginning not with a play but with a dramatic disquisition recently delivered by Laurie Anderson at Harvard's Sanders Theatre. Miss Anderson is a performance artist celebrated for synthesized renditions of eerie hi-tech musical numbers. Aroused by what she perceives to be the growing suppression of the arts along with a deepening hatred of minorities in America, she has now marshaled her talents into a defense of First Amendment privileges, delivered in a free-ranging stand-up commentary not unlike the monologues of Spalding Gray or Eric Bogosian or Jackie Mason. The piece is in development and still needs work. All of it is polemical, much of it is rhetorical and shrill, unmediated by ambiguity or complexity. An extended video section featuring Miss Anderson's male alter ego—a stature-altered, voice-enhanced turkeycock, three feet tall with size one shoes—could profitably be cut (it was previously aired on PBS's *Live from Off Center*). But Miss Anderson's ironic shafts of satire occasionally pierce their targets with laconic accuracy. On the defunct Red Scare: "Everyone said 'The Russians are coming, the Russians are coming'—not a single Russian ever showed up." On Bush: "He asks us to do with the economy what we did with the war—now wait a minute, does he mean destroy it?" On Reagan: "He's always happy, like he's always singing 'When You Wish Upon a Star.'" On the senses: "You can close your eyes but not your ears—that's a defect. Still, the eyes are primitive—they pan badly, no zoom, bad dollies." On sitcoms: "The American version of the Greek chorus is the laugh track." On Puritans: "They weren't allowed to punish people on Sunday, so they came to America to exercise that glorious right." On Jesse Helms: "He saw a black dick sticking out of a business suit, so he made a law.... Now that black dick has reappeared as Long Dong Silver."

Miss Anderson finds us in a real emergency—ideas can be crushed and people silenced—which has temporarily impelled her to abandon music in order to sound alarms about the threat to free speech. Still, she has difficulty defending 2Live Crew, even though she believes they were singled out because they were black ("a bunch of guys bragging about the size of their dicks—I mean, what else is new?"). When she parses their lyrics she finds them vicious, even dangerous. She used to think that art couldn't hurt you. Now she's not so sure. Throughout the country the politics of greed have escalated into the politics of violence. "We hate kids, we hate women, gay people, black people, old people. ...We got caught in some dark version of *Father Knows Best*, where Dad has forgotten how to talk."

These are important issues which require more subtle treatment than Laurie Anderson is able to provide with her technological equipment and synthesized voices. What is significant is the way this spirited, spiked-hair, dimple-cheeked artist has been goaded into politicizing her performance art. For her, as for many others, the censorship issue "is making people ask, What does it mean to create art?"

Paula Vogel is more concerned about another contemporary scourge, namely AIDS. Her play, *The Baltimore Waltz* (Circle Repertory Company), was inspired by a trip the playwright failed to take with her brother who, she learned too late, was HIV positive. Miss Vogel's surrogate heroine, Anna, undertakes that European journey—but it takes place only in her mind. Anna riffles through her Berlitz guide and practices foreign phrases while her brother Carl displays a pink slip to the library students he teaches, having been sacked for wearing a pink triangle to class. An officious doctor diagnoses Carl's affliction in incomprehensible technical terms, but it is Anna who imagines herself contracting a fatal infirmity—ATD or Acquired Toilet Disease. ATD, or course, is her mordant substitute for AIDS (it is contracted in dirty lavatories), and Anna's imaginary illness is inspired by the same motives as her imaginary trip abroad—to expiate the sin of omission through a process of identification. Never actually leaving Baltimore, she travels through a variety of countries, clutching Carl and her Berlitz guide, practicing French, German, and Dutch, seeking the Third Man (Harry Lime now traffics in illegal drug cures), encountering various species of Eurotrash, until, at the end, finding her brother dead, she dances the Baltimore Waltz with his corpse, a stuffed rabbit clenched under his arm. It is a touching rite of loving exorcism, personal yet transcendent, tenderly written by Miss Vogel and sensitively performed by Cherry Jones (Anna), Richard Thompson (Carl), and Joe Mantello (Third Man).

Suzan-Lori Parks is a most unusual addition to the growing ranks of female playwrights, a black woman writer of avant-garde plays. As Alisa Solomon has noted, only Adrienne Kennedy has preceded her in exploring this strange terrain, though Miss Parks is also influenced by such white experimentalists as Gertrude Stein and Richard Foreman. She represents a radical departure in African-American theatre—a writer with more on her mind than race. Distinguishing her work from what she calls the "I'm gonna-get-you-plays of the seventies," she is as much a product of Western postmodernism as of black consciousness. "It's insulting," she said in a postperformance discussion quoted by Solomon, "when people say my plays are about what it's about to be black—as if that's all we think about, as if our life is about that. My life is not about race. It's about being alive," adding, "Why does everyone think that white artists make art and black artists make statements? Why doesn't anyone ever ask me about *form.*" This is refreshing to say the least. But although her play, *The Death of the Last Black Man in the Whole Entire World* (recently performed at Yale's Winterfest in New Haven, along with plays by two other women writers, Maria Irene Fornes and Colette Brooks) is a weird and woolly exercise in form, it is, as the title suggests, also an essay on race.

The characters, costumed and made up as fictional types and mythical stereotypes—Bigger Thomas, Uncle Tom, Topsy (who sometimes sounds like Butterfly McQueen), Hazel the maid, a Bantu warrior—are endowed with names like Black Man with Watermelon, Black Woman with Fried Drumstick, Queen-then-Pharaoh Hatshepsut, Old Man River Jordan, and so forth (suggesting that still another dramatic antecedent for the play is Jean Genet's *The Blacks*.) Like other members of the postmodernist school, especially Joyce and Stein, Suzan-Lori Parks is preoccupied with deconstructing language: *The Last Black Man* is partly an effort to exalt black English into a kind of poetic code. It is also an effort to adapt English words to the black experience. As the play jerks the audience through history in nonsequential nightmare fashion, a character named "Before Columbus" reflects on a time when the world was flat, while another insists that the world was "roun'" until Columbus made it "round" with a "d." Noah's African son, Ham, reconstructs *Genesis* from the black point of view ("Yes Suh Mistuh Suh breeded with hisself n gived us Wassername"), as cries of SOLD chronicle the marketing of slaves at auction. "Where he gonna go now that he done dieded?" becomes a kind of mournful refrain when Black Man undergoes a series of executions, including electrocution and lynching, watermelons accumulating at his feet.

In short, Miss Parks deconstructs language as a means of

establishing the place of blacks in recorded history. "You will write it down because if you don't write it down then we will come along and tell the future that we did not exist. You will write it down and carve it out of rock." This is another way of endorsing Milan Kundera's definition of art as the struggle of memory against forgetting. Black Man dies over and over again, but he dies asking Black Woman to "Remember me."

The play, directed by Liz Diamond with a talented cast of actors, is too densely written for one mind to absorb at a single sitting. Miss Parks's literary influences are not always the clearest indices in the theatre, and her dialogue seemed glutted with (to my ears) uncoded dialect. The playwright avoids the conventions of black victimology, but her play remains engaged with issues of racial oppression. Turning this familiar subject into metaphorical form is a daring and original idea. Somehow it still seems somewhat familiar. It must be said, however, that the problems with *The Last Black Man in the Whole Entire World* are of a kind that inspire keen interest in Miss Parks's future. It is refreshing indeed to come upon an African-American play that values poetry over realism, that is not located in a tenement or a backyard (Michael Vaughn Sims's abstract metallic setting is a distinct asset here). It is even more refreshing to discover another woman playwright who refuses to be submerged in feminist issues.

If one were to rephrase Freud's controversial query and ask, "What do women playwrights want?" the answer might be: freedom from the kind of ignorant assumptions that inspire such questions. Laurie Anderson's jaundiced look at censorship, Paula Vogel's remorseful essay on the loss of her brother to AIDS, Suzan-Lori Parks's experimentalist probe into black history, all share an effort to throw off not just traditional male assumptions about the role of women, but recent feminist assumptions as well. Independent, idiosyncratic, and alive, these works—whatever one's caveats or strictures—are significant for exploring what is shared by all humanity.

[1992]

'Cause Jelly Don't Shake Like That
(Jelly's Last Jam; Guys and Dolls)

THE sweet comfit platter being offered on the stage of the Virginia
Theatre is called *Jelly's Last Jam*, a succulent musical spread of
acting, dancing, and singing that represents a genuine advance in
black theatrical expression. George C. Wolfe's previous productions—*The Colored Museum* and *Spunk* (his adaptation of stories
by Zora Neale Hurston)—reverberated with an original, if not
yet fully formed, artistic voice, while his staging of Brecht's
Caucasian Chalk Circle (in an adaptation by Thulani Davis)
signaled access to wider cultural references than are usually
expressed in African-American plays and productions. Wolfe's
new jazz musical, *Jelly's Last Jam*, confirms and advances the
theatrical promise of this young playwright-director. It is a
completely realized manifestation of musical theatre, exciting not
only for itself but for the roster of talented new performers Wolfe
has lined up on the Broadway stage.

Like Spike Lee's *School Daze*, *Jelly's Last Jam* is less concerned
with recruiting a litany of past and present oppression than in
probing prejudices found within the black community itself,
usually based on differences of ancestry, income, and education.
Wolfe's subject, in short, is not racism but classism—the more
widespread, if less publicized, problem of our times, since it is an
issue that involves Americans of every ethnic type. Intraracial
class prejudice among blacks is sometimes related to shades of
skin color (just as Jews used to discriminate against each other
according to accents). But instead of dealing with issues of race
or the resentments blacks feel toward whites, Wolfe concentrates
on how his hero's loyalties and prejudices, if not his musical
tastes, are determined by family background.

The "jam" in Wolfe's title has three distinct meanings—as a riff
on Jelly's name, as a reference to his music, and as a description
of the circumstances in which he finds himself at the beginning of
the play. We first see Jelly—born Ferdinand Le Menthe Morton
into a New Orleans family of Creole gentry—on the eve of his

death, rising on an elevated platform, his back to the audience. Jelly is being arraigned by a Mephisthophelean figure known as the Chimney Man for betraying his own people. Declaring that the jazz movement Jelly helped to create was the expression of messengers "torn from their native soil," the Chimney Man indicts Jelly as a "messenger who thought he was the message," for exalting his own role while denying the race that inspired his music. Now it is time for Jelly, standing at the corner of "Cadaver Avenue and Last Gasp Lane," to tell his tale and save his soul before being doomed to perpetual damnation.

As a young man Jelly is torn between the demands of his aristocratic family, who make him practice classical piano, and the more colorful enticements of Storyville, a world of washboard music, street dancers, and high-yeller women—on the one side, his picture-framed ancestors and domineering Grandmother, on the other, Miss Mamie (the Queen of Rampart Street) and Buddy Bolden, who "played notes only colored folk in heaven could hear." To his and our delight, this proper boy is soon debauched by black sin, "jammin' with niggers and messin' with whores." Circulating through pool rooms, dance halls, and brothels from Chicago to East Saint Louis, "lover of women, inventor of jazz, and owner of twenty-seven suits," he is eventually featured in supper clubs as "Jelly Roll Morton and his Red Hot Peppers," where he falls for a club owner named Anita. The obstacle to their love is Jelly's disdain for negritude. Anita believes that "the blacker the berry, the sweeter the juice," but the light-skinned Jelly, consumed by jealousy, insults his closest friend by handing him a red bellboy coat and telling him to open doors for white folk "like a good li'l nigger."

Eventually, despite some success in Tin Pan Alley, Jelly's music is supplanted by the new sounds emanating from the horn of Louis Armstrong and others. But by play's end the Chimney Man—"the concierge of my soul"—redeems him as a figure of myth, despite the harm he has caused by "the black self-hatred thing," establishing Jelly in the pantheon of great jazz musicians along with Ellington, Waller, and Armstrong. His roots are stronger than his prejudices: "Inside every note of his is what he came from, who he is."

Jelly's Last Jam is more morality play than musicalized biography, but despite the insistence of its theme it is crammed with meat, spice, and juice. Because Jelly is played by Gregory Hines, he makes an impression as a dancer rather than a piano man—but what a dancer! In two-steppers with his younger self, brilliantly performed by the agile Savion Glover, Hines has choreographed numbers of such dazzling virtuosity they join the great tap-dance tradition of Bill "Bojangles" Robinson and Charles "Honi" Coles, which reached its apogee in vintage musicals of the thirties and forties. (My very first theatre experience, as a child of nine, was *Swinging the Dream*, a jazz version of *A Midsummer Night's Dream* with Robinson, Maxine Sullivan, and Louis Armstrong—it closed in four days and determined the course of my life.) With his mournful demeanor and vaguely ophthalmic insinuating eyes, Hines establishes a relationship with the audience that is nothing short of illicit. And when his feet start moving, he is into a dimension of sheer animal grace. Mesmerizing too is the Chimney Man of Keith David, a species of strutting basso usually played by Geoffrey Holder, and enacted here with menacing intensity and virility.

But the women on stage are equally sensual and alluring. Mamie Duncan-Gibbs, Stephanie Pope, and Allison M. Williams as a singing-dancing group called the Hunnies maintain the dignity of Thompson gazelles while delivering such ribald numbers as "Lovin' Is a Lowdown Blues" ("Lovin' is a fuck you blues"), while Mary Bond Davis, belting "Michigan Water" as Miss Mamie, possesses the raunch and grit of a latter-day Ma Rainey. The real find in the distaff cast, however, is Tonya Perkins as Anita, whose gumbo is served "hot—and over a bed of rice." A splendid actress and a fine musician, she sings "Play the Music for Me" and "Last Chance Blues" with the caustic melancholy of one who knows every last secret of sexual relations. These jazz numbers, by the way, are by a variety of composers—not only Jelly Roll Morton but King Oliver, Walter Melrose, and Luther Henderson (who did the fine musical adaptation), while Susan Birkenhead's new lyrics are seamlessly woven in with traditional blues. A final word of praise for the designers—Toni-Leslie James for costumes, Jules Fisher for lights, and Robin Wagner for sets (possibly the only Broadway setting this season not designed by Tony Walton). They provide a surround of energy and color that are further testimonies to George C. Wolfe's exhilarating command of the stage.

After *Jelly's Last Jam, Guys and Dolls* (at the Martin Beck) is something of a letdown, not because the Frank Loesser score and the Jo Swerling–Abe Burrows book are anything less than the classics we remember, but because Jerry Zaks's revival is considerably inferior to the original show. We have been awaiting a major American version of this fabled musical for many years now, sustained only by a clunky movie (which miscast Marlon Brando and Frank Sinatra) and reports of occasional revivals abroad. Zaks, who alternates between cosseting the customers (*House of Blue Leaves*) and pleasing himself (*The Marriage of Bette and Boo*), is back in an audience-kissing mood with *Guys and Dolls*. He delivers a lusty, animated, well-paced show, but a show without an underlife. Damon Runyon's grifters, gangsters, and gamblers are treated like characters out of the movie version of *Batman* and *Dick Tracy* (Lieutenant Brannigan even wears Tracy's electric yellow overcoat and fedora), while New York—in Tony Walton's arch design of humanoid skyscrapers and winking subway stations—resembles nothing so much as the Toon Town of *Who Framed Roger Rabbit?*

Take the character of Nathan Detroit, originally played by Sam Levene as a gravelly, world-weary sharpster with a pencil-stripe moustache and a pinstripe suit. In the hands of Nathan Lane, the stripes have widened but the performance has narrowed. Lane is an appealing actor who knows how to zing Burrows's proto-Mamet dialogue with one-liner expertise, but he lacks the seasoning for this part, the life experience. Whatever his age, he seems too boyish. Faith Prince has been widely praised for her performance of Adelaide, and she certainly knows how to belt her songs, especially "Take Back Your Mink" and that syncopated celebration of postnasal drip called "Adelaide's Lament." But her quarrels with Lane make them sound like the Mertzes in "I Love Lucy." Vivian Blaine brought more womanliness to the part and considerably less sourness. Josie de Guzman as the Salvation Army lass, Sarah, has a speaking voice like a car alarm system and a singing voice like a klaxon. Hard-edged and mechanical, she turns the love scenes with Sky Masterson into peanut brittle. As Masterson, Peter Gallagher alone makes an effort to invest his character with inner life. Not ideally cast as a working-class New Yorker, he nevertheless manages to evoke the world-weariness of a young Bogart and—despite a costume (blue pinstripe suit, blue suede shoes, white tie, and black fedora) that tries to create him in the image of another cartoon—he's the only one on stage that seems to have walked real streets.

Still, *Guys and Dolls* is probably actor-proof and director-proof (it's certainly critic-proof), and this revival undoubtedly has its charms. Shamelessly looted from the Bertolt Brecht–Dorothy Lane–Kurt Weill musical *Happy End* (which in turn stole a page from Shaw's *Major Barbara*), this tale of a gambler redeemed by a Salvation Army lass is basically irresistible, and the Loesser music remains one of the best scores in American musical comedy history. Few people since the premiere in 1950 have been able to shoot dice without humming "Luck Be a Lady," and, though Walter Bobbie lacks Stubby Kaye's rotund charm as Nicely Nicely Johnson, "Sit Down, You're Rockin' the Boat" remains a vibrant showstopper. If I appear less than wild about this revival, it's because I don't much like seeing it through the mist of movies, television, and other screens that have since been beclouding our apprehension of human life on this planet.

[1992]

Awards Versus Achievements
(The 1992 Tony Awards; Fires in the Mirror)

THE 1992 Tony Award ceremonies confirmed once again that the heart and blood, though surely not the brains, of the Broadway theatre is the musical. This magnetic force field is not only expected every night of the year to draw thousands of out-of-towners to the island of Manhattan. It has also been charged with the added burden of keeping millions of television viewers glued to their screens every spring for an evening of awards. As a result, the great bulk of Tony prime time is invariably devoted to extended excerpts, complete with sets and costumes, from all the nominated musicals, making them the main focus of the event, the source of the most tumultuous applause. To further persuade Nielsen-baked couch potatoes that theatre can be as popular as cable TV or network sitcoms, the presenters are almost invariably movie and television stars, some of whom may have actually acted once on stage.

It is true that a number of Tonys also go to straight plays, but compared with the riotous fervor reserved for musical offerings, such awards generally seem like an obligation. They are also something of an embarrassment, considering how few serious plays actually open on Broadway each season (this year's award went to Brian Friel's *Dancing at Lughnasa*—perhaps Tony voters thought it was a play about a hoofer). Glenn Close, functioning as hostess for the event, even felt obliged to remind the glittering Minskoff audience that "many of the most famous musicals came from plays." On Broadway, Shakespeare is sanctioned for providing the inspiration for *Kiss Me Kate* and Shaw for contributing the book to *My Fair Lady*.

Miss Close, wearing a variety of shimmering gowns for the occasion, including a blue-and-green number which made her look as if seaweed were growing up her arms, was a Tony winner herself (for a part in *Death and the Maiden*). Her acceptance speech credited Amnesty International with helping to foster a world community "where cruelty and abuse don't exist any more"—she helped a little herself with the zinger of the evening, a paraphrase of Herb Gardner to the effect that "There *is* life after Mr. and Mrs. Rich" (neither the *New York Times* critic nor his theatre columnist wife, Alex Witchel, had shown much appreciation for her performance). Miss Close nevertheless seemed to share Miss Witchel's weakness for Hollywood hunks, whinnying like a mare over Alec Baldwin (and perhaps inflaming feminists further by introducing Michael Douglas as "my fatal attraction").

The Tony event had its occasional entertainments, few of them rehearsed: Carol Channing squinting like a snow owl in the giant black-rimmed glasses she used to read the teleprompter, Liza Minelli (who sloshes her sibilants) being forced to speak the name of a choreographer with three esses in it, William Finn giving two largely incoherent acceptance speeches for *Falsettos*, Vincent Gardenia extolling the virtues of "Dancing at Lasagna" (a title nobody could pronounce), Faith Prince commending "the unsustained love" of her husband, the camera's way of catching virtually all the nominees applauding themselves when their names were mentioned. It was the usual display of egoism, ecstasy, and entropy. But for reasons I'm still trying to understand, I couldn't work up my usual quotient of rage over the ceremony. Perhaps the Tonys have gotten too predictable for sustained indignation.

Although many performers displayed red ribbons symbolizing their sympathy for AIDS victims, there was more implied concern over that problematic patient, the ailing city of New York, which inspired a variety of pep talks both from presenters and winners. Significantly, three of the four nominated musicals were set in the city, and the fourth—*Jelly's Last Jam*—had New York scenes. Everybody's favorite show, obviously, was the nostalgic paean to a more innocent Manhattan, *Guys and Dolls*, excluded from Best Musical because it wasn't new (it won for Best Revival). Through reasoning that escapes me, *Crazy for You* collected the prize, despite the fact that its Gershwin score is almost sixty years old. But nothing about the Tonys makes much sense. It's not just that the judges are self-interested theatre people voting their opinions and prejudices, or that the prizes are so clearly designed to boost box office, or that internecine competition is incompatible with a creative process based on difference. By recognizing only shows produced within a fourteen-block area, the Tonys manage to exclude (except for a single award to a resident theatre—this year the Goodman) about 99 percent of the nation's theatrical activity from consideration. This includes the most interesting works being produced in New York.

Among these is *Fires in the Mirror*, a one-woman evening conceived, written, and performed by Anna Deavere Smith at the Joseph Papp Public Theater. Miss Smith has accomplished the remarkable feat—through tape-recorded interviews with twenty-six diverse characters, most of them fiercely antagonistic to each other—of capturing their opinions and personalities in a way that goes beyond impersonation. Even more remarkable, she has dealt with one of the most incendiary issues of our time—the confrontation of blacks and Jews following the accidental death of Garry Cato in Crown Heights and the retaliatory murder of an innocent bystander, Yankel Rosenbaum—in a manner which is thorough, compassionate, and equitable to both sides.

Anna Deavere Smith is associate professor of drama at Stanford and Bunting Fellow at Harvard. She is also a sensitive sociologist and a gifted actress and mimic. Donning a variety of hats, caps, yarmulkes, cloaks, and accents, she manages to move easily among a large number of people from vastly different backgrounds and temperaments. And although the Crown Heights incident is the detonating cap, it is by no means the only explosive subject in the show. *Fires in the Mirror* is part of a series to be called *On the Road: A Search for American Character*. The title suggests her ambition to bring to the stage a wide spectrum of contemporary types, both celebrated and obscure.

The first half of the evening is devoted to some of those who make up the American character, most of them Brooklyn residents: the playwright Ntozake Shange expounding on the nature of the desert with a kind of stoned imperturbability, Gittel Lazerson, a preschool teacher, talking in high nasal tones about how she has to get a black kid to turn off the radio on Shabbus, the playwright-director George C. Wolfe describing how he could be treated as an extraordinary child and a "nigger" at the same time, and an anonymous thirteen-year-old girl reflecting on how black people are really into hair styles. As if to confirm this, the Reverend Al Sharpton materializes to claim that he copied his own coiffure from James Brown ("the father I never had"), while a Lubavitcher woman named Rivkah Siegal tells of the five wigs she must wear as a woman among Hassids.

Reflecting on race, Angela Davis surprises us by saying she now believes that "race is an increasingly obsolete way to construct community," while a female rapper named "Big Mo" takes after her male counterparts for failing to understand rhythm and poetry. One character who offers no surprises is Leonard Jeffries (Miss Smith collapses into a chair and dons a green African kepi to play him). He boasts about how he was hired by Alex Haley to keep *Roots* honest, and then was betrayed when Haley went off to make a series on Jewish history. Jeffries claims to have been tired when he made his Albany speech, yet displays his usual paranoia in charging Arthur Schlesinger, Jr., with suggesting "this [Jeffries] is the one to kill" just because the historian devoted a full page to him in *The Disuniting of America*. Nation of Islam Minister Conrad Muhammed (in a red bow tie) affirms that the Jewish Holocaust was nothing compared to 200 million people killed on slave ships over a three-hundred-year period. Not only do African-Americans win Muhammed's prize for competitive suffering, but "we are the chosen...the Jews are masquerading in our garments." Letty Cottin Pogrebin reflects on how if you want a headline, "you have to attack the Jews," though "only Jews regard blacks as full human beings."

The Crown Heights section collects all these tensions into an overpowering conclusion. Through the use of Wendel K. Harrington and Emmanuelle Krebs's graphic projections, a series of photographs capture the contorted world of violence, accident, grief, and revenge. Rabbi Joseph Spielman sadly describes how, though Gavin Cato was killed through no malicious intent, angry blacks began running through the streets, shouting for Jewish blood. Their anger was fired by rumors that the Jewish ambulance wouldn't help the child along with charges that "they" never get arrested. One anonymous black man sees significance in the fact that the blue-and-white colors of New York police cars and Israeli flags are the same. Michael Miller of the Jewish Community Relations Council, while expressing sympathy for the dead child, agonizes, "But 'Heil Hitler' from blacks? 'You better warm up the ovens again' from blacks?"

The incendiaries stoke these fires. Smug and self-satisfied, Sonny Carson warns of another "long hot summer," and Al Sharpton, flying to Israel in a media-savvy effort to arrest the driver, announces, "If you piss in my face I'm gonna call it piss, I'm not gonna call it rain." A sharp-tongued Brooklyn yenta attired in a spangled woolen sweater asks, "This famous Reverend Al Sharpton, which I'd like to know, who ordained him?" She adds that black people have nothing to do with their time, "so somebody says, Do you want to riot?"

People on both sides of this conflict can claim to be victims of injustice and prejudice, but the scariest thing about the incident, aside from the absence of leadership and the appalling mismanagement by the city, was the tinderbox nature of the community, a condition magnified in Los Angeles. In both riots the condition can be ascribed to hopelessness and lack of opportunity. One anonymous black boy tells us there's only two choices for kids like him, to be a D.J. or a "Bad Boy," and with disc jockey jobs in short supply, the Bad Boys form the armies of the rampage. The most harrowing words, though, belong to the survivors of the dead. Norman Rosenbaum shouts at Yankel Rosenbaum's funeral, "My brother's blood cries out to you from the ground." And Carmel Cato, a spent exhausted Caribbean, tells of how the death of his child was "like an atomic bomb." The simile is apt in describing his grief and rage, not to mention the grief and rage being expressed throughout the country in these inflamed times, however misdirected. *Fires in the Mirror* dramatizes those emotions, and tempers them, with an eloquent dispassionate voice.

[1992]

Wilson Lights Stein's Lights
(Doctor Faustus Lights the Lights; Richard III)

IN JULY, Robert Wilson made one of his rare appearances in this country with his Hebbel-Theatre production of Gertrude Stein's *Doctor Faustus Lights the Lights*. It is only one of many Wilson projects now in workshop, in rehearsal, in performance, and on tour. His latest calendar—a mimeographed document he distributes semiannually to friends and collaborators—not untypically records seven productions over seven months in twenty-five different cities. Most of these will be stages in Europe where Wilson usually spends his creative time. Apart from a handful of projects originated by American theatre companies (like Wilson's forthcoming production of *Danton's Death*, now being prepared with Houston's Alley Theatre, and a touring revival of *Einstein on the Beach*), the Texas-born artist usually appears before native audiences through subsidized foreign exchanges. Our country simply does not have the resources—or, I fear, the sense or sensibility—to support his epic imagination with any continuity.

Doctor Faustus Lights the Lights, which opened the Serious Fun Festival at Lincoln Center's Alice Tully Hall, is not one of Wilson's more grandiose creations. It lasts but ninety minutes—

about 167 hours short of the seven-day *KA MOUNtain and GUARDenia Terrace*—and employs only twelve actors. Two of these are professional. The rest are students in training at the Ernst Busch Theatre School in East Berlin (many are taking their first trip beyond a border once barred by the Wall). Wilson's work with these student actors is an extension of his lifelong interest in young people. His very first piece, *Deafman Glance*, was inspired by a deaf black child named Raymond Andrews; succeeding works were made in collaboration with Christopher Knowles, an autistic youth; and his celebrated *Hamletmachine* was developed with undergraduate theatre students from NYU.

Wilson's task in the current production was not only to train bodies unskilled in his meticulous choreographic demands but, with the aid of elocutionist Bernd Kunstmann, to drill foreign tongues in the eccentric Basic English of Gertrude Stein. This language they articulate in a flatly accented Germanic style, adding an exotic piquancy to the already distanced activities on stage.

I can't say I've been a great fan of Stein's later writings, which strike me as weighted down with repetitive preciosity. It was reputedly Stein's intention to make nonsense so intrusive it begins to approximate sense. Sometimes this works—her famous "A rose is a rose is a rose" is a good shorthand way of warning writers to avoid flowery symbolic connotations. More often her repetitions seem to me a lazy method of keeping her motor idling. One cannot, on the other hand, deny Stein her place as a pioneer of postmodernism, which makes Robert Wilson the perfect director for her plays. What Wilson does with *Doctor Faustus Lights the Lights* is integrate many of the traditions of the American postmodernist school, from the prepared sounds of John Cage to the spasmodic choreography of Merce Cunningham to the Eastern-inspired minimalism of Philip Glass to the eerie compositions of Meredith Monk to the elaborate technology of Laurie Anderson, mixing them all with his own genius for precision lighting, furniture design, and stage setting, and adding a hint of German expressionism for good measure.

The production features a Wilson-lettered stage curtain which subjects Stein's title to the same repetitions as her play ("Thank You Doctor Faustus Lights the Lights the Lights Doctor Faustus

Lights the Lights Or Faustus Lights the Lights," and so forth). After raising the curtain on a man holding a pair of calipers to his head, he multiplies these repetitions by splitting the characters: three actors perform Doctor Faustus, three play Marguerite Ida and Helena Annabel (Stein's name for Goethe's Gretchen), and two enact a Red and Black Mephisto. Other characters include a barking dog who snaps its jaws and says "Thank you," a little boy in white, a Mr. Viper who kills Marguerite and sends her to hell, and a Country Woman on stilts who carries a scythe. Originally planned as an opera, but lacking a composer, the work has found a brilliant one in Wilson's frequent collaborator Hans Peter Kuhn, who contributes a striking sound score consisting of the shattering of broken glass, comic bleeps, snippets of oompah band music, and synthesized flourishes reminiscent of computer games like Super Mario. Both the frisky music and Wilson's own whimsicality endow the text with continuous playfulness.

Since it was Stein's intention to create a literature without logic, this dense and gnomic work defies interpretation. As the title suggests, however, the author was apparently intrigued at this time with the invention of electricity. Stein's Faustus, more akin to Goethe's than to Marlowe's, possesses an overweening passion to achieve the unknown, and being modeled also on Edison, sacrifices his soul to see the light ("Oh Doctor Faustus, do say that you are the only one who can turn night into day"). A wizard of lighting, Wilson has chosen to make electricity the central image of his production, not an inconsiderable feat considering the limited technical resources of Alice Tully Hall. At one point a large number of globular incandescent light bulbs actually float down from the flies, but the stage is always awash in rays of every color and size, including suspended neon booms and illuminated rectangular beams.

What plot there is concerns the effort of Faustus to join Marguerite in hell after the viper has ended her life. Before death separates them, the two have plighted their troth ("I am the only he and you are the only she and we are the only we"). Mephisto tells Faustus that a man without a soul can only go to hell by killing someone, and Faustus responds, to an ineffably sad piano accompaniment, by drawing his index finger first across the throat of the Boy, who falls slowly to the ground, then of the

Dog who expires with a silent scream. Though Mephisto endows him with the gift of youth, Marguerite does not recognize the rejuvenated Faustus because she knows he is old and cannot go to hell. He speaks his last words, "Leave me alone," isolated on stage as the rectangular screen behind him diminishes to nothing.

This description cannot begin to convey the actual theatrical experience, its visual beauty and aural delights, its uncannily precise choreography and continuous surprises. Without Wilson's unifying imagination, Stein's text would be a series of arbitrary effects, lacking a coherent animating idea. But by treating *Doctor Faustus Lights the Lights* as an avant-garde musical comedy, reinforced by the high spirits and daring of his young cast, Robert Wilson has redeemed a difficult play and again confirmed his place as one of the most original theatre artists of our time.

Another overseas company recently visited our shores: the Royal National Theatre, touring with its celebrated *Richard III*. Opening at the Brooklyn Academy of Music on the tour's first leg, this production was graced with three major contributions—a demonic performance by Ian McKellen in the role of Richard, a powerful concept by Richard Eyre as director, and a striking minimal set by Bob Crowley. The rest of the touring company was merely competent, yet serviceable enough to support a riveting though virtually uncut interpretation of the play. In London during the same season, the National Theatre produced *The Resistible Rise of Arturo Ui*, a Brecht work dealing with the ascension of Hitler and partly inspired by *Richard III*. It did this badly. As if in atonement, the National's *Richard III* has been inspired by *Arturo Ui*, and comes off very well.

This is, in fact, one of the best simile productions I have yet seen (a simile production being one that updates a classical play in order to establish an historical "as if"). It takes up where Ingmar Bergman's *Hamlet* left off, with a political monarchy succumbing to virulent fascism. McKellen's Richard, I suspect, is modeled on Oswald Mosley, a British blackshirt who was also a peer. But where Mosley failed to persuade his countrymen of the virtues of totalitarianism, McKellen's Richard succeeds all too well, leaving us convinced that it *can* happen here.

An act curtain emblazoned with the name of Edward IV rises on a series of explosions; Richard emerges out of the smoke wearing the khaki greatcoat of a British officer in the "piping time of peace" between the wars. His reading of "Now is the winter of our discontent" is a shocker, delivered at it is in the ripe, fatuous tones of an overly cultivated Royal addressing the House of Lords. This Colonel Blimp may be pompous and effete, but is he capable of murdering children?

Yes. McKellen does not overstate Richard's evil any more than he exaggerates his physical deformities. But in time his persona somehow becomes more terrifying than Olivier's tenor snarls, half-closed eye, conspicuous hump, and wizened arm. McKellen illustrates his opening speech with significant ellipses (he is a master of the telling pause). Squinting like a nearsighted Mr. Magoo, he calls attention to his slight limp on the word "deformed," to the useless hand he hides in his pocket on the word "unfinished." Removing his peaked cap, he reveals that one side of his head is partially bald, decorated with stray wisps of hair. The whole left part of his body has been scorched by some monstrous stroke at birth.

Richard's scene with Ann is less persuasive. Her swift capitulation to the man who killed her father and her brother is hard enough to play convincingly, but it's impossible to believe that this fashionably dressed flapper could ever be attracted to such a patrician fop, even when he unbuttons his tunic with one good hand, bares his breast, and offers her his bayonet. Although McKellen's Richard is insufficiently sensual, however, he hardly lacks for menace or cruelty. While Queen Margaret rants on about the death of her husband, he concentrates indifferently on dinner, and after she leaves, lights a postprandial cigarette off one of the candles.

Slowly, subtly, Richard and his followers begin to exchange their khaki uniforms for blackshirts, armbands, and jackboots. In a scene staged like a Nuremberg rally, Richard, barking into a mike from a raised platform, denies all interest in the throne, despite roars from an enthusiastic crowd. Finally accepting the crown, he rips off his armband in a gesture that ends in a Nazi salute as a curtain bearing the name Richard III in German Gothic type descends over tumultuous cheers.

The second part does not possess equal theatrical power, largely because Shakespeare's play deteriorates from a fascinating character portrait into desultory scenic pageantry and battle scenes, ending with Richard's defeat at the hands of Richmond. Eyre fails to find a convincing contemporary analogy for the ghost scenes, and the battles are routine. But that's no matter— McKellen's Richard remains vivid and compelling. An actor I have often considered a mannered star personality, substituting elocution for depth, McKellen succeeds here in making verbal affectations the basis for a powerful political personification.

[1992]

The Theatre of Pain
(Les Atrides)

THE level of discomfort at Ariane Mnouchkine's ten-hour Greek tetralogy *Les Atrides* has only been surpassed, in my experience, by Peter Brook's nine-hour Sanskrit marathon, *The Mahabharata*. These two epic productions share a similar Asian aesthetic, but a more striking similarity is their calculated desire to make the spectators pay for theatrical satisfaction with physical hardship and spiritual denial—like yogis squatting on a bed of nails. In 1987 Brook persuaded the Brooklyn Academy of Music, at a cost of five million dollars, to renovate the Majestic Theatre so it resembled the crumbling, peeling conditions at the Bouffes du Nord in Paris. BAM spent only one million to remove jeeps, artillery, and ordnance from Brooklyn's Park Slope Armory and turn it into a replica of the Bois de Vincennes armory used by Mnouchkine for the Théâtre du Soleil. This expenditure is a bargain by comparison, and the armory's backed wooden chairs are comfort itself compared with the spine-crunching benches Brook insisted on. But the controlling impulse is the same and so is the motive behind these imperious mandates—to transform well-padded bourgeois theatregoers into butt-weary acolytes of arcane Eastern mysteries.

The danger is that, conforming to the frailties of your class, you may leave these intermissionless presentations remembering the pains more than the pleasures. Standing on a round-the-block line for an hour (thank heaven it wasn't raining) to be admitted into the vast tenebrous building. Groping in the dark on another line to enter a nonreserved bleachered seating area. Being banned from the theatre if you haven't arrived on the stroke to watch a play that begins twenty or thirty minutes late. Restrained and rebuked by stern Gallic guardians if you dare leave your chair before the final curtain call. Mnouchkine, in a more friendly gesture, invites the audience to visit the dressing room area before the show to watch her actors applying their paint. But with each makeup table scrupulously decorated, and every actor on display, the effect is not unlike that of looking through the windows of the red-light district in Amsterdam.

My ungracious grumbling admittedly reflects the aches of an aging body, and is in no way meant to lessen my gratitude to Harvey Lichtenstein and BAM for their Herculean efforts to move *Les Atrides* to Brooklyn. This is the legendary Mnouchkine's first visit to the Eastern United States (she brought three Shakespeare plays to the Los Angeles Olympic Theatre Festival in 1984), and while the overall impression is somewhat disappointing, *Les Atrides* is clearly the work of a major artist. Like Brook, Ariane Mnouchkine has committed her life to transforming the ways in which we think about the stage.

Both directors create works based on religious myths in order to urge the holiness of theatre in a world without God. The absence of belief made the glorious swirling spectacle of *The Mahabharata* look largely decorative, and *Les Atrides* often runs the same risk. For half its length these Greek tragedies seem to have been directed by a supremely gifted but essentially clueless costume designer and choreographer. Some savvy theatre people abandoned the armory in irritation after the first two plays, which is a shame because *Les Atrides* grew progressively better. At the climax of *The Libation Bearers*, a defining metaphor finally began to emerge, and *The Eumenides* proved an extremely strong rendering of a difficult work.

But it took some time for Mnouchkine to recover from an initial conceptual mistake, which was to patch on Euripides' *Iphigenia in Aulis* as prologue to Aeschylus's *Oresteia*. It is harsh to say that this was like using passages from Erich Fromm or Karen Horney as a preface to Genesis, but the result was not dissimilar. Aeschylus is a profound religious poet whose *Oresteia* is a meditation on the triumph of the Olympian order of gods. Euripides, writing fifty years later in a more humanistic age, was an agnostic rationalist with essentially social-psychological interests. It was precisely because of his differences from Aeschylus that Nietzsche hated this "civic mediocrity," calling Euripides a "poet of aesthetic Socratism" who banished Dionysian ecstasy and heroism from the drama: "Through Euripides the average man forced his way from the spectator's benches onto the stage itself."

Although this makes Euripides more acceptable to contemporary tastes (he is the true ancestor of Ibsen, Shaw, and Arthur Miller), he is also the dramatist least likely to provide any insights into *The Oresteia*. *Iphigenia in Aulis* is essentially about the victimization of women. It centers on the agony of Clytemnestra when she learns that her husband, Agamemnon, is preparing to sacrifice their daughter, Iphigenia, to Artemis in exchange for favorable winds to Troy. It is, in short, an Abraham and Isaac story as seen through the eyes of Abraham's wife Sarah. Agamemnon, sitting stone-faced before the audience with his legs crossed like a samurai warrior, remains deaf to all appeals to pity or moderation, while other principals and the chorus describe the pain of losing a beloved child. The play is strong in pathos, and no Greek dramatist better understood the psychological state of women in distress. But poignant as *Iphigenia* is to modern ears, it runs the risk of making Aeschylus's *Agamemnon* into a linear one-motive play about human fallibility rather than divine command.

Mnouchkine's *Iphigenia* ends (as all plays but the last end) with the ominous sound of barking dogs. *Agamemnon* picks up the story ten years later and on the same simple setting—a large raw wood arena resembling a bull ring with cattle doors upstage and matador escape areas where the chorus hovers when it's at rest. The Watchman, who begins the play squatting "doglike" on the roofs of Argos, spots the beacon light that signals the return of Agamemnon from Troy, and joyously ululates like an African tribesman. Whereas the chorus of foreign women in *Iphigenia* were splendidly Asiatic in their Rajasthani brocades, the chorus of old men in *Agamemnon* look vaguely Mesopotamian (even

Ozian—like ancient Munchkins) with their stylized beards and long staves. And whereas the *Iphigenia* women pummeled the stage with athletic Kathakali dances, the old men, exhausted by minimal movement, collapse upon each other, breathing heavily. The primary function of the chorus in *Agamemnon*, aside from offering hymns to Zeus, is to wander over the events of the Trojan War, a campaign as controversial to the Greeks as Vietnam was to us. When Agamemnon enters on his chariot (a moving platform modeled on the Greek *eccyclema*), he is enjoined by his ululating wife to tread upon a purple carpet.

The murder of Agamemnon is partly motivated by that hubristic act. It is also motivated by Clytemnestra's affair with Aegisthus, by her resentment over Cassandra (Agamemnon's Trojan courtesan), by the curse on the house of Atreus, and by several other reasons aside from the sacrifice of Iphigenia. Clytemnestra, in fact, offers as many motives for her act as Iago does for destroying Othello. (Unlike contemporary ideologists, great classical dramatists rarely adduce a single explanation for any crime.) By the time a mattress bearing the bloody bodies of Agamemnon and Cassandra is dragged on stage, the scene is set for a perpetual saga of eye-for-an-eye vengeance.

Until this point, it is true, Mnouchkine's *Les Atrides* seemed like an exercise in monotony. The heavy masklike makeup (pastewhite faces, darkened eyes) was an obstacle to facial expressiveness; the *Gestus* vocabulary was limited; the international cast of five principals mostly lacked vocal command though they doubled many roles and every speech was delivered to the audience; the lighting was general; even the galvanic choral dances began to seem repetitive. Jean-Jacques Lemetre's percussive music was more interesting to watch than to hear, as the bearded, pigtailed composer scooted back and forth among more than a hundred instruments in full view of the audience. But *The Libation Bearers*, which always struck me as the weakest of the trilogy, proved to be the play that most engaged the director, and at last a comprehensive overview began to emerge from the sequence of discrete images.

Here the aggressive, scornful chorus of young serving women mock their sartorial splendor with blackened teeth, black hands, and eye sockets dripping blood, testifying to their participation in the agonies of this family. Orestes, enjoined by Apollo to avenge his father, cannot sustain a dance, forcing his sister Electra to prop him up. The same actor who played Orestes (Simon Abkarian, who also played Agamemnon) leaves the stage to return as Orestes' old Nurse, lamenting his putative death and, in the most realistic speech of the trilogy, describing his toilet training. A scream issues from the pit and a servant enters with blood on his face; Orestes has killed Aegisthus. Wielding a bloody sword, Orestes threatens to kill Clytemnestra on stage, despite her appeals to spare the breast on which he slept. He grabs his mother's trembling hand and throws her on a moving platform, standing above her menacingly as they disappear from sight. Following a leaping dance by the chorus, the steaming waxen figures of Aegisthus and Clytemnestra are hauled in on a mattress. Orestes dances around the corpses in an ecstasy of blood lust before sensing the gorgons poised to pursue him ("You don't see them, but I see them. They push me—I can't stay here"). Two Noh-like supernumeraries in black vainly try to pull the mattress from the stage. Electra vainly tries to help them. The entire chorus vainly tries to pull the bodies—an eternal presence. The lights fade on the sound of barking dogs.

In *The Eumenides*, where the chorus reemerges as a principal character, the barking assumes physical form in the shape of Furies—apelike figures with doglike snouts and leonine manes. Exhorted by the ghost of Clytemnestra, they have driven Orestes mad, and now they want his blood. *The Eumenides* traces the development of Greek religion from the pre-Hellenic chthonic deities, with their tribal system for punishing family crimes, to the Olympian system of justice and order. In the first trial in recorded history, Orestes is brought before the Court of the Areopagus, composed of twelve Athenian citizens, for the murder of his mother. When the jury splits, this matricide is saved, ironically, by a woman. Athena casts the deciding vote for acquittal on the argument that, since she sprang full-blown from the brain of Zeus, a mother is not necessarily the blood relation of a child! Although feminists would hardly appreciate Athena's decision "to favor the male side in everything," it is to Mnouchkine's credit that she does not "interpret" this scene. The Errinyes or Furies, punishers of blood crimes, are transmogrified into the

Eumenides, patrons of the hearth (and family values). And thus these "difficult divinities," these matriarchal remnants, are absorbed into the new masculine order.

In *The Eumenides*, Mnouchkine largely abandons her Eastern influences to suggest an evolution into Western modernity. The actress playing Athena, for example, wears no makeup. The chorus of Furies, fitted with lupine prosthetic snouts inspired by *The Howling* and leaping up and down on padded fists like the apes in *2001*, are led by three ragged women who could be female Jacobins out of Mnouchkine's *1789*. Apollo is played by a tall, handsome, perpetually smiling actor capable of being a heartthrob for Gaumont studios. And just as the choreography changes from the graceful to the grotesque, so the acting evolves from Kathakali to Brecht.

Although the individual actors—apart from the versatile Simon Abkarian and the dynamic Catherine Schaub (who plays most of the Chorus leaders as well as staging the dances and designing the makeup)—sometimes seem inadequate to Mnouchkine's monumental design, the strength, discipline, and dedication of the entire troupe are ultimately what linger in the mind. Your body may sag but your soul is lifted, for if *Les Atrides* subjects you to theatre of pain, it has its moments as theatre of imagination and majesty as well.

[1992]

The Editorial Play
(The Destiny of Me; The Sisters Rosensweig;
Spic-O-Rama; Danton's Death)

ART and journalism may not be natural bedfellows, but ever since Euripides social-minded dramatists have been inclined to write editorials instead of plays. Against his better nature, Ibsen composed a few such editorials himself (notably *A Doll's House* and *Enemy of the People*), which made Bernard Shaw, that supreme journalist, wrongly assume "discussion" to be the quintessence of Ibsenism. You can always tell that a playwright is in an editorial mood when his language turns declarative: "I am angry against the Gods" (Euripides); "He is strongest who stands alone" (Ibsen); "Maybe we'll fix it so life won't be printed on dollar bills" (Odets); "Attention, attention must finally be paid to such a man" (Miller). This kind of broadcast prose usually indicates that the writer, caught up in an urgent issue, has momentarily become indistinguishable from his protagonist in pursuit of radical change.

Editorial drama can be a lively and useful form of playwriting, but it's not the most textured or profound. F. Scott Fitzgerald famously called the mark of a really fine mind the ability to keep at least two opposing ideas in your head at the same time. Since conflict (whether of thought or action) is the very essence of drama, you might say that command of dialectic is also the mark of a really fine playwright. Editorial writers, on the other hand, usually stop at thesis without encountering antithesis, which is to say, they are content with only one idea.

I suspect that Larry Kramer would be perfectly happy with a column on the op-ed page of the *Times*. His earlier play, *The Normal Heart*, in fact, was mainly about the rage of his autobiographical hero, Ned Weeks, over that newspaper's inadequate coverage of the AIDS crisis when compared with articles devoted to Legionnaire's Disease. Kramer is an AIDS activist—more recently (and lamentably) an AIDS victim. His playwriting has consisted almost exclusively of an effort to raise media awareness of this plague so as to shame the government into committing sufficient resources to a cure.

This is a noble cause which he has pursued with force, constancy, and eloquence. He's not alone. AIDS-related plays now constitute a whole subsection of modern American drama—*As Is*; *Eastern Standard*; *The Baltimore Waltz*; *Lips Together, Teeth Apart*; *Falsettos*; and, preeminently, *Angels in America* are only a sampling. Sometimes, as in the case of Scott McPherson (*Marvin's Room*), the playwrights don't outlive the run of their plays. It is almost as if this dreadful scourge, which is killing so many gifted theatrical friends, has assumed a presence in our drama similar to that of fate in *Oedipus* or venereal disease in *Ghosts*.

But AIDS is not only a lurking tragic inevitability; it represents an unsolved medical mystery in need of attention. And therein lies the critic's difficulty. How do you assess the artistic qualities of such an urgent social agenda? If the editorial function dominates Kramer's new play, *The Destiny of Me* (at the Lucile Lortel Theatre), that is because the author sees AIDS exclusively as proof of an unjust society which must be shamed into action. Set, like so many modern plays, in a hospital room (is disease now the metaphor of our times?), the play begins with Ned Weeks engaging in clinical tests while the gay activists he leads picket outside. In his own mind at least, Ned has now assumed the role of homosexual messiah ("I can't save the world with my mouth shut"), enduring experimental treatment while awaiting his obit in the *New York Times*. His enemy is "they"—the vast American majority that wants to "kill off all the faggots and niggers and spics.... Too many of us have been allowed to die. There's not one person out there that doesn't believe a genocide is going on." In this vaguely paranoid conspiracy fantasy, "they" even include the doctor and nurse who are trying to help him, whom he abuses for "rat-shit" cures and for being unwitting pawns in a homophobic American plot. Told that President Bush is eager to find a cure, he retorts, "He's brain-dead and you're brainwashed," while offering to donate to the president some of his tainted blood.

Running parallel with this hospital drama is a memory play about Ned's Jewish family—his brutal unfeeling father, his bustling possessive mother, his sympathetic straight brother, and himself as a waggish, sensitive young gay. This too is a story of injustice and insensitivity. Dad punches him out for being a sissy ("I never wanted you, I should have shot my load in the toilet"), Mom is too passive, even brother Ben sends Ned to a shrink to "cure" him of his sexual condition. At the end, facing his death, Ned informs his younger self of his blighted HIV-infected future, and they join in singing "Only Make Believe."

It is the makeup of this family, and probably the excessive length of the evening (three hours), that has led critics to compare Larry Kramer with Eugene O'Neill. His true kinship, however, is with Arthur Miller (with blood lines out to Clifford Odets, Tennessee Williams, and David Rabe as well). O'Neill, like most great dramatists, knows that no one is free from responsibility, and *A Long Day's Journey* concludes with the author's understanding and forgiveness for all his benighted characters, including the author's surrogate. But there is very little self-examination in *The Destiny of Me*, aside from the uninvestigated idea (first mentioned in *The Normal Heart*) that gays have trouble finding love because they're always seeking sex. Kramer's enemy is invariably the Other, and his constant purpose is to induce, excavate, and heighten the audience's sense of guilt.

What the play lacks, in short, is O'Neill's existential tragic rhythm, a quality Dennis Potter also managed to capture in yet another work about disease, *The Singing Detective*. Still, for all its self-absorption, self-exoneration, and self-importance, *The Destiny of Me* is never boring. Ned Weeks displays much the same vital energy as Osborne's Jimmy Porter, another relentless kvetch whose endless grievances kept his blood pulsing through his veins—though, in the case of Ned Weeks, his blood may be killing him.

Marshall Mason's Circle Repertory Company production, however, has too much vital energy. Instead of cutting *The Destiny of Me*, he has raced it, creating the technical clatter of a farce marathon. I found the tone and pace incongruous with a reflective memory play. Jonathan Hadary, as the older Ned Weeks, rattles his lines in a manner appropriate to the Broadway musicals that poster his hospital walls, and John Cameron Mitchell as his youthful self, though ingratiating, is sometimes stuck in show-time. The ripening, red-haired, dark-voiced Piper Laurie is seriously miscast as a Jewish mother. David Spielberg as the father has convincing early moments, but his violent rages are embarrassingly staged. Peter Frechette as brother Ben ages well and manages the difficult feat of creating irregular details inside a square character. Oni Faida Lampley as Nurse Hanniman possesses authority and humor. But I never believed for a moment that Bruce McCarty's callow Dr. Della Vida had ever seen more than a few weeks of medical school. As for John Lee Beatty's setting, it is serviceable as an antiseptic hospital room but transforms clumsily and unconvincingly in the domestic scenes. The same might be said for this editorialized play.

Wendy Wasserstein's *The Sisters Rosensweig*, newly opened at Lincoln Center, has quickly been announced for Broadway where it should have opened in the first place. It is the female equivalent of *Conversations with My Father,* Neil Simon for the college set, a sitcom *Three Sisters,* already destined for Critics Circle Awards and anthologies like *Best American Plays of the Year.* My heart sank a little when the witty one-liners began popping ("Multiple divorce is a splendid thing, you get so many names to choose from" "Love is love, gender is merely spare parts"). I had hoped, after *The Heidi Chronicles,* that my very gifted former student was shaking her witticism habit. *The Sisters Rosensweig* has a lot of charm, but it is a regression. I guess it's hard, in the precarious circus of American theatre, to give up your trapeze.

Wasserstein's wit is not cruel, which makes her play at the same time endearing and somewhat toothless. Her technique is to create a character that looks at first like a stereotype, then to show the more complicated workings of the human heart. One can't help liking the person who creates this kind of material, even when it seems thin and predictable, so by its own internal measure, which is to be likable, *The Sisters Rosensweig* is a success. People will be entertained and will leave the theatre feeling warm and wise, which are the requisites of a commercial hit.

The play is primarily about Jewish identity. Three sisters gather together in London to celebrate the eldest's fifty-fourth birthday. Sara (Jane Alexander) is a haughty, loveless banker who, scorning her religious background, is now seeing a vaguely anti-Semitic Englishman. Gorgeous (Madeline Kahn) is a New England housewife from West Newton, currently "schlepping the sisterhood around London." Pfeni, the youngest (Frances McDormand), is an activist journalist in love with a bisexual English stage director. Of these only Gorgeous is remotely satisfied with her sexual lot. The main action concerns Sara's reluctant attraction to a shamelessly Jewish furrier named Mervyn from Roslyn (Robert Klein) who prefers to call her Sadie. Although Pfeni's stage director eventually decides he prefers men, Sara gets to sleep with Mervyn ("That furrier has some very special skills—just call it fun fur"). And the character who once called herself "a cold bitter woman who has turned her back on her family, her religion, and her country" finally gets to acknowledge her Jewish roots.

The director, Daniel Sullivan, has mismatched three actresses who really don't seem like sisters, which makes the simulated

Moscow Art Theatre poses appear even more artificial. But the performances are creditable enough—in the case of Madeline Kahn even wonderful. Edgy, nervous, and slightly hysterical, with a voice that slides into bat shrieks, she invariably finds both the comedy and the poignancy in a character who could easily have become a suburban housefrau caricature. I found Jane Alexander's Sara, though womanly, a trifle too coiffed, but so is the role. And his colorful character tempted John Vickery's English stage director into too much show biz rodomontade. Robert Klein's Mervyn, on the other hand, was a congenial loudmouth, a good-natured version of Alan King.

I've left no room for more than a mention of John Leguizamo's *Spic-O-Rama* at the Westside Theatre, but it's brilliant. This is a one-man show about a dysfunctional Hispanic family ("Not representative of all Latin families.... If your family is like this one, please seek professional help") where Leguizamo plays all the male and female characters. It instantly hoists him into the pantheon of such sharp-eyed chroniclers of contemporary character as Eric Bogosian, Lily Tomlin, and Anna Deavere Smith. Let me also briefly cite my colleague Robert Wilson's production of Buechner's *Danton's Death* at the Houston Alley Theatre—one of the most beautiful (and surprisingly textual) events he has ever staged. The acting in this extended death scene about French revolutionaries ranges from powerful to woeful, and the sound score is uneven. But Robert Auletta's haunting adaptation, John Conklin's gorgeous period costumes, and Wilson's sets, furniture, and lighting (with Stephen Strawbridge) combine to create exquisite verbal and visual images, evoking David, Ingres, and Daumier. The production also captures the timeless sense of what it means to be human in an editorial age.

[1992]

Nothing to Declare
(An Inspector Calls; Carousel; The Deep Blue Sea;
The Rise and Fall of Little Voice)

THANKS to an incorrigible need to generalize, I usually return from a visit to English theatre with a satchelful of opinions about the state of English society. This trip I sailed through customs with nothing to declare. While our own stage, though uninterested in defining a national character, has grown preoccupied with racial, sexual, and ethnic identities, current English theatre is virtually mute on the subject of what the nation is and where it's going, suggesting a contemporary culture that has not yet found a voice.

To judge by most of the productions I saw in the course of a week, in fact, the English may have decided that the pleasures of nostalgia are presently preferable to the ardors of self-definition, which is to say the nation is looking toward more confident periods of history. (This may explain why Arthur Miller is currently England's favorite national playwright.) While the Royal Shakespeare Company is still focusing on classics, the Royal National Theatre is giving superb productions to plays from the forties and fifties, lavishing sumptuous resources on projects either stuck in their time or arguably not worth reviving.

Take J. B. Priestley's *An Inspector Calls* (composed in 1944 and first performed in Moscow in 1945). Written partly to help ensure a Labor party victory in the 1945 elections, the play functions as an indictment of the moneyed classes for their indifference to the suffering of common people. A poor young woman has committed suicide by swallowing disinfectant, and a police inspector named Goole arrives to question a wealthy Yorkshire family about the death. After his relentless interrogation reveals that every member of the family was somehow implicated in her fate, Goole tells them that "we are members of one society, responsible for each other," and that "if men do not learn this lesson they will be taught it, with sword and fire." Blame and responsibility as manufactured and distributed in the Yorkshire branch of the Arthur Miller Guilt Factory.

The son and daughter are eager enough to accept their portion of blame ("if there's nothing else, we have to share our guilt"). The others are more recalcitrant about learning this "lesson," especially when they discover that the inspector is an impostor and there is no record of the girl's suicide. Just as they are celebrating their own complacency, they are told that a young woman has poisoned herself and another inspector is coming to interrogate them.

For all its supernatural paraphernalia, *An Inspector Calls* is a conventional exercise in the Theatre of Guilt, and it suggests how far socialist drama had departed from the paradoxes of Shaw, how clumsy bourgeois drama had become after the exhumations of Ibsen. The characters are judged, in Marxist fashion, almost entirely according to class, and the plot is entirely predictable from the start. But if the audience usually keeps ahead of the writing, it must pant to keep up with the production. Stephen Daldry's direction and Ian MacNeil's design at the Lyttleton provide a totally mesmerizing experience which almost succeeds in validating the play.

Daldry begins the action in front of an old-fashioned red-curtained proscenium arch. A pile of junk sits there, including a red English pay phone, fallen out of the perpendicular, and an abandoned table radio. One of a group of ragged children, climbing through a trap onto the stage, kicks the radio, which emits scary Gothic music. The ragamuffins then push open the curtain and invade the stage. It is a bizarre mystic landscape, backed by dark clouds, strewn with potholes and rubble, in the midst of which, adjacent to a crooked gas street lamp, sits an Edwardian house on stilts. (In the distance sits the model of a similar house, next to an identical street lamp.) We look at the inhabitants through the window of a tiny dining room, celebrating the daughter's engagement. When they emerge to speak to the Inspector, they must cross the crumbling pavements, just as modern city dwellers are forced to navigate a rotting infrastructure when they leave the comfort of the hearth. Near the end of the play they are confronted by a mob of the poor, their jury, mute accusers, glowering witnesses.

In short, this supernatural landscape is peopled with political ghosts, reminding us of the chasm between wealth and poverty, between complacency and suffering, between material gain and its human consequences. And at the climax, when the family has been charged and indicted, the house literally blows up and falls apart. Daldry's surrealist approach, coupled with the penetrating acting of the cast, create the poetic metaphor that the text so sorely lacks. But for all the theatrical wizardry and invention, we are ultimately left with the creaky mechanics of a crudely written polemic.

Upstairs at the Olivier Theatre, another brilliant production is enhancing another odd choice for a subsidized theatre, Rodgers and Hammerstein's *Carousel*. As a note tells us, it was possible for the National to mount *Carousel* on this monumental scale only "through a lavish and inspired grant from the Cameron Mackintosh Foundation," which will support other "classic musicals" in coming years. I'll say the grant's inspired. Guess who will probably get first crack at producing these shows when the commercial cash registers start ringing.

Let me affirm my sometimes suspect respect for American musicals and revues. I consider their composers and lyricists among the finest talents our country has produced: Gershwin, Berlin, Kern, Porter, Rodgers and Hart, Loesser, Bock and Harnick, Hamlisch, Styne, Bernstein, Sondheim, the list is only partial. If I have been less enthusiastic about some of the "book musicals" that followed the first collaboration of Richard Rodgers and Oscar Hammerstein II (*Oklahoma* in 1943), that is because they achieved "artistic" status by adulterating their already middlebrow source material. (Some, admittedly, like *Gypsy*, *Guys and Dolls*, and *Jelly's Last Jam* enhanced their source material.) Hammerstein, in particular, enjoyed smuggling into Rodgers's lush music capsule messages about the various liberal issues of the day when he wasn't celebrating imaginary rural American virtues (inspired no doubt by the farm this New Yorker owned in Pennsylvania). Substituting artificial blood sugar for the unpretentious, robust, acerbic energies of the thirties musical, Rodgers and Hammerstein manufactured a *lehrstuck* dipped in treacle which was merchandised to the public as a "native American artform."

Carousel, their second musical collaboration, written in 1945, is generally taken more seriously because it is based on a serious play—Ferenc Molnar's *Liliom*. While *Carousel* does derive some strength from the Middle European wit and sophistication of the play source, Hammerstein cannot refrain from pasting a toothy smile on Molnar's sardonic features. The program note cheerfully documents the "improvements." For example, the Hungarian play is set in Budapest, the American version on a fantasy New England coast. The one ends darkly, with Liliom, given one more chance at salvation after a life of crime and wife abuse, failing his opportunity. The musical's Billy Bigelow succeeds in redeeming his one day on earth by inspiring his rebellious daughter to sing "You'll Never Walk Alone" during graduation (the program reminds us that the more cynical Molnar believed you *always* walk alone). Liliom is arraigned before a heavenly police court; Billy exchanges homilies with a twinkly Starkeeper. These changes, combined with all the interpolated clambakes, fishermen jigs, community sings, and everyone's irrepressible high spirits, not to mention inspirational exhortations to keep hope in your heart when you walk through the wind and the rain, create a Rotarian atmosphere congenial to audiences who seek not reality but escape from reality, not truth but respite from truth.

In short, it is American skimmed milk of the postwar variety, but Nicholas Hytner's production serves up the pabulum with extraordinary energy and verve, and even some edge, to an obviously delighted audience. Once again an inspired English director has been joined with an inspired English designer, Bob Crowley, whose sets reinforce one's sense that British scenic artists are now among the best in the field. Crowley has carefully studied the New England landscape, along with such indigenous American painters as Andrew Wyeth, John Kort, Kib Bramhall, and Neal Welliver. The results are exquisite: Cape Cod perspectives of crowded shacks decorated with lobster traps and marker buoys, maternal mounds of earth supporting a model of an enchanting steepled house, a sandy beach backed by undulating beach grass, and the Mullins Carousel itself, circling wildly on a revolving stage.

Hytner begins his production with an interpolated scene, the women in Bascombe's Textile Mill working at their shuttles and looms. It is an image of perfect symmetry reinforced by harmonious choral singing and by the lively choreography of Kenneth

MacMillan (who died a month before the show opened). The English render the mechanics of "June Is Bustin' Out All Over" and similar rustic hosannas as rousingly as any American production I've seen. The National's nod toward nontraditional casting involves an African-American in the part of Mr. Snow, whose eight children by Carrie Pipperidge are a multiracial brood of six blacks, one Caucasian, and an Asian (my, that woman must have been a caution). All the actors are fine, but Joanna Riding as Julie Jordan is wonderful. The half-anguished, half-exalted look on her face when she senses the ghost of Billy in the room is worthy of a much greater play. She is transfixed and so, for a moment, are we.

The most adventurous theatre in London, at present, is the Almeida. It has featured a number of interesting new plays as well as powerful productions of *All for Love* and *Medea*, both starring Diana Rigg, so when friends urged me to see a production there of Terence Rattigan's *The Deep Blue Sea* I overcame my skepticism and went. This play was written in 1952 and, like all of Rattigan's work, continues the despair-among-teacups tradition that the Osborne revolution was designed to end. The production is, indeed, a finely modulated piece of theatre—empathetically directed (by the Czech filmmaker Karel Reisz) and acted with depth and sensitivity by a first-rate cast. Yet here was another of those evenings when you wished that all that talent had been lavished on a more cogent play.

Rattigan was inspired to write *The Deep Blue Sea* as result of the suicide of a former male lover. In conformance with the mores of the time (pre–Joe Orton) Rattigan turned the man into a woman. Hester Collyer doesn't succeed in killing herself, though she tries twice. She has left her stolid husband, a jurist, and taken up with a raffish RAF pilot who doesn't love her enough, and much of the play is her explanation of why she prefers unfulfilled passion to safe domesticity. These people talk at each other very earnestly and they suffer a lot in solitude. They also display the most sympathetic British qualities—understanding without sentimentality, quiet control, the capacity to endure. Rattigan can draw small moments of truth, and he's not afraid to be depressing. Penelope Wilson as Hester brings extraordinary depth and anguish to her role. The rest of the cast is excellent. Why couldn't I like this more? Perhaps because, as in all such sensitive domestic relationship plays, you end up pitying the characters through a well-insulated fourth wall.

But compared with *The Rise and Fall of Little Voice*, *The Deep Blue Sea* is a masterpiece. Jim Cartwright's new play is a big hit at the Aldwych, having transferred from the National Theatre. I am totally bewildered by its appeal. It has, first of all, one of the most hideous sets in my theatregoing experience, and I've seen a few. Secondly, it is badly overacted, crudely directed, and written with clubbed fingers. And thirdly, it is debased by an *Edward Scissorhands* plot about a sensitive artist destroyed by the coarse commercial world. Mari Hoff, played by Alison Steadman with a voice that sounds like static in a broken CB radio and continually tugging her girdle, has a daughter (Jane Horrocks) who can impersonate every belter in the business, from Edith Piaf to Liza Minelli, though her own voice is scarcely audible and she's terrified of crowds. Mari professes to love her ("She's all I got beside my ass and tits") but allows her spiv lover to exploit the girl's gift, thus exposing Little Voice (or LV) to nervous collapse when she has to face an audience. Furious over the desertion of her lover, Mari throws LV's beloved records out of the window. Eventually, LV is rescued from despair by a telephone repair man who brings her back to the deserted nightclub and restores her self-esteem. By the end she can sing in her own voice.

This is the sort of thing that turns intelligent people off the theatre—a play pretending to depict the vulnerability of the artist (and celebrate the indomitability of the working classes) but written in a style more appropriate to a network TV series like *Roseanne*, with running gags about smelly fridges and blown fuses and sick drunks and clumsy fat people, with the audience functioning as a laugh track. It made me despondent, probably because it confirmed a sense of England in social drift and cultural confusion.

[1993]

Akalaitis Axed
(Wings)

A MUSICALIZED version of Arthur Kopit's *Wings,* produced by the Goodman Theater in Chicago, opened recently at the Public Theater in New York. Although virtually all the other notices (including that of the *Times* Sunday reviewer) were enthusiastic, it got a predictably sour reception from Frank Rich who called it "cerebral" and "intellectual." A few days later the Public's artistic director, JoAnne Akalaitis, was summarily dismissed, following only twenty months as Joe Papp's handpicked successor (her replacement is the gifted George C. Wolfe). The two events, if not exactly causative, are symbolically related.

It does not take a conspiracy theorist to conclude that some role was played in this affair by the *Times,* which had conducted an unrelenting campaign against Akalaitis ever since her appointment was announced. But whatever the pressures on the board, the dismissal of Akalaitis was unusually brusque and humiliating. She was given twenty-four hours to clean out her desk and vacate the premises, behavior more appropriate to corporate raiders than to nonprofit managements. Still, it cannot be said that the decision was unexpected. Ever since her brief tenure began, there had been rumors that Akalaitis's days were numbered, even that Papp himself had changed his mind before he died and tried to replace her.

It is true that, for a number of reasons, Akalaitis was not well cast as the leader of a large multiplex institution. For one thing, she often intruded a forbidding political agenda into her classical deconstructions. For another, she was not overly diplomatic in a role requiring tact and mediation. For a third, she wasn't proving too successful at fund-raising. But these are ways of saying that Akalaitis is an artist rather than an administrator, and artists are notoriously singleminded and tunnel-visioned. (For that reason, the more entrepreneurial George C. Wolfe may well prove an effective successor.) It is difficult enough to focus your energies on a single production, much less fill a number of other theatre spaces with continuous activity over the course of a season. Papp's solution was to leave most directing assignments to protégés. Akalaitis chose to fill the smaller stages with one-person shows and stage almost all the major productions herself.

This probably hampered her administrative duties. It certainly left the perception that little was happening down on Lafayette Street compared with the storied days of glory. Although I agreed with this criticism, I must also admit that the glory days were something of a myth. Papp often left many of his stages dark, particularly in the first five months of each season, while incubating his spring projects. But although Akalaitis was learning on the job, developing a group of Artistic Associates who would surely have increased activity at the Public in time, the impression of comparative inertia was difficult to overcome. Worse, it attracted undue attention to the few things she produced, which subjected the Public to hit-flop criticism and focused a harsh spotlight on her own personality instead of dispersing commentary over a number of people and projects.

Some subscribers complained that her choices were "grim." In a characteristic kick-the-corpse Sunday piece, Frank Rich called these choices "academic"—"plays by writers on Ms. Akalaitis' short list of Drama 101 modernists" (meaning Brecht, Lorca, Beckett, and Buechner, "the avant-garde of the 1960's and 1970's"). Conveniently forgetting he'd regularly expressed a similar disdain for Papp's choices, and had been particularly ferocious about the Shakespeare Marathon, Rich asserted that while this now infallible figure might have tolerated such "avant-garde" works as *Woyzeck* (1837), he "would have combined them with other, more substantial offerings, such as a diet of original new American plays and musicals, not to mention frequent mountings of Shakespeare." Actually, Akalaitis had herself directed the Public's *Cymbeline* and the two parts of *Henry IV* (as well as the Jacobean *'Tis Pity She's a Whore*), and was not only persisting with Shakespeare in the Park but planning her own production of *Henry VIII* this summer.

And no other projects in her two seasons were incompatible with traditional Public Theater fare. Anna Deavere Smith's powerful *Fires in the Mirror* originated at the Public under Akalaitis. And although Rich charged that Akalaitis became a cosponsor of

Tony Kushner's *Angels in America* and Jose Rivera's *Marisol* "only after other theatres had developed them or given them their imprimatur," the fact is, as Alisa Solomon noted in a hard-hitting *Village Voice* piece, that Akalaitis had sponsored these plays from the beginning. Her scheduling problems were due to simple bad luck. She lost *Angels in America* when the Mark Taper decided to bring it directly to Broadway, and she lost *Marisol* only after the author elected to open it first in Hartford (no doubt to avoid premature death at the hands of New York reviewers).

The savagery of Rich's postmortem (he even attacked the bookstore she set up in the lobby) is more than a personal vendetta. It can be better understood in the context of the New Aesthetic Populism, a condition threatening virtually every theatre in the country and causing many similar artistic upheavals. The causes are social, political, and economic, with pressures to compromise and conform coming from critics, audiences, foundations, and government alike. The result is that theatres these days are not being led so much as administered, the power of artistic directors having been transferred to managers and boards: "We have always been more comfortable with management structures ... than with the troublesome intangibles of the creative imagination," I wrote some years back in "Boards versus Artists," and the crisis has only deepened. The artistic result is a common centerpiece of *A Christmas Carol* surrounded by critically sanctioned, recycled Broadway and off-Broadway hits.

This explains why so many second-generation artistic directors, following the death or retirement of strong-willed founding artists, have lost the capacity to hold a nervous board at bay (much less to disband it if it exceeds its powers). In the past few years these boards have fired a number of adventurous theatre leaders, usually for failing to please the audience or attract enough contributed income—not only Akalaitis at the Public but Liviu Ciulei at the Guthrie, Adrian Hall at the Dallas Theatre Center, and Anne Bogart at the Trinity Repertory Theatre, among others. The fact that two of these are women (and that Carey Perloff, the new artistic director at the American Conservatory Theatre, may be in similar trouble) has raised cries of sexism that would seem to confirm Akalaitis's recurrent theatrical theme of female victimization. But the condition goes deeper. All of these were artists on the cutting edge in theatres grown more dependent on popular approval. None was given sufficient time to develop a policy or a following after early audience defections.

In short, our culture is still in the grip of Reagan-Bush conservatism, despite the recent change in administration, and a bottom-line mentality continues to rule our art. Instead of educating audience taste, once-independent theatres have now begun to follow it, and the visionary gleam is dimmed. Of course there are sound financial reasons for cautious management, since the survival of an institution is a crucial goal. It is a goal second only to its survival as a creative force. For what profits a theatre to gain the world and lose its own soul?

To me the most disturbing thing about the New Aesthetic Populism is the alliance of mainstream critics like Rich with fiscally conscious board members and hit-happy consumers against the artists who provide the inspiration. Rich indicts the theatre community for not ganging up on Akalaitis, and he indicts Akalaitis for criticizing the taste of her own subscribers (something the feisty Papp often did too, especially at the Beaumont). He reserves his praise for the board, which should "be applauded for ending the misery with relative promptness."

I'm not questioning the Public Theatre board's decision, and I don't underestimate the difficulty of supporting controversial theatre artists in a declining economy. I do question its callous procedures, and particularly what many perceive to be its buckling before critical intimidation. I once described a war on the arts from the left (political correctness), from the right (moral correctness), and from the center (aesthetic correctness). This is clearly an attack from the center. It is bad enough for one newspaper to control the destiny of commercial production, but when a powerful critic begins to arbitrate the conduct of nonprofit institutions, a shudder passes through the entire theatre community. Who next will lose her job through the *New York Times*?

Frank Rich's insistence that the Public concentrate on more musicals like *A Chorus Line* and more new plays that might attract a wider audience exposes not only his inability to distinguish between the values of the commercial theatre and nonprofit structures but his continuing indifference to art with any depth or daring. Papp used a production like *A Chorus Line* as a means of supporting his more serious work, not as an end in itself. Rich apparently believes the resident theatre to be valuable only as a breeding ground for Broadway or for the latest Yuppie fashions.

JoAnne Akalaitis will survive these indignities. In time she'll even begin to enjoy the advantages of being a free artist with no institutional responsibilities. A more serious worry, under present conditions, is whether there'll be any institutions left where such free artists would want to work.

I've left precious little space for a review of the last production at the Public under her auspices, but it is a condition of the age that politics consumes the energies once reserved for art. Anyway, *Wings* is wonderful, though I must preface my review with the admission that Arthur Kopit's play, which began as a radio piece, was first produced at my theatre in New Haven. Now it's at the Public on the very same stage we visited on tour in 1978, and I must admit the present version is an improvement. A musical about a stroke must sound as appealing as a ballet about muscular dystrophy. But Kopit's work is not about disease or affliction so much as it is about language—the effort of an aphasiac to understand the function of words.

Kopit wrote this play after the death of his father from a similar affliction. His central character, however, is a woman, Emily Stilson (a Freudian might conclude that, though the author has lost a parent, he is *still* a *son*). Fiddling with the controls of her radio one morning, Emily falls to the ground in a faint, and the progress of the action is her long slow recovery back to a state where language regulates thought. A former barnstormer and aerial acrobat, she thinks of her condition in aeronautical images—the stroke was an air crash and the hospital is a prison in Rumania ("How it came to pass that I was captured?").

Emily is like an aging Alice caught in a Wonderland where she invents her own gibberish and absurdities. But the interesting thing about Kopit's work is how it turns prattle into poetry, much the same way Robert Wilson in his earlier work made poetry out of autistic language. What Emily remembers is how she "used to walk on wings," how she would "bank and soar and spin," and, finally, soon before her death, how she had an out-of-body flight, floating up to the ceiling.

The play is very moving, but the musical version is affecting in the extreme. Michael Maggio has devised an eloquently simple production with scenery and projections by Linda Buchanan, employing Foreman-like strings across the stage to essentialize entrapment and loss. Linda Stephens, though not quite as penetrating as Constance Cummings who originated the role of Emily, is nevertheless a noble and commanding presence, and I also much admired Ora Jones as a nurse and Hollis Resnik as the therapist who helps Emily recapture lost time and lost words (like "snow" and "tears"). Although there are Sondheim influences, the music and lyrics by Jeffrey Lunden and Arthur Perlman are more indigenous to opera than to musicals—and the title song is guaranteed to exalt and enthrall you. Try to catch *Wings* before it closes. You may never see its like at the Public again.

[1993]

Angles in America
(Angels in America)

TONY KUSHNER'S *Angels in America*—or rather the first of its two parts, *Millennium Approaches*—may very well be the most highly publicized play in American theatre history. It is certainly one of the most peripatetic. Originally planned for a 1989 opening at San Francisco's Eureka Theatre, then performed in full workshop at the Mark Taper in Los Angeles, later produced by the Eureka Theatre in San Francisco in 1990, still later by the Royal Shakespeare Company in London in early 1992, then staged along with its second part by the Mark Taper in Los Angeles in late 1992, and now mounted on Broadway after bypassing one of its scheduled sponsors (the New York Public Theater), *Angels in America* has received unanimous praise at every step in its journey, while its author, Kushner, and latterly its Broadway director, George C. Wolfe, have been inspiring feature stories in countless newspapers and magazines. Awarded a Pulitzer Prize before it even opened in New York, the play will doubtless win multiple Tonys, the Critics Circle Prize, the Outer Circle Award, and any other honors still being stamped by theatrical trophy factories. A hungry media machine collaborating with a desperate industry has turned the second dramatic effort of a relatively young playwright into that illusory American artifact, The Great American Play.

In short, *Angels in America* is being regarded less as a work of the imagination than as a repository of high cultural hopes and great economic expectations. And burdened with such heavy baggage, it virtually invites close scrutiny at the customs desk, which is to say, a classic critical debunking. This will surely come, but don't expect it from me. I have a few reservations about the script and more about the New York production. But for all the hype and ballyhoo, and granted one is judging an unfinished work, I must join in welcoming the authoritative achievement of a radical dramatic artist with a fresh, clear voice.

Indeed, the real question is how such a dark and vaguely subversive play could win such wide critical acceptance. Compare how long it took Mamet to find success on Broadway, and consider how many gifted writers such as Sam Shepard, David Rabe, Maria Irene Fornes, Christopher Durang, Wallace Shawn, and Craig Lucas, among others, have still failed to reach majority audiences. As noted, Kushner's new play satisfies special extra-dramatic needs. More intrinsic appeals are suggested in the subtitle, "A Gay Fantasia on National Themes." *Angels in America* is, first and foremost, a work about the gay community in the Age of AIDS—urgent and timely subjects fashionable enough off-Broadway, now ripe for the mainstream. It is also a "national" (i.e., political) play in the way it links the macho sexual attitudes of redneck homophobes in the eighties with those of Red-baiting bullies in the fifties. It is a "fantasia" not only in its hallucinated, dreamlike style but in the size and scope of its ambitions (O'Neill, among others, has accustomed us to associate greatness with epic length and formal experimentation). And it is a very personal play which distributes blame and responsibility as generously among its sympathetic gay characters as among its villains.

In short, despite its subject matter, *Angels in America* is not just another contestant in the Theatre of Guilt sweepstakes. Compare it with any recent entry on the same subject and you will see how skillfully Kushner navigates between, say, the shrill accusations of

Larry Kramer's *The Destiny of Me* and the soggy affirmations of William Finn's *Falsettos*. It is Kushner's balanced historical sense that helps him avoid both self-righteousness and sentimentality, and so does his balanced style—angry but forgiving, tough-minded but warmhearted, ironic but passionate, mischievous and fantastical. Kushner is that rare American bird, an artist-intellectual, not only witty in himself but the gauge by which we judge the witlessness of others. His very literate play once again makes American drama readable literature.

Kushner takes his title from one of his more memorable lines, "There are no angels in America, no spiritual past, no racial past." But if our country offers few figures of saintly virtue to satisfy our hopes for history, the author provides plenty of hallucinations, dreams, apparitions, ancestral ghosts, even a mute tutelary deity who, to the accompaniment of beating wings and garbed like a figure in a grammar-school pageant, comes crashing through the ceiling at the conclusion of the play. (Sam Shepard's unfinished *War in Heaven* is about another angel who crashes onto the American landscape.)

While they are no angels, most of Kushner's characters have their positive side. What he wishes to celebrate is the joy and courage with which they pursue their sexuality in a dangerous world. His main subject is how people display, discover, and affirm the fact they are gay (only one of his major characters isn't homosexual, and she's having a nervous breakdown). But despite Kushner's sense that America is essentially a queer nation in every sense of the phrase, his dramatis personae is a fairly representative grouping of contemporary American types: Joseph Pitt, a Mormon lawyer, Harper, his Valium-addicted wife, Louis Ironson, a Jewish computer technician, Prior Walter, his Brahmin lover now dying of AIDS, Belize, a former transvestite now turned male nurse—and Roy Cohn.

The presence of this malignant conservative icon heightens the political dimension of the play. As Joe McCarthy's former henchman, Cohn proudly assumes credit for the execution of Ethel Rosenberg (a phantom who appears near the end). But although he identifies homosexuality with subversion, he suffers from Karposi's sarcoma himself. Cohn stubbornly refuses to admit he is gay ("Roy Cohn is not a homosexual. Roy Cohn is a heterosexual man...who fucks around with guys"), mainly because gays have no *political* power. But it is another sign of Kushner's achievement that he is almost able to make this monster appealing (the warmhearted, totally confused Joe Pitt even expresses love for him). Roy Cohn is a classical dramatic villain who remains the play's most fascinating figure, a feat worthy of Racine who, tradition tells us, wrote his *Phédre* in order to prove he could make an audience sympathize with a criminal character.

Alternating between intellectual debates and theatrical hallucinations, *Angels in America* lacks an animating event or action, which is a major structural flaw in such a long (three-and-a-half-hour) work. The compensation is a gallery of wonderful characters, thirty in all, played by eight actors. The pivotal figures are Cohn and Prior, two men dying of AIDS, with two other men, the married Mormon Joe Pitt, discovering his own homosexuality, and Louis, discovering his own cowardice, revolving around these contrasting poles in various attitudes of guilt and sympathy. Louis abandons Prior when his disease reaches an advanced stage, though he seeks a pickup in Central Park in punitive disregard for his own physical health. And it is Louis, deploring the marginality of gays, who reflects on the difficulty of love in a country on the edge of serious nervous breakdown ("In the new century, I think we will all be insane").

This ominous premonition regarding the new century, the expectation of divine retribution, sends shivers through this play. The fatality is Greek but the prediction belongs to Ibsen who believed that "all of mankind is on the wrong track" and that the ghosts of the past and the future would retaliate for all our failed ideas and broken promises. As the ghost of Ethel Rosenberg says to the dying Cohn, "History is about to break wide open. Millennium approaches." *Angels in America* foreshadows these future schisms by dramatizing racial and sexual strife, the failures of liberalism, the absence of a genuine indigenous culture—and at the same time, curiously, manages to offer a trace of redemption. One redemptive feature, certainly, is a strong-voiced, clear-eyed dramatic artist capable of encapsulating our national nightmares into universal art.

The good news is the play. The not so good news is the New York production. In his notes Kushner wrote that "the play benefits from a pared-down style of presentation, with minimal scenery," though he wanted the magical effects to be "amazing." But at sixty dollars for an orchestra ticket (the highest price ever established for what we can no longer call a "straight" play), it was inevitable the physical production would be lavish. Robin Wagner's setting is made up of cold blue marbleized panels that seem appropriate only when one of the characters lands up in Antarctica. Usually the design chills an otherwise warm-blooded work. More disconcerting is the designer's literalism in displaying a New York skyline outside Roy Cohn's window and the canyons of Utah for a brief (cuttable) scene about a character moving from Salt Lake City, even glaciers and ice floes when the action moves to the South Pole. And far from being amazing, the special effects could use some help from Industrial Light and Magic.

I saw the production a few days before its postponed opening, and it has undoubtedly improved since. But I wasn't certain that George C. Wolfe, though extraordinarily gifted as a showman, possessed the temperament to realize such a subtle play. The evening contained a few touching scenes (particularly Louis dancing with the stricken Prior at the end), but the staging often seemed more appropriate to musical comedy than to serious drama (two scenes played simultaneously by four characters reminded me of the Jets and Sharks chorus in *West Side Story*).

And much of the acting lacked depth. Admittedly, most of the gay characters are highly theatrical (they make continuous references to Broadway shows), but if they don't possess a solid core of truthfulness, it is hard to identify their humanity. I much admired Joe Mantello as the suffering ironist Louis Ironson, Stephen Spinella as the cadaverous Prior Walter, and Ellen Mc-Laughlin in a number of doubled roles, all from the original California cast. But many of the major characters were either too bland or too frenzied to be credible. Suspended between keyed-up show biz and toned-down domesticity, the production lacked command, which is a shame because this is a play that requires a director as authoritative, and actors as intelligent, as the author. As for Ron Leibman's Roy Cohn, it is clearly over the top. Leibman, who has the mouth and teeth of a barracuda, and a nasalized vocal instrument which sounds like Jerry Lewis blowing a klaxon, plays the part as a Jacobean monster or Dickensian caricature, shouting, screaming, barking, stabbing his finger and slapping his thighs. He's so apoplectic you fear for his health, but he carries you along by the sheer force of his personality. I couldn't help admiring his outrageous audacity, and I also liked the Restoration fop he played in one of Prior's hallucinations (Leibman would be terrific as the brutal Manly in Wycherly's *Plaindealer*).

For me the central concern is not the quality of this production (there will be many more in future), but rather how its talented author will cope with all our deadly critical embraces and still continue his creative development. To be frank, the signs thus far are not exactly promising. The moment commercial interest surfaced for *Angels in America* there were enough personal betrayals, expedient decisions, fractured loyalties, and postponed promises to confirm the playwright's conviction that there are no angels in America—only angles. The Broadway producers, risking millions, are of course expected to protect their investment. But very few of the creative people involved acted with honor in this undertaking—not the director who broke his commitment to another theatre in order to take on the assignment, nor the author who agreed to drop his original designer, members of the original cast, and the original director (also his close friend), after the L.A. production. The decision to bypass the Public Theater may even have hastened JoAnne Akalaitis's departure.

Perhaps to compensate for all the shattered friendships and broken agreements, Kushner has insisted that eight hundred seats each week be sold at Public Theater prices (thus passing the moral debt to his producers in the form of reduced revenue). But one suspects that for all his professed loyalty to nonprofit theatres and "downtown audiences," he is rationalizing for the sake of a Broadway splash. We have had enough theatre history (notably, Tennessee Williams's career after *Cat on a Hot Tin Roof*, when he reluctantly allowed Kazan to soften the ending) to tell us that personal deception is not compatible with artistic development. Still, I have enough faith in Kushner's intelligence and self-knowledge (after all, he created Louis Ironson) to believe he won't deceive himself long and may even turn this experience to creative advantage. The great theatrical subject, which O'Neill pursued all his life and only captured when he created the character of James Tyrone, Sr., is how the bitch goddess success blights the life of the American artist. Who is presently learning more about this theme—or is more qualified to write about it—than the author of *Angels in America?*

[1993]

Aftermath: My review of this play provoked a long and angry letter from the author, charging me with slander, inaccuracy, and self-interest, since I was trying at that time to obtain *Angels in America* for my own theatre. The two inaccuracies, which I derived from an article in the *New York Times* Magazine, concerned the number of tickets reserved at discount prices and the chronology of the replacements of director, designers, and cast members (I had repeated the *Times*'s imputation that these came *after* the Frank Rich review). The misstatements have been corrected in the current version of my review, though I am still not entirely convinced of the time sequence for the replacements—John Conklin, the set designer, for example, has testified that he learned of his firing in a *Times* piece following the Rich review. As for self-interest, my criticism of Kushner's conduct was hardly likely to increase my chances of obtaining the play.

Despite Kushner's protests, the Broadway move left a lot of human debris in its wake. As I wrote in reply to Kushner's letter, that's not unusual, and no one questions a dramatist's right to change his personnel, but it's delusionary to believe, as the author apparently does, that all the victims are happy sacrifices to his career. The breach of a prior agreement with the Public Theatre was an action that led the soon-to-be-dismissed JoAnne Akalaitis to dub the whole affair "a study guide on what's happening to the not-for-profit theatre." And George C. Wolfe's decision to cancel his agreement to direct a play at the Hartford Stage Company in order to undertake the Broadway production was called "reprehensible" by Hartford's artistic director, Mark Lamos.

Kushner also criticized my reference to "the bitch goddess success" as "misogynistic." I have resisted the temptation to change that phrase to "morally challenged deified personhood."

The Great Work Falters
(Perestroika)

AT THE conclusion of *Millennium Approaches*, the first part of Tony Kushner's *Angels in America*, an angel crashes through the ceiling of Prior Walter's bedroom and announces: "The Great Work Begins." At the start of Part II, entitled *Perestroika*, a doddering Bolshevik complains that humankind cannot function without the equivalent of Marxist theory. *Perestroika* makes a heroic, if partly ironic, effort to furnish that alternative theory through the conception of a totally sexualized universe. But despite its admirable ambitions and for all its extraordinary qualities, *Perestroika* seems more a repetition than a culmination of the Great Work promised by the initial design. Like *Millennium Approaches*, it is alive with fierce intelligence and sharp scenes. It contains the same engrossing conflicts and engaging central characters. A kind of extraterrestrial soap opera (akin to *Twin Peaks*), it continues to mix reality and dreams—personal relationships and supernatural shenanigans—in a dazzling display of style. It features the wittiest writing and brightest sensibility of any play in memory. But it not only has little in the way of structure, it lacks the important dramatic component of a central action or animating event to push it forward. Most serious, it fails to prove its thematic premise, that an insistently homosexual perspective can be the basis for a universal worldview.

Even more than *Millennium Approaches*, *Perestroika* looks at politics and metaphysics almost entirely through the prism of sex and interpersonal transactions. The ailing Prior Walter ejaculates when the Angel first descends and experiences erection whenever she reappears. While she chants *"Ectasis in Excelsis,"* he humps a sacred text (the stage direction reads: "If they had cigarettes, they'd smoke them now"). He learns that "Heaven is a City much like San Francisco," where many of the angels are gays or lesbians, engaging in perpetual copulation and producing a Proto-matter (called "Angelic Spooj") which glues the universe together. Even Hannah, the stern mother of the gay Mormon, Joe

Pitt, gets turned on to the point of orgasm by the lesbian angel. Similarly, Conservative Joe and Liberal Louis discuss their political differences while making out in Jacob Riis Park ("The more appalling I find your opinions the more I want to hump you," Louis admits), and Roy Cohn's reactionary politics are almost entirely explained by his being a closet queen.

Then there is the specter of AIDS, which surrounds this play like an evil miasma, with its attendant horrors of emergency rooms and IVs, diseased tissues, lesions, sarcomas, pneumonia, and blindness. Though Prior is still alive at the end of the play, he and Cohn are dying of the disease throughout the long evening, inspiring Kushner to write at least four death scenes and two resurrections. (Cohn's dying is presided over by his arch-nemesis Ethel Rosenberg, who later prompts Louis in his recitation of the Kaddish over Cohn's body.) Kushner comes perilously close to suggesting that this plague is heaven-sent—not, as the fundamentalists would have it, as a punishment for sin, but as a sign of God's abandonment of humans around the time of the 1906 San Francisco earthquake (in heaven, Prior enjoins the Angels to take this deadbeat Dad to court for desertion). Prior's refusal to despair, or to let us avert our faces from this ghastly specter, are the qualities that anoint him as the Prophet of *Angels in America.*

In the conclusion, he, Louis, and Belize are sitting near the Bethesda Fountain in Central Park, presided over by a stone statue of another angel. The Bethesda Angel is associated with healing properties, and when the millennium comes, all who are afflicted will be enabled to bathe in her fountain. After Prior and Louis argue over Gorbachev and *perestroika*, and Louis and Belize dispute the rights of Palestinians, Prior reflects on the scourge that is killing him, and his comments are worth quoting: "This disease will be the end of many of us, but not nearly all, and the dead will be commemorated and will struggle on with the living, and we are not going away. We won't die secret deaths any more. The world only spins forward. We will be citizens. The time will come."

It is a moving statement on behalf of all who suffer the torments of this deadly affliction, and for once Kushner's mordant jests in the face of the horror modulate into pure feeling. But the swelling inspirational tone of his coda takes a sharp turn toward bathos with Prior's concluding lines, delivered directly to the audience: "Bye now. You are fabulous creatures, each and every one. And I bless you. *More life.* The Great Work Begins." The "Bye now" is unfortunate enough. But unless Kushner is assuming that everybody in the theatre is gay or HIV positive, there is more than a trace of audience-stroking in these curtain lines. To be blessed as "fabulous creatures" after watching three and a half hours of painful death scenes, sexual betrayals, corrupt politics, and cynical metaphysics in a "terminally crazy and mean America" suggests that sentimentality is the down side of Kushner's rhetoric, just as high camping is the flip side of his wit. For every surprising conjunction of clauses or skillful interlapping of scenes, there is a vaudeville skit or a gay wisecrack to trigger the laugh machine (Kushner has a particular weakness for gags about hairdressers and Fabergé cologne better left to the Theatre of the Ridiculous). Those lapses are frequent enough to prevent *Angels in America* from fulfilling its extraordinary potential, and so is our growing realization that the play's length is less a sign of richness than of the author's incapacity to edit out repetitions or focus on an integrated action.

For the subject of AIDS does not readily accommodate itself to any single worldview. It is an appalling disease which has claimed many of our close friends in the arts, but it does not lend itself to metaphor any more than cancer or tuberculosis, and is no more reducible to moral outrage than bubonic plague or syphilis. "I am dying. Why doesn't somebody help us?" asked the *Times*'s Jeffrey Schmalz before he succumbed to AIDS himself. Who but that absent God can answer his heartbreaking question? Like most viruses, AIDS has yet to find a cure, but until a cure is found, the disease has reality to us helpless humans less as a moral or political issue than as a particularly miserable and recalcitrant biological fact. Among the many AIDS plays, only Paul Rudnick's whimsical *Jeffrey* seems to recognize the practicalities of the problem, since it concerns a gay man who doesn't waste his time assigning blame but rather determines (though he fails) to stay celibate to save his life.

Kushner indicts his straight characters less for remaining indifferent to AIDS than for failing (*vide* Roy Cohn) to acknowledge their own homosexuality. And he condemns the gay world not for spreading the disease so much as for failing (*vide* Louis Ironson) to remain loyal to the friends who contract it. Personal loyalty and mutual support remain the lodestones of this author's public compass. Nevertheless, a pervasive sense of victimization wraps around his play like a shroud. The bleeding finger writes, and having written, fails to move on.

My main criticism of George C. Wolfe's direction of *Millennium Approaches* was that it applied Broadway accessories to a serious play. Oddly, these accessories seem entirely appropriate to the more commercially inclined *Perestroika*. Robin Wagner's scene design is now considerably more modest, and therefore considerably more effective, than his sets for Part I, consisting of simple furniture strategies rather than large location pieces. And the extravagant acting fits better inside a play with large theatrical gestures. I found Ron Leibman's shrieking and kvetching Roy Cohn just as impressive in Part II of *Angels in America,* though he is still on the outlandish side of reality. His mercurial shifts in tone and volume, his incredible rattling pace, mark him as the only actor alive who can interrupt himself. Stephen Spinella's feverish, spasmodic, emaciated Prior Walter is still enormously affecting, and David Marshall Grant's Joe Pitt remains a model of tortured propriety. Ellen McLaughlin is compelling both as a butch nurse and as the gyrating calisthenic Angel, Jeffrey Wright is a marvelously bitchy Belize, and Kathleen Chalfant is dignified in a variety of older male and female roles. Only Marcia Gay Harden's Harper Pitt remains embedded in sitcom, though Joe Mantello's Louis Ironson, vocally whiny and physically itchy, began to pall on me a little this time too. But then the actor is charged with playing so many sex scenes in front of an audience that he's probably a little strung out.

[1993]

Return of the Master
(Peer Gynt; Madame de Sade)

INGMAR BERGMAN has returned to the Brooklyn Academy of Music to consolidate his supreme position in world theatre—also, inadvertently, to highlight the poverty of the New York stage. Do we have to travel down Flatbush Avenue these days to find genuine examples of integrated theatrical art on brief visits from Sweden? Broadway can boast of award-winners and media favorites, but in Manhattan's showshops either dazzling staging is compromised by preposterous plotting, as in *Tommy*, or, as in *Angels in America*, powerful playwriting is obscured by hyperactive directing.

Bergman's visions of *Peer Gynt* and *Madame de Sade* highlight everything that's wrong with our theatre—its clamor for audience and critical attention, its financial insecurity and aesthetic bankruptcy, its rickety commercial values, its anxious and unstable nature. There is surely an appetite here for theatre of high ambition and consummate artistry—at both Bergman productions the overflowing BAM audience was rapt. It's just that we don't trust the public any more. We're no longer convinced that a truly serious theatre has any future.

No such doubts trouble Ingmar Bergman, who proceeds along his artistic path with high confidence and total dedication. His four-hour *Peer Gynt* is spellbinding in its various components, not least impressively the way it displays the certainty of a master. Bergman's recent treatment of classical writers almost amounts to co-authorship. Faithful to the spirit of the plays, he nevertheless invents fresh metaphorical entryways into their mysteries. For Henrik Ibsen, the Beethoven of modern drama, he has devised a symphony of brass and kettle drums, staging the entire action of *Peer Gynt* within a domestic Scandinavian room dominated by a central wooden platform that rises, flips, and falls to accommodate a variety of settings.

When the boyish Peer first appears to chivy and charm his adoring mother Ase, he is played by a middle-aged actor—Börje Ahlstedt, the memorable lead in *Fanny and Alexander*, as well as Bergman's Claudius in *Hamlet*. Directors have found various ways to cope with Peer's radical physical changes (he ages some fifty years in the course of five acts). Some, like Liviu Ciulei at the Guthrie, have used three different actors. Others, like Patrice Chereau in the Thêatre de Ville production, have stuck to one young actor and grizzled him. Others, like Mark Lamos at the Hartford Stage, have cast a young man without bothering to age him at all. Bergman's Peer is having a midlife crisis throughout the entire play.

Ahlstedt's oafish physique and buffoonish features at first make him look like an extra in a Hal Roach comedy, but when he slaps on a rumpled black felt hat and hunkers down, he transforms into Beckett's Estragon (Chereau's Peer, Gerard Desarthe, had affinities with Beckett's Lucky). Ahlstedt's ample belly burgeoning under a boiled shirt and his oxlike carriage endow him with a carnality seemingly at odds with conventional notions of Ibsen's charming fabulist. Yet by contrast with his boorish neighbors he's almost ethereal. Bergman has imagined a savage, animalistic rural society not unlike the Breughel-like world of *Virgin Spring,* where rape and violence are endemic. Peer is a rapist too, but at least he has a large imagination (he could have been an artist were he not so self-infatuated). As for Ase (played by Bibi Anderson, lovely and youthful despite a mop of spiky grey hair) and Solveig (played by the tender Lena Endre), these women are islands of innocence in a coarse, threatening firmament.

It is a world where trolls are only a natural extension of the general inhumanity. The Troll King's daughter, like the rest of her clan, is bathed in an eerie green light and sports a phallic tail. Pulling a rubberized penis out of his trousers, Peer takes her brutally from behind (she shortly gives birth on stage to a full-grown monster). Later, when she accosts him by grabbing his balls, he sinks an axe in her head. Still, the curious thing is how Bergman's depiction of this rampant bestiality conceals a deeper tenderness, as if extremes of feeling could only coexist with extremes of cruelty. Ase's death—Peer drives her to heaven like a coachman (and characteristically doesn't stay for the funeral)—is by far the gentlest and most compassionate rendering of this famous scene I have yet to witness.

In Act IV Ahlstedt embodies perfectly Peer's development into a callous capitalist, selling arms to the Turks in their war against the Greeks. Ahlstedt remains comically complacent right up until the madhouse encounter, when lunatics are declared sane because "what we call common sense expired yesterday, at 11 p.m." (a fair description of America in the nineties). It is there Peer discovers that absolute absorption with self, which we call narcissism, is a form of absolute insanity.

Bergman's final act is not as compelling or surprising as the first four. The pacing decelerates into a series of monologues, and the Button Molder is presented, not very originally, as an old man in uniform carrying a huge casting ladle (I preferred Chereau's image of a skinny wraith paring his long fingernails). Still, the final Pietà is exquisite, with Peer curling up in (blind) Solveig's lap while the Button Molder is backlit in the doorway. It is women who save Peer, just as women have always saved Bergman, and it is women who drop the anchor of compassion into these turbulent, inhuman seas.

Women also take center stage in Bergman's treatment of Yukio Mishima's *Madame de Sade*, five noblewomen and a servant giving performances of incomparable grace and majesty. I have always considered this piece unplayable, the static declamations of a writer with no real feeling for the stage. Mishima boasted that he "felt obliged to dispense entirely with the usual, trivial stage effects, and to control the action exclusively by the dialogue; collisions of ideas had to create the shapes of the drama, and sentiments had to be paraded throughout in the garb of reason." What he is describing is closet drama. Bergman, without disguising the disquisitory nature of the play, has skillfully managed to pull it out of the closet.

Mishima's theatrical objective was to speculate on why Madame de Sade, devoted to her husband during his eighteen years of imprisonment, abandoned him at the moment he was freed. His philosophical purpose, however, was to probe the beliefs of a famous historical figure without ever bringing him on stage (at the door near the end, he is turned away by his wife). Clearly Mishima felt some deep affinity with this sacred monster who established sexual cruelty as a new divinity.

Alphonse, Marquis de Sade, "a kind of music with only one theme," engages in the most exquisite forms of torture and perversion. He corrupts the sister of his wife. He can only enjoy sex through pain, in groups of threes and fours, or by profaning religious sacraments. Mishima's fictional Countess de Sain-Fond describes how she participated in a black mass with a crucifix between her breasts and a chalice between her thighs while the blood of a lamb cascaded over her body. Like her counterpart, the Marquise de Merteuil in Choderlos de Laclos's *Liaisons Dange-*

reuses, she is the female embodiment of the link between refine-
ment and corruption: "Alphonse is myself," she realizes, "the
bloodstained abortion of God, who can become himself only by
escaping from himself." His wife suffers all this, and even abets it,
because she is determined to be as devoted as he is debauched—
until he memorializes his crimes in a series of shameless novels.

The way Bergman approaches this decadent philosophical trea-
tise is by turning it into parallel forms of art—a Bourbon
painting, an eighteenth-century saraband, but also an exercise in
Japanese theatre. For just as Mishima projected his samurai
imagination into French history and culture, so Bergman projects
his back into the Orient. The setting by Charles Koroly is a series
of simple arches, with Japanese prints of flowers, fire, and clouds
projected on a cyclorama. Koroly's lovely brocaded gowns are
sometimes adorned with Japanese ideograms (the nuns wear obis
under their habits). The music is played on Japanese instruments.
And the acting proceeds in that stately deliberate mincing style
associated with Japanese theatre. When a character raises her fan
overhead, she could either be an actor on a Kabuki stage or a
figure in a painting by Watteau.

Bergman, in short, has found that undiscovered country where
one culture merges gracefully with another. He has also managed
to merge periods and centuries. As the action proceeds through
eighteen years—years which take their toll on the young and old
women alike—we are catapulted into modern times. Madame de
Sade's sister enters in a mink coat and hat and lights a cigarette
off a coal-burning stove. And the pastel silk gowns of youth are
replaced by heavy dark wools, almost Slavic in their style. The
Bastille has been stormed. The Revolution has begun. The Countess de Sain-Fond, killed in a demonstration masquerading as a
prostitute, becomes the legendary whore of the Revolution, like
Genet's Chantal. And the housekeeper, who has been hovering
discreetly in shadows throughout the play, either awaiting service
or eavesdropping on the family, has now turned surly and inso-
lent, preparing to deliver these tainted aristocrats over to the
guillotine.

All this, as Mishima promised, is pure dialogue. Physical action
is usually limited to a character raising a fan or striking a riding
crop against her palm. The women speak facing the audience, like

a chorus line of porcelain statuettes, or circle each other like panthers, and if anyone makes a sudden move, it's a violent event (the audience starts visibly at the exposure of an ivory breast). We grow intent on the curl of a smile, the raising of an eyebrow, a ruby at the base of a neck, the well-coiffed wigs, the variety of physical insults performed by the Marquis. Bergman has created this subtle stillness as a way of making us look and listen.

And we are attending to six truly accomplished actresses, some young, some old, all beautiful except the sullen servant, who radiate an inner calm and tranquility. Mishima's feminine world of elegance and sophistication represents a vivid contrast to the brutal masculine world of *Peer Gynt*. Yet both works illuminate the dark corners of the human heart, a purpose amounting almost to an obsession in Bergman's later years. That he has the will to concentrate on this theme makes him the ideal interpreter of Ibsen and Mishima as well as Strindberg, O'Neill, and much of Shakespeare. To enjoy the privilege of having him on our shores again restores our faith in a provisional art.

[1993]

Diversity and Unity
(I Am a Man; Marisol)

THE contemporary surge in racial, sexual, and ethnic consciousness-raising popularly known as "cultural diversity" has resulted in a tremendous outpouring of works by minority artists. Some of these are of genuine significance. Others have importance mainly as calling cards—demands for seats at a national banquet from which a lot of hungry people have long been excluded. And since our liberal culture—amorphous, uncertain, and continually in the process of defining itself—is more than eager to welcome new guests to the table, invitations are sometimes extended merely on request.

It is a practice that can lead to confused standards. White male critics are being asked to subscribe to a relativist code which decrees that, not being members of minority groups, they are disqualified from making judgments on minority art (unless, of course, the judgments are positive—separatists rarely refuse praise, prizes, and subsidies from the people they claim can't comprehend their work). It's disarming, in all senses of the word, to say we don't share common experiences that are measurable by common standards. It's also defensive nonsense. But the growing number of truly talented minority artists with more universal interests, like Anna Deavere Smith, John Leguizamo, Suzan-Lori Parks, George C. Wolfe, and others, suggests that we may soon be in a position to return to a single value system.

Two recent off-Broadway productions reinforce this hope: José Rivera's *Marisol* at the New York Public Theater, and OyamO's *I Am a Man*, which recently concluded a run at the Classic Stage Company. Both are written by dramatists of genuine power and imagination whose perceptions go beyond sectarian racial or ethnic agendas.

I Am a Man is a rousing play about a strike by Memphis sanitation workers in 1968. I recognize that a docudrama about garbage collectors in the sixties must sound about as intriguing as *Waiting for Lefty*, the thirties agitprop play it most resembles. Two things give it more immediacy than Clifford Odets's dated tribute to taxicab drivers—all the Memphis workers were African-American, and their strike immediately preceded the assassination of Martin Luther King.

There is a third dynamic activating *I Am a Man*—the Working Theatre's powerful production under the direction of Bill Mitchelson. Simply set in a confrontational style, the evening has all the color, infectiousness, and musicality of a prayer meeting, and it is performed by actors who display an almost familial relationship with the audience, which responds in kind. Beginning with some projected verses by the Greek poet Alceus ("a city stands or falls by its men"), the play proceeds to create a gallery of civic heroes and villains, meanwhile drawing religious analogies between the sanitation workers, some of whom lost their lives under dangerous conditions, and another "garbage collector who died trying to clear away rubbish," namely Jesus Christ. The analogy with Christ is even more striking in regard to Martin Luther King, whose rolling rhetoric, hypnotic voice, and saintly image form a ground bass for the action. A projection of da Vinci's *Last Supper*

is occasionally illuminated to underline the Easter parallel, fore-
seen by King himself, when he broke bread with disciples and
predicted his own death just before his assassination (in April no
less).

King, however, is a background figure until the last few
moments of the play. The real hero is T. O. Jones (Paul Butler)
who, after founding the union in 1963, was summarily dismissed
for illegal actions against the municipality. Jones is far from a
spotless figure. His wife kicks him out of the house for philander-
ing, and he grows increasingly self-important as the action proceeds. On the one hand he is fearless in facing down Memphis
Mayor Loeb, rejecting his bribe of a foreman's job and slapping
his face when the mayor calls him "nigger" (Jones's reply gives
the play its rather clumsy title). On the other hand Jones is
extremely susceptible to the flattery of a Swahili-speaking black
militant group called the Invaders (a thinly disguised version of
the Panthers). He accepts them as bodyguards and imitates their
swagger and salutes. Thus the play features a struggle not only
between striking workers and city officials but also between the
violent "by any means necessary" tactics associated with Malcolm
X and the passive nonviolence of King.

As King prophesies "a storm coming in Memphis," the forces
group for battle. A salty representative of the national union,
himself a Jew, arrives to confront Mayor Loeb (he calls him a
"putz" for denying his own religion). He also chides the sanitation workers for calling a cold-weather strike at a time when the
garbage is unlikely to rot. The workers are maced, beaten, and
arrested by rioting police. One man is killed. In this atmosphere
of turmoil and hatred, after announcing a massive civil rights
demonstration in Memphis, King is assassinated at the Lorraine
Motel.

The dramatized murder of this "poor dead leader" has all the
power and poignance of the episode in Joyce's *Portrait of the
Artist* when Simon Dedalus breaks down over the death of
Parnell. In both cases history was irreparably altered, which is
why King's death still evokes the same shock, rage, and despair
the country felt in 1968. One small victory emerges from this
colossal catastrophe—the union is recognized, the first of its kind
in the history of Memphis.

The whole thing is splendidly acted by the entire cast and engrossingly dramatized by OyamO. The playwright's style is at times a little too raw, at times a little too declarative. But he has a sense of balance that puts his play in a class with such discriminating studies of racial conflict as Anna Deavere Smith's *Fires in the Mirror* and J. Anthony Lukas's *On Common Ground*.

Puerto Rican–born José Rivera is a rather more sophisticated writer than OyamO. His *Marisol* strives to go beyond documentary realism into spiritual and transcendent realms. Because it features an angel, *Marisol* has been compared with *Angels in America*. There is another striking parallel with Tony Kushner's play: *Marisol* is driven by a similar millenarian imagination, which identifies the year 2000 with events of apocalyptic magnitude.

The action takes place in various boroughs of New York, a city so riddled with frenzied demonic events that it becomes a metaphor for the infernal regions (as in Adrian Lyne's profoundly spiritual film *Jacob's Ladder*). Marisol, the Latina heroine, is first discovered on a subway, about to be attacked by a mugger wielding a knife. She is saved by the Angel, but for much of the play it's uncertain whether or not she's already dead. Back in her Bronx apartment she festoons her bed with necklaces and jewelry to protect herself against demons, goes to sleep, and is informed by her angelic companion that the apocalypse is coming. No one has seen the moon in nearly nine months, and New York will soon experience an "evacuation followed by fire on a massive scale."

The universal body is sick, earth is running a temperature, and "God is old and dying and taking the rest of us with Him." It is the angel's job to stop this hemorrhage by declaring war on "our senile God," a heavenly rebellion which will bring on the millennium. When she returns to her scientific publishing job, Marisol learns of newspaper reports that "Miss Puerto Rican yuppie princess of the universe" (as she is called in the *New York Post*) has been bludgeoned to death. In an undead condition, in a world where "logic was executed by firing squad," she encounters a number of even stranger phantasms, all of them caught up in the coming war in heaven.

By the second act the angels have shed their wings and equipped themselves with tommy guns while the derelict landscape has been gutted of all civilized forms of life. The city has become a kind of celestial Vietnam with God and the angels in mortal combat, and all surviving civilians forced to spy for one side or the other. The narrative turns phantasmagoric. One character has been stripped of his skin, another lives on rat poison, all food groups have turned to salt. Although the angels are dying and the rebels retreating, the people start another revolt, and the first day of the new history begins with the rising of a new moon. An angel appears with a crown, and on this qualified note of hope, the play ends.

Some of the writing (particularly the second act) is not perfectly controlled. But much is shot through with fierce Baudelairean poetry of decomposition. Rivera shares with the later Strindberg not only a passion for new nonmaterial theatrical forms but also a messianic mission to replace old and dying creeds with bold new visions. He is an adventurous talent, and I look forward eagerly to his coming work.

It's a pity that Michael Greif's production muddies the play. Greif, so expert directing an efficient piece of machinery like *Machinal*, has turned *Marisol* into an exercise in flashy cyberpunk. His inspiration for the shattered city seems to be drawn from sci-fi pulp movies like *Escape from New York* and *Terminator* 1 and 2, with side glances at *Blade Runner*—generous doses of strobe, laser, and thunder effects punctuated by earsplitting rock music— and most of the actors seem to be on speed. Cordelia Gonzalez is an attractive Marisol with surprised and vulnerable eyes, but she has difficulty maintaining a continuous state of terror, while Danitra Vance, as the Angel, is too coolly laid back to be persuasive. The rest of the cast resorts to the hysterical shrieking in vogue with New York actors these days, which leaves much of the dialogue incomprehensible.

Still, these two dramatists have genuine talent, and they swell the lists of gifted writers willing to risk their careers on our problematic stage. Drenched in their own cultural juices, they are nevertheless capable of telling stories that include us all, thus proving again that theatre works best as a unifying rather than a segregating medium. OyamO and Rivera belong to the family of playwrights, which is to say they transcend ethnic, racial, and

even national boundaries to join that universal culture called
dramatic art.

[1993]

Hillbilly Blues
(*The Kentucky Cycle*)

ROBERT SCHENKKAN's Pulitzer Prize–winning *The Kentucky Cycle*,
now stopping at the Kennedy Center's Eisenhower Theatre in
Washington before it goes to Broadway, is in nine acts and two
parts, consuming about six hours' playing time. Aside from any
values it might have as a work of the imagination, *The Kentucky
Cycle* is yet another sign that American dramatists are beginning
to fashion their plays into protracted journeys at the very moment when audiences are apparently losing patience with sitting
in the theatre at all.

Marathon plays, of course, have been a commonplace of dramatic literature since *The Oresteia*. One thinks of Marlowe's
two-part *Tamburlaine*, Goethe's two-part *Faust*, Ibsen's *Brand* and
Peer Gynt, Strindberg's trilogy *The Road to Damascus*, and Shaw's
"metabiological pentateuch," *Back to Methuselah*, among others,
all of which attempted to endow the drama with something
approaching epic form. But until the last few years there was
little evidence that American dramatists had a similar appetite for
theatrical giantism, apart from Eugene O'Neill, whose monumental works culminated in a projected eleven-play cycle about
American materialism. O'Neill's cycle was left unfinished (*A Touch
of the Poet* and an early draft of *More Stately Mansions* are the only
surviving remnants), but there have recently been a number of
American efforts to achieve O'Neillian scope, among them *The
Texas Trilogy*, *Angels in America*, and Robert Wilson's early large-
scale extravaganzas (one of which took seven days to perform).
Now comes *The Kentucky Cycle*, designed to be precisely what
O'Neill originally envisioned—an epic study of American materialism as seen through the prism of family life.

Whatever one thinks of Schenkkan's achievement, one has to

admire his nerve. *The Kentucky Cycle* is a construct of domestic plays endowed with the dimensions of a national saga. In the program, Schenkkan provides a genealogical chart to help us follow the extended progress of three different families tied to one another by marriage and hatred. Beginning with the Indian Wars of 1775, the play ranges through two hundred years of American life, touching on the Civil War, the unionization of coal miners in the 1920s, the compromises of the United Mine Workers in the 1950s, and the conclusion of the Korean War in 1954, finally ending in 1975 with an epilogue devoted to tying up the strands of plot and theme. Although the references to recorded history are often muted, and the canvas is geographically narrow, it is clearly the author's intention to provide a general historical overview of this continent through the device of specific familial events.

Schenkkan's central theme is the despoliation of the American landscape by greed and rapine. There are virtually no heroes in this work, only plunderers and their victims. The one pure element, aside from a few black characters, is the land itself, and that is gradually reduced to mud and rubble. To reinforce this point, most of the action takes place in Howsen Country, a Cumberland area of eastern Kentucky marked by a thick forest and a magnificent oak tree which serves as the central symbol. Neither the forest nor the oak survives the ravages of rapacious men. The property belongs to the Rowen family after its patriarch, Michael, procures it from the Cherokees in exchange for guns (though the Indians believe that "no one owns this land, it cannot be given"). It is entirely consistent with Rowen family behavior throughout the next two hundred years that Michael also trades the Indians contaminated blankets which will infect most of the tribe with smallpox.

Although Schenkkan's Indians are not exactly noble savages, they are contrasted with the white man in a manner clearly influenced by the racial assumptions of the movie *Dances with Wolves* (there is even a howling wolf to begin and end the play). "Here the savage was taught his lessons in perfidy by masters of the trade," reads the epigraph by Harry Caudill, whose *Night Comes to the Cumberlands* was the inspiration for Schenkkan's research. The Cherokees stick to their bargains; the settlers are invariably mean and treacherous. Treachery, in fact, is almost a leitmotif of the play, and its repeated reversal device is an offer of friendship followed by a particularly savage murder. Rowen even betrays his own wife, an Indian woman named Morning Star, first by cutting her tendon to prevent departure, then by killing their infant daughter, and finally by fathering a child with a slave girl he bought at auction (thus initiating a related black family line). He is rewarded in kind when his half-breed son, Patrick, stabs him to death in a tub.

The only vaguely moral figure in this murderous family is Patrick's grandson, Jed, but even he is involved in a series of grisly actions. After the rival Talbert family, though also related by blood, has reduced the Rowens to sharecroppers on their own property, the Rowens take delayed revenge by slaughtering all but the Talbert womenfolk. Jed joins Quantrill's Raiders during the Civil War and participates in the ambush of Union soldiers.

After the war Jed makes the mistake of selling mining rights to his recovered land for a dollar an acre, where Standard Oil, strip-mining for coal, creates a sulfurous scene of havoc and pillage that more than compensates for the sins of the family. The unionization of the coal miners is marked by similar acts of treachery. Mary Anne Rowen's husband, Tommy, characteristically betrays a friendly union agitator who is gunned down by the owners.

When their son, Joshua, eventually becomes president of the district union, he betrays his own local by compromising on safety standards. In the inevitable catastrophe, his own son is killed. The play ends with Joshua recovering a two-hundred-year-old infant corpse, wrapped in buckskin, which happens to be the murdered baby daughter of his ancestor Michael.

As my synopsis might suggest, this remorseless depiction of the white settler's duplicity and meanness eventually grows tiring, even to a spectator with no particular illusions about the benevolence of human nature. Occasionally a character, usually a woman, will detach herself from the contemptible crowd to express a decent emotion. But for the most part everyone acts like a survivalist, sacrificing friend and foe alike for the sake of personal gain. It's as if only Snopeses inhabited Yoknapatawpha County. There is no sentiment in this play, but, curiously, Schenkkan's endless parade of basehearted men eventually becomes a reverse form of sentimentality. One leaves the theatre persuaded of the human capacity for evil but also confirmed in a sense of one's own virtue.

Where the author excels is in his storytelling. Despite its length, the play is never boring, and despite its growing predictability, it is often engrossing. The scene in the first part called "Ties That Bind," where Patrick Rowen is dispossessed of his land by a venal judge and a vengeful neighbor, is a subtle portrait of relentless retribution, as satisfying as a morality play. Even here, however, where a suspenseful plot carries the action forward, one wishes for language that would deepen it as well. Schenkkan's dialogue is never less than serviceable, and his hillbilly dialect usually sounds authentic. What is missing is the poetry that could plumb emotions beyond vengeance and hatred.

In short, for all its ambitions *The Kentucky Cycle* rarely escapes from melodrama, and its panoramic sweep suggests it would be most comfortable as an epic film or a television miniseries. I don't say this patronizingly, only as a way of suggesting how its limitations might be better disguised by authentic locations and rural landscapes. Schenkkan's laudable desire to universalize his theme is often trivialized by domestic two-handed scenes and table arguments. And the importance he attaches to the land as a central symbol is not reinforced very well by a set composed of wood platforms and steel pipes.

Given these limitations, however, Michael Olich's abstract scene design is very flexible, and Warner Shook's direction is a model of energy and economy. The eleven-member cast, supported by a seven-member chorus which acts as townfolk, scene changers, and silent witnesses, transforms into a variety of characters with considerable authority. Stacy Keach, playing a medley of blackhearted Rowen characters, gives his most ferocious performance since Macbird. Jeanne Paulsen displays towering strength in a number of matriarchal roles. And Gregory Itzin, Randy Oglesby, John Aylward, Jacob (Tuck) Milligan, and Ronald Hippe create a range of colorful Kentuckians, making Howsen Country seem a lot more populated than it really is.

So, with all my cavils, and with no small doubts about how it will fare in the commercial theatre, I wish this epic well on its journey to New York. Evolved by a system of resident theatres, it is a testimony to the creative health that sometimes manages to flourish there, against all odds.

[1993]

A Theatre Marking Time
(Medea; Tamburlaine; The Tempest; King Lear)

AT ANY given historical moment a nation's theatre is a dependable barometer of its cultural life. Whether that culture is moving forward or backward is related to whether the stage is dominated by playwrights or by directors and actors—which is to say, whether by new plays or by classics. To judge by my most recent visit to England, the British theatre presently belongs more to its interpretive than to its creative artists. Lacking enough new works of any real quality, England is now primarily devoted to renewing its traditions through fresh looks at the great texts of the past.

This is an entirely honorable alternative to theatrical stasis, but it signifies a culture marking time. Harold Pinter and David Hare are still capable of giving the stage a jolt from time to time, and Caryl Churchill has just opened a (problematical) new work at the National. But the really big events this season are not new plays but rather classical masterpieces dominated by star performers and resourceful directors. The productions I saw were of varying quality, which sometimes made me nostalgic for remembered glories. Still, it was a joy to be again in theatres whose central objective was creating compelling works of art rather than delivering community services or undertaking audience development projects.

The event that truly enthralled me on this visit was Diana Rigg's ferocious performance in Euripides' *Medea* at the Wyndham. This production, under the direction of Jonathan Kent, had originally opened at the Almeida Theatre in Islington where, in addition to new plays by Pinter and revivals by Rattigan, Kent and his partner Ian McDiarmid have been producing such arcane star-activated classics as Dryden's *All for Love* (also with Rigg) and Ibsen's *When We Dead Awaken* (with Claire Bloom). For *Medea,* Kent chose a stark simple style of presentation, reducing the chorus of Corinthian women to three ladies in black sitting on chairs and alternately chanting and singing. Together with the Nurse, they reminded me of the keening Irish women who mourned the drowned Bartley in Synge's *Riders to the Sea.* And there was a lot to keen about here, given the shattering events of the play. Peter J. Davison's burnished steel-panel setting reinforced the cruel sense of moral disintegration by literally bursting apart with a great racket at the bloody climax.

All the performances were strong, though Tim Woodward's Jason was a bit too external to respond convincingly to the horrible death of his children, a scene as difficult to enact as Macduff's grief over losing "all my pretty chickens and their dam at one fell swoop." But Diana Rigg more than compensated with a Medea that stands with the most riveting performances of our time.

I started applauding Miss Rigg's artistic progress in the early seventies when she first gave up the easy celebrity of *The Avengers* to explore the deeper demands of classical theatre. Her Medea confirms my conviction that an actor grows in proportion to the way she embraces the great repertory roles. To be sure, Rigg's feline grace had always seemed to me more appropriate for wit comedy than for classical tragedy. But although her Lady Macbeth with Anthony Hopkins and her Regan in Olivier's TV *Lear* had been admirable, I was not prepared for the scorching power of her Medea. The cat has been transformed into a panther who roars and lacerates rather than purrs and scratches. Like few English actors of her generation, Diana Rigg now pulls her voice out of her internal organs, producing a sound of almost primitive savagery. The last Medea I saw was Judith Evans in the 1946 Robinson Jeffers version (I believe John Gielgud was her Jason) where she skulked and scowled as if still playing Mrs. Danvers in *Rebecca.* Diana Rigg restores to the role its terrifying animal nature.

In a red dress, long ponytail, and bare feet, Rigg greets us with a piercing cry of pain. All her sacrifices for Jason have been rewarded with treachery, since he is preparing to contract a cynical match with Creon's daughter (the almost feminist theme of male advancement at the expense of women is heightened in Alistair Elliot's new translation). Describing her indignities and sense of abandonment, she coils like a snake, growls, hisses and croaks like a fury, calling up images from jungle mythology. Perhaps inspired by how Olivier had trained his voice for *Othello,* Rigg has obviously worked hard to develop deeper vocal registers for this role. Yet her Medea remains consistently womanly, even when she materializes near the end, drenched in the blood of her slaughtered children. (By comparison with the way Medea repays her husband for sexual abuse, Lorena Bobbitt's revenge is almost merciful.) At the conclusion Rigg disappears, not through a *deus ex machina* but in a swirl of angry clouds, leaving us in the aftercalm of an emotional storm one rarely experiences on the stage these days.

Anthony Sher tries to kick up the same sort of dust in the Royal Shakespeare Company production of *Tamburlaine the Great* at the Barbican. And for five of the ten acts, he manages quite effectively. Although Christopher Marlowe's marvelous two-part epic of imperial conquest is the first English play by a literary genius, it is very rarely produced, perhaps because the staging requires tactics and logistics cultivated less by theatre directors than by military strategists. In the first professional revival since the early seventeenth century, Brigadier General Tyrone Guthrie led his troops in a 1951 production starring Donald Wolfit and a huge supporting army (all I remember of that is a lot of swirling figures impaled by arrows). Terry Hands has now directed a big, boisterous, bludgeoning version of the show which allows Anthony Sher full scope to bellow and bluster.

Tamburlaine is Marlowe's first essay on the nature of aspiring minds. He is drawn to heroes who, in Berlioz's words, "make all barriers crack"—in *Tamburlaine* through world conquest, in *Doctor Faustus* through forbidden knowledge, in *The Jew of Malta* through absolute evil. The most modern of the Elizabethans, a government spy and uncloseted homosexual, Marlowe fathered a genealogical line of rebels leading to Sade, Genet, Orton (whom he resembles in the violent manner of his early death), and the Theatre of Cruelty. An Artaudian bloodbath, *Tamburlaine* is a play that exults in butchery and carnage. In his thirst for glory the hero is loyal only to the captive Zenocrate. He scourges and pillages, batters and strangles, hangs up the slaughtered carcasses of virgins on a wall, even murders his own cowardly son. At the conclusion he is preparing to storm the heavens—"to set black streamers in the firmament to signify the slaughter of the gods" —and is stymied only by his own mortality. Through the character of Pistol, Shakespeare makes fun of Tamburlaine's extravagance and hyperbole, but Marlowe is the only contemporary for whom he expresses admiration in his plays.

The most American of English actors, Anthony Sher makes Tamburlaine into a cross between Al Pacino and Douglas Fairbanks. Sporting a Cherokee haircut, bare arms, and a huge black moustache, he gives the most calisthenic of performances, complete with tumbles and handsprings, climbing a rope backward, shambling loosely around the stage like a boxer. Unlike some of his supporting cast, who often sound more like elocutionists than soldiers, Sher is capable of savoring Marlowe's swelling verse without sounding like a RADA graduate. And he has a really good time battling a variety of enemies, including four Turkish kings on mechanical stilts.

Ultimately, however, all the clanging music and bravura acting, not to mention the constant heavy smoke of the production, begin to wear you down a little. And after Sher's Tamburlaine turns fat and sluggish in the second part, his physical agility can no longer compensate for a certain lack of inner strength. Following the death of Zenocrate, having burned the Koran to signify his superiority to Mahomet ("on earth there's none but me"), Tamburlaine suddenly falls ill, and in truth it's time to die. We're left exhausted by the bombast, though grateful to have seen the play.

At Stratford I witnessed the final performances of two productions, the first being the new RSC *Tempest* under the direction of Sam Mendes. It was the most disappointing experience of my visit. Alec McCowen, playing Prospero, still appeared to be reciting *The Gospel According to St. Mark* (his one-person show), contributing a sonorous milk-fed performance that not only put Miranda to sleep but half the audience. If McCowen's milk was homogenized, that of Simon Russell Beale, playing Ariel, was curdled. Sour, sullen, and sulky as an ill-tempered Regent Street window dresser, Beale's Ariel was not only imprisoned against his will but beneath his class. Set free, he thanked Prospero by spitting in his face. Usually a capable actor, Beale in this role looked like the type that only does scornful parts.

There were two engaging performances in this deadly *Tempest*, those of David Bradley as Trinculo and Mark Lockyer as Stephano. Lockyer played the drunken butler with an Oxbridge accent (enunciated through a set of protruding false teeth) like a fantastical Bertie Wooster, and Bradley turned Trinculo into a red-wigged vaudevillian in a checkered suit and long shoes. Brandishing a ventriloquist's dummy dressed in the same clothes and sharing some of his lines, Bradley managed to contribute the few moments of real delight in an otherwise torpid production.

Finally there was Robert Stephens as King Lear, also at Stratford, in a heartbreaking performance, and I mean this in a number of ways. In his powerful debut in the Osborne-Creighton *Epitaph for George Dillon* in the late fifties, Stephens showed the sardonic power of a great English actor, but for years an alcohol problem severely limited his potential. Having freed himself of this affliction, he brings a ravaged persona to the most difficult role ever written, and the results are poignant and penetrating, though ultimately lacking in sufficient stamina to make the performance unforgettable.

In Stephens's hands, Lear's exhaustion is evident from his first appearance. Limping slightly, large-nosed, gaunt and hollow, though endowed with an ample belly, the actor looks like a homeless wretch dressed up in a bright red coat. With his wispy beard and desperate eyes, he evokes the vague mental wanderings, the mad melancholy, of a derelict Don Quixote. His feelings for Cordelia do not constitute his most tender relationship, not surprisingly considering Abigail McKern's Yorkshire pudding appearance in the part. She's too heavy to carry (most Lears demand a lightweight Cordelia), so he allows some soldiers to bring in her body. Enraged at her death, he kicks her over on her stomach.

Lear's warmest feelings are reserved for his Fool. And in Ian Hughes's beautifully modulated performance, these feelings are wholly reciprocated. I have not seen a more affectionate, touching engagement between these two characters since Louis Calhern and Norman Lloyd played the roles in John Houseman's production more than forty years ago. The seat of Lear's affliction, in Stephens's bittersweet rendering, is the heart. He suffers from angina pains, and his "hysterico passio" or "climbing passion" is something close to cardiac arrest. The Fool, leading Lear away, holds his master's heart as if to keep it from breaking. He hugs and fondles him, sharing moments of remorse and regret. For all his goading and nagging, Hughes's Fool expresses an almost physical love for Lear. He can't let Lear out of his sight, and when he disappears, a crucial link is broken. I have never seen the relationship played so much like a marriage.

Adrian Noble directs this production with the same meticulous attention to detail and fresh approach to language that he showed in last year's *Hamlet*. Anthony Ward's design is dominated by a huge hanging sphere that opens after the blinding of Gloucester, like a cracked moon, to spill a mountain of sand on the stage. If this is a literalized realization of Lear's desire to "Crack Nature's molds, all germains spill at once, / That makes ungrateful man," it has more impact than the hoarse thunderings of Stephens, who is dampened by the drenching rain, both physically and emotionally. Stephens has beautifully rendered the ruefulness of the role, but ultimately fails to convey its majesty and size.

A number of the supporting performances are disappointing, but David Bradley's painful Gloucester (especially seen in repertory with his jaunty Trinculo) identifies him as one of the strongest and most versatile members of this company. Bradley will undoubtedly be next in line to play this part. It is actors like he, along with Stephens and Rigg, who keep the English stage alive in its process of marking time.

[1994]

The Rehabilitation of Edward Albee
(Three Tall Women; The Family Business)

A NUMBER of years ago, while praising Edward Albee's much-reviled stage adaptation of *Lolita*, I commented on the startling reverses in the fortunes of this once lionized American dramatist:

"The crunching noises the press pack makes while savaging his recent plays are in startling contrast to the slavering sounds they once made in licking his earlier ones.... If each man kills the thing he loves, then each critic kills the thing he hypes... brutalizing the very celebrity he has created."

I was generalizing not only from Albee's career but from that of Miller, Williams, and Inge, for although I had often depreciated works by these playwrights myself, it struck me as unseemly that mainstream reviewers were displaying such fickleness toward their favorite Broadway sons. This may sound territorial, but it's not. Readers expect highbrow critics to express dissent about an overinflated dramatic work, but it is an entirely different matter when those with the power to close a show become so savage and dismissive in their judgments. If it is a function of the weekly critic to try to correct taste, it is the function of the daily critic to guide theatregoers, not to trash careers or demolish reputations.

Fortunately, Albee's stubborn streak has kept him writing in the face of continual disappointment, a persistence he shares with a number of other artists battered by the New York press (Arthur Miller, David Rabe, Arthur Kopit, Christopher Durang, Philip Glass, and so on). I call this fortunate because Albee has a vein of genuine talent buried in the fool's gold, and, as I wrote then, there was always a hope, provided he was not discouraged from playwriting, that this would appear again in a world of some consequence. That work has now arrived in *Three Tall Women* (Vineyard Theatre), and I am happy to join his other former detractors in saluting Albee's accomplishment.

Three Tall Women is a mature piece of writing, clearly autobiographical, in which Albee seems to be coming to terms not only with a socialite foster parent he once satirized in past plays but with his own advancing age. Three women are discovered in a sumptuously appointed bedroom decorated with Louis Quatorze furniture, a rare carpet, and a parquet floor. They are called A, B, and C, which suggests a Beckett influence, though on the surface the play appears to be a drawing-room comedy in the style of A. R. Gurney. The oldest of the women is an imperious rich invalid (A) who appears hobbling on a cane, her left arm in a sling. She is attended by a middle-aged companion (B), an angular woman with a caustic tongue and a humped back, and a young politically correct lawyer (C) who has come to discuss A's business affairs.

The first of the two acts examines some scratchy transactions among this symbiotic trio, consisting of A's recollections (clearly not in tranquility) and the shocked reactions of her companions. A has turned sour and abrupt in old age, and there are traces of Albee's celebrated talent for invective in her rage against life. Her spine has collapsed, she has broken her arm in a fall, and now the bone has disintegrated around the pins. Likely to wet herself when she rises from a chair ("A sort of greeting to the day—the cortex out of sync with the sphincter"), she is inordinately preoccupied with the aging process—"downhill from sixteen on for all of us." She even wants to indoctrinate children with the awareness that they're dying from the moment they're born, and anyone who thinks she's healthy, as C does, had better just wait.

In short, A is an entirely vicious old wretch, with a volatile tongue and a narrow mind, but it is a tribute to the writing and the acting that she gradually wins our affections. Although prejudiced against "kikes," "niggers," "wops," and "fairies" (among them her own son), she is a model of vitality and directness when compared with the humor-impaired liberal democrat C, who protests A's intolerance. A remembers a past of supreme emptiness, of horse shows, dances, and loveless affairs, and particularly of the time her husband once advanced upon her with a bracelet dangling from his erect penis ("I can't do that," she said, "and his peepee got soft, and the bracelet fell into my lap"). That arid marriage, and the son who brings her chocolates but doesn't love her ("He loves his boys"), represent memories that can bring her to tears. They also bring A to a stroke at the end of the first act, as she freezes in mid-sentence describing her deepest family secrets.

Act II begins with A lying in bed under an oxygen mask. By this time B has been transformed from a sardonic hunchbacked factotum, slouching toward Bethlehem like Igor or Richard III, into a stately middle-aged matron in pearls, while C has become an elegant debutante in pink chiffon. Before long they are surprisingly joined by A, newly rejuvenated (the figure in the bed is a dummy), and the play shifts gears into a story of one woman at three different moments in time (A at ninety, B at fifty-two, and C at twenty-six). Just as B has shed her hump and C her primness, A has lost her feebleness. All three share the same history, the same child, the same sexual experiences, but A and B are united against C in their hatred of illusions. They warn C that her future will be one of deception and infidelity: "Men cheat a lot. We cheat less, but we cheat because we're lonely. Men cheat because they're men."

The prodigal child, now a young man carrying flowers, returns to sit by the bedside of his dying mother ("his dry lips on my dry cheeks"), silent and forlorn. None of the women will forgive him, nor will they forgive each other. A dislikes C, and C refuses to become A, while B bursts out bitterly against "parents, teachers, all of you, you lie, you never tell us things change." The inevitability of change is responsible for the obscenities of sickness, pain, old age, and death, but A, having accepted her fate, affirms that "the happiest moment is coming to the end of it." Taking a deep breath, she allows the action and her life to stop.

Beckett was the first dramatist to condense the past and present lives of a character into a single dramatic action, and *Krapp's Last Tape* is a play to which *Three Tall Women* owes a deep spiritual debt (it was also the companion piece to Albee's first New York production, *The Zoo Story*, in 1960). Beckett compressed youth and age through the device of a tape recorder; Albee uses doppelgangers; but both plays evoke the same kind of existential poignance. Lawrence Sacharow's direction reinforces this mood with a performance of considerable grace. Myra Carter as the aged A combines the classic calm of Gladys Cooper with the snappish temper of Bette Davis. She can move from meanness to winsomeness and back again in nothing flat. (When C, coolly played by Jordan Baker, accidentally hurt A's shoulder, Carter threw her a look of such ferocity I expected the younger actress to shatter.) Marian Seldes, angular and inscrutable as B, her hands thrust deeply into her cardigan, plays the part as if she is continually tasting something bitter, screaming "Bad girl!" when A breaks a glass in the sink. Most of us have encountered horrible old women like A, fuming over their pain and helplessness. It is

Albee's personal and professional triumph to have made such a woman fully human. His late career is beginning to resemble O'Neill's, another dramatist who wrote his greatest plays after having been rejected and abandoned by the culture. Happily, unlike O'Neill, he may not have to wait for death to rehabilitate him.

Ain and David Gordon's *The Family Business* (Dance Theatre Workshop's Bessie Schonberg Theater) is about another formidable old woman with a family of an entirely different sort, one that writes, directs, and (with Gordon's wife, Valda Setterfield) acts in its own drama. The action chronicles the hospitalization and eventual death of Annie Kinsman, an elderly Jewish kvetch who has fallen in her kitchen. Tante Annie is played by the barrel-chested, moustachioed David Gordon with barettes in his flowing hair, and his son, Ain, plays the flustered great-nephew who is forced to take care of her. In Pirandello fashion, Ain is currently writing the very play in which he appears as her reluctant caretaker, Paul. Donning a false nose and spectacles, he also plays his own father, Phil (presumably based on David Gordon).

Paul is entrusted with bringing his great-aunt to a hospital where she is examined by Dr. Piranha, Dr. Devour, and Dr. Paymore. Following each visit with this whining, troublesome woman, he loses another part of his anatomy—his pinkie, his left ear, a piece of his nose. She is literally eating him up alive, besides ruining his (gay) sex life. "Is there some medication I can take to prevent this woman from being the most important thing in my life?" he asks. She is a complete pain in the ass but nevertheless represents his continuity, "my last link to history."

Tante Annie would run the risk of becoming one of those unforgettable characters you'd like to forget were she not such a nattering nag and irresistible tummler. When she tells a doctor that Paul wants to become a "play writer," Paul corrects her, "Playwright. One word," to which she replies "Two words. *No money.*" Annie goes through all the agonies of illness and old age. Before she dies she also goes through dozens of nurse's aides. Grown abusive and obscene, she can't stand companions who talk and talk and talk. At the end she appears as a ghost to ask Paul what's happening with his show ("You make money yet?").

The production has a charming crudeness, the set consisting of moving clothes racks and transparent shower curtains, and it is acted with goofy unpolished verve and absurdist humor. Ain Gordon has a nice hangdog charm, Valda Setterfield (playing a variety of parts, including the ambulance siren) displays engaging simplicity, and David Gordon, looking like Trudeau's Megaphone Mark with his generous nose and brush moustache, makes an enchanting old yenta. I should mention that David Gordon will soon be directing a play at the American Repertory Theatre, so you can discount my opinion as collegial prejudice. But a lot of us had a helluva time at this show.

[1994]

PC—or Not PC
(Twilight: Los Angeles 1992; Politically In*Correct)*

THE most cogent commentators on our stormy times have unquestionably been not the columnists but the cartoonists, which is another way of noting that representational satire has more capacity than political or social commentary to relieve the pressures of a fractious age. On stage, two inspired performers have recently been offering their own perspectives on the issues that divide us, and while the African-American Anna Deavere Smith and the Jewish Jackie Mason seem worlds apart in tone, attitude, focus, and ethnicity, they each provide more perspective on the nature of our discords than an army of op-ed pundits.

It is true that Anna Deavere Smith might be more accurately described as a sociologist than as a satirist. Both in her previous *Fires in the Mirror,* which covered the Crown Heights affair, and in her current piece at the Joseph Papp Public Theater, *Twilight: Los Angeles 1992,* which deals with the riots in South Central L.A., she has drawn her material from interviews with the actual participants in those events. Still, Smith is not only an objective ear but a characterizing voice, and just as she shapes her text through editing and selection, so she achieves her emphasis through gesture and intonation. In the course of the evening the actress impersonates forty-six different people, capturing the essence of each character less through mimetic transformation, like an actor, than through the caricaturist's body English and vocal embellishments. Just look at her photographs—you'd never guess from any of those contorted head shots that she's an extremely handsome young woman.

Smith's subjects divide essentially into victims, victimizers, and viewers, though it is sometimes difficult to determine which is which. If Former Police Chief Daryl Gates (defending himself against charges that he permitted the riots to rage while attending a fund-raiser) and Sergeant Charles Duke (complaining that Officer Powell was "weak and inefficient with the baton" because he wasn't allowed to use the "choke hold") are clearly the patsies of the piece, the rioters, looters, gang members, and assailants often appear more sinned against than sinning. A white juror in the first Rodney King trial, asked by a reporter, "Why are you hiding your heads in shame," is appalled to receive approving calls from the KKK. Keith Watson, one of those acquitted of beating Reginald Denny, justifies his rage and the burnt-out vacant lots by saying, "Justice didn't work," while Paul Parker, chairperson of the "Free the L.A. Four Defense Committee," charges, "You kidnaped us, you raped our women...you expect us to feel something for the white boy?" One gringo-hating Latino, ranting against the "peckerwoods" and "rednecks" who have persecuted his family, expresses pleasure in the way Mexicans are able to terrify whites. Another Latino is encouraged by a policeman to "go for it, it's your neighborhood." A black woman, "touring" in the white neighborhood, loots I. Magnin's because she finds it "very offensive" that rich stars should feel protected from rioting.

Then there are the other victims—the Asian shopkeepers who, in those tumultuous days, lost 90 per cent of their stores and a number of their family members. At the same time a spokesperson for a young black girl shot by a Korean shopkeeper (who was acquitted) is raging against Asians, Mrs. Young-Soon Han, a former liquor store owner, speaks of her disenchantment with blacks. There were none in the Hollywood movies she saw in Korea; she thought this country was the best. Now "they" have destroyed the shops of innocent merchants simply because "we have a car and a house.... Where do I find justice? What about victims' rights?" Another store owner, inveighing against shoplifting and looting, remarks, "After that, I really hate this country, I really hate—we are not like customer and owner but more like *enemy*." "Enemy" and "hate" are the operative words of *Twilight*. With each ethnic group bristling at the other, one might think "cultural diversity" had become a euphemism for race war. A Mexican woman reporter, told her life is in danger, replies: "How could they think I was white?" The African-American Paul Parker boasts how "we burnt down the Koreans—they are like the Jews in this neighborhood." And this is countered not by appeals for tolerance but by counsels of caution, like those of Elaine Brown, formerly Black Panther, reminding the gun-brandishing swashbuckling looters about America's willingness to use its power: "Ask Saddam Hussein."

To judge by the interviews in *Twilight*, however, the Los Angeles riots caused a lot of soul searching and considerable guilt among some white Americans. The experience certainly stimulated considerable generosity from Reginald Denny, who, pleading for recognition as a person rather than a color, expresses profound gratitude to the black people who risked their lives to save him. By contrast, others, like a reporter named Judith Tur, wonder why South Central blacks can't be more like Magic Johnson or Arthur Ashe, adding that "white people are getting so angry, they're going back fifty years." A suburban real estate agent named Elaine Young, who has had thirty-six silicone surgeries on her face, whines that "we don't have the Freeway, we can't eat anywhere, everything's closed," meanwhile defending her decision to hole up in the Beverly Hills Hotel.

These are easy targets, and it is true that *Twilight* sometimes lacks the dialectical thickness as well as the surprise and unpredictability of *Fires in the Mirror*. Lasting over two hours, it seems at the same time too long and too short for its subject. The L.A. riots were a response to violence and injustice through acts of violence and injustice, and the paradox still to be explored is how looting and burning Korean stores and destroying your own neighborhood, not to mention racial assaults on innocent people, could be considered acceptable means of protest against inequity and racism. With most of them still in shock, few of Smith's respondents are in a position to examine the irrationality of such acts unless, like Shelby Coffey, they cite "a vast, even Shakespearean range of motives."

Smith makes some effort to penetrate these motives by ending her piece with a poetic reflection by a gang member on the "limbo" twilight of crack addicts, but the metaphor somehow seems inadequate. Still, if she has not always gone beyond the events of this tragedy, she has powerfully dramatized a world of almost universal tension and hatred. George C. Wolfe's elaborate production, with its videos of Rodney King's beating and films of Los Angeles burning, is probably more appropriate for the coming Broadway move than for the stage of the Public. But it leaves us with a shocking sense of how America's hopes for racial harmony were left burning in the ashes of South Central L.A.

Jackie Mason's *Politically InCorrect* (John Golden Theatre) is bound to fan these fires further. It is totally inflammatory, offensive in the extreme, brazen, cheeky, reckless, unapologetic. It is also painfully funny, though Mason uses no obscenity, in that rude unbuttoned manner first patented by Lenny Bruce, then developed by Richard Pryor and Eddie Murphy. Still smarting from the abuse he suffered—mostly from white liberals—for using the word *shwartzer* in the first Giuliani campaign, Mason is now delivering a ferocious assault on all the PC fortresses, not only black power but feminism, gay pride, affirmative action, Hillary and Bill, a sensation-hungry press, and those stupid enough to blame the media for crime and violence ("The Three Stooges poke out each other's eyes—do you do it to your brother Irving?"). Mason is tempting fate and knows it. The real purpose of his show, he says, is to tell the truth as he sees it, and for that "I can get killed"—or at least clubbed in the knees for satirizing Tanya Harding. I was reminded of Lenny Bruce, after questioning Jackie Kennedy's motives for climbing out of the presidential limo in Dallas, pointing at the chandelier and saying it was going to explode. Like Bruce, Mason has turned himself into a sacrificial object. At the preview I saw, he was roundly heckled by a woman in the balcony whom he referred to throughout as "that sick stupid *yenta*." Having once identified himself as the "hit of the building," he now expects to be hit by the building.

This may account for the slightly nervous manner of his delivery. His dyed red hair topping his half-closed eyes and masklike face, a guided missile in a double-breasted suit, Mason seems terrified of silence. Even when he dries, he still keeps spritzing. The perfect embodiment of the Jewish anxiety which is his theme, he's confident only when he stays on Jewish subjects. Entering the stage announcing that "this is one of the great thrills of all time to be able to see me in person," he immediately begins badgering the few gentiles in the audience ("Do you understand this, Mister?" "Who am I talking to?"). His safety zone is Jewish-gentile contrasts. Jews always have the biggest doctors in the world—the head of the hospital. Rising from his chair, he kvetches and moans: "Did you ever see a healthy Jew?" Jews have no desire to be in rodeos while gentiles love to fly off broncos ("I say, Shmuck, use the other hand"). Jews won't become jockeys because they could never weigh eighty-five pounds ("A Jew is not going to give up coffee and Coke just to sit on a horse").

This is familiar stuff from an entertaining insult comedian, but for most of *Politically* In*Correct* Mason has considerably less ingratiating things on his mind. One of them is to defend the Jewish civil rights record against anti-Semites like Farrakhan. He rejects the charge that Jews were slave traders. They came from Kiev, not plantations, carrying matzoh balls, not cotton balls. Mason is enraged by the whole notion of what constitutes a "minority" in America. Jews, who are lumped with the majority, are "the most persecuted minority in the world." He therefore would like affirmative action for Jews, starting with a lower basketball net. Whites get fired for saying that blacks make better athletes, but blacks are allowed to make movies called *White Men Can't Jump*.

Indeed, it is reverse discrimination that really shivers his kishkes: "Only the majority is allowed to be persecuted." Because of rules barring previous knowledge of a case, the judicial system is a total fraud—you have to be mentally retarded to get on a jury. The proof: the Menendez brothers "admitted that they killed their parents and the jury said: They didn't." To be guilty of sexual harassment, all you have to do is show up: "You're not looking, you're leering; you're not walking, you're stalking." And no matter how lazy or incompetent she is, you can't fire a woman from a job—employ a black homosexual female and "you'd better close your business in a second." As for homosexuals, they're always parading. "Not only that, they demand to be in *your* parade. At the Mafia party, do you invite women from the Hadassah? Never!"

As if this were not enough to alienate him from the Broadway audience, Mason spends most of the second half of his show attacking President Clinton, largely because of what Mason considers his wayward treatment of the truth. "Washington couldn't tell a lie; Nixon couldn't tell the truth; Clinton can't tell the difference." Nixon used to shvitz when he lied; Clinton only shvitzes when he tells the truth. "He says he smoked marijuana but didn't inhale. Would you put a pastrami sandwich in your mouth if you didn't want to eat it?" Whether on the subject of Bosnia, Haiti, Whitewater, or his own health plan, Clinton can do nothing right. The only thing, in fact, that Mason will defend about Clinton is his alleged adultery, a subject on which he finds the press to be totally hypocritical. Still, Mason can't resist his own digs at Clinton's sex life. The president is always in shorts because he doesn't have time to put on his pants, and Hillary selects the women he appoints on the basis of their unattractiveness (Ruth Ginsburg was chosen because she was so skinny Clarence Thomas wouldn't bother her).

I may be wrong, but as a commercial venture I think the new Mason show may be a serious miscalculation. Certainly the tepid applause at the conclusion of the evening did not augur well for future ticket sales. The liberal Jewish spectators whom Mason usually attracts are hardly the likeliest audience for satire on minority groups, and *Politically InCorrect* will undoubtedly be charged with sexual and racial intolerance. Still, it's not more restraint we need in a time when free speech is being muzzled— let's leave that to Catharine MacKinnon and the professional sensitivity trainers—so much as the freedom to hear the unmentionable, even when it hurts. Mason may be wrongheaded at times, but he's fearless and frontal, and that makes for an exhilarating, if disturbing, evening in the theatre.

[1994]

PROFILES

Strindberg to the Life

THERE has been a surge of scholarly interest recently in the Swedish dramatist August Strindberg, without any particular enhancement of his public reputation. Strindberg has small appeal in an era of normalcy. He belongs to a more irrational age than our own—to people in the grip of tumultuous love affairs, psychic breakdowns, romantic literary movements, radical social currents, ecstatic religious sects. Apart from the odd revival, he is rarely performed on our stages, and while students dutifully read his plays in modern drama courses, they really don't like him.

I don't think Michael Meyer likes him much either. His *Strindberg* is thorough and rigorous, based on painstaking research of primary sources including many unpublished letters. But while it fills many lacunae in the dramatist's life, the biography is not terribly sympathetic to its subject. True, Strindberg can certainly be repellent at times, and his accumulated fits, hysterics, recriminations, rages, prejudices, hatreds, and paranoid panics—not to mention his ferocious love-hatred of women—are pretty trying in large doses. Still, Meyer's temperament is more attuned to the comparatively sensible radicalism of Ibsen (the subject of a previous three-volume biography) than to the wild-eyed fanaticism of his current subject. He is forever chastising Strindberg for diffusing his energies in extraliterary pursuits instead of writing plays; he patronizes his occult studies, rationalizes his supernaturalism, and shows no real understanding of his excursions into hallucination and dream.

What is more, out of scholarly infatuation with primary sources, he scants the work of those who *have* investigated this important side of the playwright's temperament, and entirely ignores the major critical studies. Evert Sprinchorn's *Strindberg as Dramatist* and Harry G. Carlson's *Strindberg and the Poetry of Myth* are acknowledged in his select bibliography, but there is no mention in the text of Sprinchorn's explorations into Strindberg's unconscious or Carlson's insights into his mythopoeia, while Elizabeth Sprigge's sketchy, gossipy, inaccurate, but fascinating pioneer biography, *The Strange Life of August Strindberg*, is not even listed. It is Meyer's habitual method to correct Strindberg's feverish and hysterical interpretation of the events in his life with the authentic facts, as if every time Strindberg starts raving in the next room we have to be reminded of soundness and sanity. In order to get inside this demented genius it is sometimes necessary to be as mad as he, but Meyer's orderly *Strindberg* emerges as a respectable study of a disreputable artist, with no arresting insights into either the man or his work.

Still, however juiceless and flavorless, this is the most factually complete account of Strindberg's life we are likely to get, indeed a treasure house of priceless material for future explorers. Everything is there: his three miserable marriages to successively younger women, with a fourth—to seventeen-year-old Fanny Falkner (when Strindberg was already in his sixties!)—prevented only by the girl's instinct for survival; his scurrilous assaults on women and marriage which exposed him to lawsuits in various countries; his growing hatred of Ibsen (that "decrepit old troll") who nevertheless remained fascinated with his rival's "violent strength"; his sojourn in Berlin and Paris where he communed with Gauguin, Edvard Munch, Stanislaw Przybyszewski, and other bohemians; his bizarre correspondence with Friedrich Nietzsche, both of them cooking with lunatic gas until the philosopher signed off as "Nietzsche Caesar" and "The Crucified One"; his long exile from Sweden, culminating in the *Inferno* period when Strindberg imagined he was being pursued by imaginary enemies and electrocuted by regiments of monstrous witches; his "scientific" experiments proving that the earth is flat, that the elements are divisible, that plants have nerves; his extraordinarily prolific output of plays, autobiographies, treatises, poems, scientific studies, paintings, histories, most of which were met with contempt or indifference throughout his life; his founding with August Falck of the Intimate Theatre, to produce plays "designed for an impatient age: searching but short"; his quarrels with the Swedish Academy over its failure to award Nobel Prizes to worthy recipients such as Tolstoy (or Strindberg); his receipt of an "Anti-Nobel" prize just before he died; his pathetic old age and painful death, wracked with stomach cancer, working to the end.

"Don't bother about me," he said to his nurse, "I no longer exist."

It is a life without peace or serenity, restless and embattled, driven by motors of mad energy. Meyer resists interpreting the events of this life; the little speculation he offers (absinthe poisoning as the cause of his *Inferno* psychosis; ulcers for the pains Strindberg himself diagnosed as stomach cancer) is unconvincing. As a book of facts, however, *Strindberg* includes a lot of detail for less reticent analysts. My own early suspicion, for example, that Strindberg's misogyny was linked to his uncertain masculinity finds ample confirmation in Meyer's research. Consider Strindberg's imagery when describing the influence of Nietzsche: "My spiritual uterus has found a tremendous fertilizer in Friedrich Nietzsche, so that I feel distended like a bitch in heat. He is the man for me!" Speaking of his attraction to the Norwegian writer Björnson, he writes, "This is the man I have sought for so long; mostly, perhaps, because I am so unmasculine myself." Looking for reasons for his first wife's alleged infidelities, he suspects his penis might be too small! ("Irritated to the roots of my testicles, I visited Geneva and took a doctor with me to a brothel. . . . I had my semen investigated which proved fertile, and was measured at full cock"). He dreams of his third wife with no breasts, then as a boy, and later charges her with undermining his manhood ("The day after the wedding you declared that I was not a man"). He develops a theory that women serve only as a bird's nest for men's eggs, and that under certain circumstances men can give birth to children. The evidence accumulates that Strindberg's antifeminism is closely linked to a genuine sexual insecurity, a weak masculine identity, and that only when he was willing to acknowledge the female qualities of his own nature was he able to control his illness, create sympathetic woman characters, experiment with the unconscious, and accept the authority of what he called the "Higher Powers."

Until then, however, he was pretty brutal to the other sex, and not only in his writing. He assaulted Siri von Essen, woke from his sleep to throttle Frida Uhl, and penetrated Harriet Bosse twice on their wedding night despite the fact that she pleaded a ruptured uterus. His savage battles with his women, not to mention his competitiveness toward rival authors, are highly reminiscent of the American writer Norman Mailer, who seems to share so many other Strindbergian qualities—his excremental vision, combativeness, occultism, diffused creative energy, romantic excess, writing facility, addiction to drink and drugs, possession by demons, multiple marriages—that he almost seems a contemporary doppelganger.

Strindberg's paranoia is also Maileresque, and contrary to the common assumption that he finally achieved calm and serenity in his older age, Meyer's book shows he never laid his demons to rest. In later years, after reading Swedenborg, he was able to regard his sense of persecution as a sign of grace, but before this it was a painful affliction which seriously affected his relationships. To a friend who never wished him anything but good, he wrote: "I sense something in your personality which oppresses me and threatens to make me sick. I also feel something menacing in your manner of behavior, a desire, possibly with good intent, to interfere with my destiny. . . . I beg you: do not seek me before I seek you." He interprets accidents in nature—such as a gull sitting on his window sill—as signs that people are out to trap him. Pianos playing in the next room, people hammering nails, leaves forming on the ground, all are tokens of conspiracies. "If a man," he wrote,

> is actually persecuted so that everything he does is torn to shreds, mocked, smeared with filth; if he is persecuted with lawsuits, threats of imprisonment, false accusations of anarchism, hunted from country to country; threatened with the madhouse, hounded by debts, harassed in public places; and when enemies turn up at the hotel where he lives and warn the landlord, etc.; if this man, who is persecuted, gets the idea that he is persecuted, then this is no illusion or mania.

Which is Strindberg's way of saying that even paranoids can be objects of persecution.

A harmless outgrowth of this persecution complex was a sense of clairvoyance which later informed his writing and influenced his life. Some of the most remarkable passages in Meyer's book are quotations from Strindberg's journals after his divorce from Harriet Bosse, when he imagined she was visiting him sexually in waking dreams. But there is also a malignant side which Meyer, I believe, is the first to have emphasized in Strindberg—his virulent anti-Semitism. Strindberg's suspicious hatred of Jews—many of whom (like the Brandes brothers and his publisher Albert Bonnier) were well-wishers and supporters—was not that lofty sniffing associated with such class-conscious literary figures as T. S. Eliot or Wyndham Lewis; it was savage and snarling, redolent of Julius Streicher. In a typical letter he writes: "If you only knew what a net the Jews have spun around the whole of Europe.... Remember: a Jew never forgives! He will not kill you, but he will take your job." In an effort to deny his prejudice, he gets even more vicious: "I am regarded as an anti-semite...." he writes to Edvard Brandes. "I do not hate the Jews, only *our* servile, medal-greedy, despotic, oppressive Jews who with all the power of their wealth (they have found it easy to cheat the stupid Swedes of their money) work, in their ruthless way, to support the reaction against us." (Brandes replied: "You speak of the hatred under which you shrink; that is just what every Jew who is not willing to abase himself before the Cross meets every day of his life.... That is exactly what every little Jewish boy or girl has to suffer, year in, year out, as my own two little girls will find.") Naturally, Strindberg was convinced of Dreyfus's guilt (partly so that Zola's naturalistic star would fall and people would be more responsive to mysticism), and when Dreyfus was finally released he noted the event furiously in his diary, declaring that documents had been falsified. Inevitably he hated black people as well ("To squander, to pinch, to pilfer, to be disloyal and show one's eyeteeth...that is nigger! Black man is bad man! Vanity without ambition!").

These are not just the ravings of a lunatic but the opinions of a respected dramatic artist, and as such are bound to color future impressions of Strindberg's work. They are prejudices not unrelated to his prejudice against women—strong illustrations, were any still needed, of how bigotry is usually seeded by paranoia. The compulsion to find an external source for your own suffering leads to the need to identify the Other as Enemy, especially if he is weak or defenseless. Not until the end of his life was Strindberg ever sufficiently large enough, as man or artist, to concede his suffering might be self-induced.

Still, it is by his incendiary work that Strindberg will be

remembered, however modified our impressions are by these depressing discoveries, and it is in his work that he remains powerful and profound. Sounder men, alas, have created less penetrating art, and rationality has never been a criterion for inspiration. Meyer's distaste for his subject is understandable, but however he denies it, it influences his attitude toward the plays and blocks his understanding of their supernatural rhythms. Meyer is an Englishman, and although Strindberg found some champions among the Irish (Shaw, Yeats, O'Casey, O'Neill), the English have never regarded him very highly. Their social sanity recoils before his psychological frenzy; their rational view of life is offended by his passion for the occult. Acknowledging this, Meyer concludes by quoting John Mortimer's observation that Strindberg was the first dramatist not to have presented himself as "the reasonable man of moderation, the sort of character of sterling common sense that his audience was flattered into believing it also represented." I'm not sure he was the first. What about Buechner and Kleist? But Mortimer finds him unique in his impact on the "irrational" characters of Osborne and Pinter, as if anger and absurdity were his most influential qualities. Perhaps they are, but there is a deeper Strindberg available than is celebrated in the Anglo-Saxon world—demented, daring, dangerous—a Strindberg who composed his own biography in every line he wrote. "My whole life seems to me to have been planned like a play," he said, "so that I might both suffer and depict suffering." Meyer's study is valuable, but I'm glad Strindberg's own long autobiography is still accessible to us as well—the ultimate record of his own suffering and the suffering he imposed on others.

[1987]

Legitimizing Kenneth Tynan

WHEN Kenneth Tynan died of emphysema in a Los Angeles hospital, at the age of fifty-three, many of us mourned the premature loss to criticism and to the theatre. Kathleen Tynan's new biography of her husband, *The Life of Kenneth Tynan,* is a protracted act of mourning—an extended obituary pulsing with heartache, pain, and subterranean rage. It is a tender but melancholy testimonial, memorializing not only the passing of a man but of the age with which he was identified, which he did so much to shape. Mrs. Tynan is not always altogether certain that Tynan's century had its head in the right place—or that her husband truly fulfilled his own role as an "influential figure in the theatre, in the evaluation of mid-century mores, and as a man of letters." But her rich, lush, sensual prose testifies to Tynan's continuing impact on her spirit and on her affections. Researching the book, she feels "an acute and evil loneliness. . . . I'm a robber—of Ken's life." Playing the role of ghoul, she also plays the sorceress. At the same time she is building a myth, she is enacting a rite of exorcism.

The general facts of Tynan's life are relatively well known; Kathleen Tynan supplies the candid supplemental details. To her, he was a jumble of contradictions—moralist and pleasure-seeker, political activist and dandy, vulgarian and aesthete, creative artist and poseur. "Was he a performer who happened to write?" she asks. Whatever the answer, she confesses to being "forever astonished" by him. Astonished, but not always content or approving. Tynan, whose relations with his first wife, Elaine, were a history of epic battles and epic adulteries, was not always faithful to Kathleen either after the first ten monogamous years. And what I find so sad about this account is how such a genuine love could be so morbidly vitiated by sexual ideology. Tynan had a bad case of that malady D. H. Lawrence called "sex in the head." Perhaps his fatal flaw, and the quality that exposed him to ridicule, criticism, and ultimate rejection, was his self-generated image as a

sexual revolutionary. He took pride in being the first to say
"fuck" on the BBC. He was an intellectual who felt no qualms
about being featured on the masthead of *Playboy*. Equipped with
glittering prose gifts, he made his major creative contributions to
the raunchy revue *Oh, Calcutta!* and to a script for a pornographic movie. He got his sexual kicks from spanking the bot-
toms of young nubile girls (at Oxford he hung a whip over a pair
of female underpants) and from "sexual ownership." He avoided
the draft by confessing to an army doctor that he couldn't have
sex without spurs. And while he proudly disclosed his extra-
marital adventures to his wives, he was shocked when they took
lovers themselves. It's hard to avoid sounding like a hindsight
moralist now that his vaunted sexual revolution has foundered on
the shoals of divorce, escalating venereal disease, sour marriages,
and AIDS. But Tynan's erotic agenda appears like the provocation of a bright but cheeky schoolboy nourishing his unlicked
sexual idiosyncrasies with intellectual and political rationaliza-
tions.

Most of Tynan's enthusiasms—politics excepted—were developed at Oxford. After his early years in Birmingham—the illegiti-
mate son of an Irish woman, Rose Tynan, and a knighted draper,
Sir Peter Peacock—he went to Magdalen College and turned into
a bit of a peacock himself. Leaving an endless trail of broken
marriage engagements, he sucked on a wine-dark cigarette holder,
wore gold satin shirts and a doeskin suit, and carried a black
umbrella tied with a red silk ribbon. He also wore makeup,
dressed in drag, and declared with Byron that "the great object in
life is sensation." He encouraged the rumor (though this was one
form of sensation he never tasted) that he was homosexual,
perhaps in an effort to imitate Sebastian Flyte in *Brideshead
Revisited*. Brilliant from birth, he soon became a legend at Oxford
for his writing, debating, acting, directing, and personal style,
and everyone assumed he was destined for greatness.

Following some aborted efforts to act on the professional stage
(the title of his first book, *He Who Plays the King*, was a reference
to his role as the Player King in Alec Guiness's *Hamlet*), Tynan
wrote a scathing letter to a hostile critic which won him a
reviewing job on Lord Beaverbrook's *Evening Standard*. From
that moment he was the darling of the city and commanded

"swinging London" from his perch as arbiter of theatrical taste (a post he later held even more authoritatively on the *Observer* after Beaverbrook fired him for threatening to sue his own paper). Unlikely as it seems today, the stage was once a very potent social instrument, especially during Tynan's years as a critic. It certainly had a powerful influence on Tynan, who claimed it was responsible for his political conversion—"I have seen *Mother Courage*," he declared, "and I am a Marxist." Tynan's Marxism was often indistinguishable from liberal humanism of his own sexual brand (he once defined a humanist as one "who remembers the faces of the people he spanks"). It was certainly more theatrical than economic, and saturated with reflexive political ideas. He fought for sexual freedom and against the bomb, protested the Suez invasion, defended homosexual rights, deplored censorship, and lent his support to Fair Play for Cuba, which earned him a subpoena from the Senate Internal Security Subcommittee. It also aroused in this former aesthete a new tolerance for propaganda plays whose "aim was to 'start you talking'"—even though he knew in his heart that the purpose of great drama "is to *stop* you talking." After championing *Look Back in Anger,* he began to measure dramatic art by ideological yardsticks, preferring the engaged dramatists—Brecht, Miller, Hansberry, Osborne, Sartre—to such metaphysical writers as Beckett and Ionesco, and what he called their "privileged despair."

Tynan's sympathy for the underprivileged and the dispossessed did not always extend to his own family, particularly his mother who died in a psychiatric hospital neglected by her son. And it did not prevent him from socializing with royalty, whether of blood or of celebrity. This opened him to charges of being a "champagne socialist." A self-admitted "talent snob," he felt compelled to fraternize with just about everyone he admired, a spectrum ranging from Orson Welles and Ernest Hemingway to bullfighters and movie stars. Kathleen was exhausted by this "diet of Great Persons." Bored with the parties, she decided to find work, at the same time becoming attracted to feminism through her friendship with Germaine Greer. Soon after, Tynan took a mistress of twenty-eight with a matching anal-sadistic fantasy, causing Kathleen to muse, "No one had thought to reveal to me the real secret of married love, which is that it comes to an end."

Although severely tested by Tynan's continuing passion for "exposing and demonstrating his sexual life," the marriage did not come to an end. Following his dazzling two-year stint as critic for the *New Yorker* and subsequent divorce from Elaine, Kathleen joined him for his difficult tenure as literary manager (later literary consultant) with the National Theatre under the founding leadership of Laurence Olivier. Tynan admired Olivier and became his effusive Boswell, but they were not a natural match. Tynan had previously been highly critical of Olivier's wife, Vivien Leigh, even of Olivier himself, and he was considerably more radical—politically and intellectually, if not theatrically—than his other colleagues at the National. Yet it is a tribute to Olivier's tolerance and loyalty that he always defended Tynan against the hostility of Lord Chandos, the chairman of the National board, and even agreed (though he later had to back out because of prostate cancer) to help Tynan produce the politically inflammatory *Soldiers* on the West End when the Tory Chandos rejected it.

Provocations and challenges of this kind were brave, but, along with his notorious personal life, they undermined Tynan's position with the National. They may also have undermined Olivier, because he was soon to be dumped unceremoniously by Chandos's successor, Max Rayne, in favor of Peter Hall. The ostensible reason for this brutal rejection was a series of four successive flops (Tynan defended the season, sounding a little like the Shuberts, by saying, "there's nothing wrong that a couple of hits won't cure"). But there was clearly bad blood between the artistic leadership and the board which Tynan—following his critical credo to "rouse tempers, goad and lacerate, raise whirlwinds" —did a lot to stir up.

A larger question was why he didn't do more to stir up the National artistically. By contrast with Peter Hall's mild tenure, the regime under Olivier today almost seems daring. But the play selection was actually pretty tame by comparison with what was happening in the more innovative theatres of the world. Tynan was responsible for commissioning some new translations of European classics, for a few novel interpretive ideas such as the all-male *As You Like It,* and for the occasional new gamble like Trevor Griffith's *The Party.* But these were only scraps on a table where the usual diet was Establishment classics, chic revivals, and mainstream new works by the likes of Stoppard and Shaffer, all in relatively orthodox productions. As Tynan later wrote, explaining his policy of having no policy, it "was partly tailored to the limitations (and strengths) of Larry's temperament—pragmatic, empirical, wary of grand designs or distant goals."

Whatever the reason, Tynan did not leave, as a dramaturge, any particularly significant mark on the practical theatre. Where his lasting significance lies, I believe, is in his prose, especially his theatre criticism. Tynan's reviews of the New York and London stage remain breathtaking in their sheer descriptive brilliance and wit. One does not have to agree with his aesthetic or his judgment to recognize that he is absolutely peerless in the way he describes a theatrical event and—perhaps because he was a performer himself—preeminent in the way he evokes a performance. He is often called the finest drama critic after Shaw. This is probably true—not because, like Shaw, his criticism emerged from a congenial and generous social-political context (Tynan correctly noted that he was more interested in words than ideas), but rather because it often achieved the quality and texture of a creative act. Tynan's affinity for performers occasionally turned into fan's notes, as in the volume of celebrity profiles he did for the *New Yorker* (later published as *Show People*). But he never lost his gift for formulating the exact verbal equivalent of the visual events he had witnessed, as if he were not just an observer but a dancer joining the dance.

He was, however, a dreadful caretaker of his talents. It was not just the smoking habit which he could not shake even when fighting for breath and taking oxygen, or the continuing dissipation even when death was a constant companion. He simply did not respect his own gifts enough to husband these resources for a larger purpose than personal pleasure. "I write to become sexually desirable," he noted in his engagement book, "now I have what I desire, why write?" Kathleen was forced to watch him deteriorate, physically and spiritually, to hear him speak drunkenly (in an interview) of his infidelities while claiming he had forgotten why he had married, to witness his growing self-hatred and accidie.

"Life itself is my enemy," he declared to her, and then, "If you don't want to come down to the bottom with me, I don't want to go anywhere with you." Tynan's slide into physical collapse and spiritual bankruptcy sounds like the crackup of F. Scott Fitzgerald, and his drunken sojourn in Puerto Vallarta, months before his death, where he turns out one sentence in six months and is plagued by roosters and mariachi bands and hallucinations, reminds one of Malcolm Lowry's alcoholic consul in *Under the Volcano*. No doubt Tynan was aware of these literary and romantic resonances too. He was always attracted to doomed talents; it was inevitable he would join them himself. Back in Los Angeles he loses control of his speech and spends his last days glued to a television set. When he dies the BBC refers only to his production of *Oh, Calcutta!* and the four-letter word he had uttered on that network. But Tynan had written an even crueler epitaph for himself in the form of a parody of prehistoric animals: "The Tynanosaur had fallen into such general atrophy and disuse that, by a process of accelerated natural selection, his brains had been eliminated altogether. All these features point to a remarkable conclusion: for the first time in the history of paleontology, we have here a creature which, long before physical death overtook it, had already been partially extinct."

Kathleen Tynan's memoir restores the Tynanosaur to life. Despite her personal suffering as a result of her errant husband's narcissism and coldness, she knows what precious relics may be salvaged from the remains of such extinct creatures. Tynan's genius survives his sexual adventurism, his political foolishness, his weakness for celebrities and show business chic, even his final wretched years, to find rich expression both in his critical work and in the pages of his wife's inconsolable remembrances.

[1987]

Vaclav Havel Disturbs the Peace

IN 1986, Vaclav Havel tape-recorded his answers to fifty questions posed by a friendly interrogator, Karel Hvizdala. The result is *Disturbing the Peace* (translated from the Czech and with an introduction by Paul Wilson), and it is unquestionably the finest work this Czechoslovakian artist has yet produced. Part autobiography, part political philosophy, part history, part aesthetics, the book finds its unity in the personal qualities that catapulted a lonely dissenter, ostracized as an enemy of the people, into prominence as the reluctant president of his country: modesty, tolerance, inner grace, courage, discriminating intelligence, and, above all, strength of principle. There may be disagreement about Havel's powers as a dramatist—Havel himself expresses doubts about his theatrical talents. But *Disturbing the Peace* leaves no room for controversy about his place in the moral pantheon of our century.

The career of this heroic literary figure runs counter to the common wisdom about the individual in mass society—a fate that Havel continually warned about in his writings. Instead of being crushed by the state juggernaut, Havel eventually triumphed over a mechanism that controlled the press, the media, and the reins of government despite continuous harassment, the banning of his books, and a long imprisonment. Havel has no ordered political program. His mission, as he defines it, is "to be a Cassandra who tells us what is going on outside the walls of the city...to speak the truth about the world I live in, to bear witness to its terrors and miseries—in other words, to warn rather than hand out prescriptions for change." Havel is obsessed with the erosion of the spirit in the modern world, continually enjoining humankind to extricate itself from "the obvious and hidden mechanisms of totality." It is a prescription that informs his plays, his manifestos, his appeals to Dubcek and Husak, even his prison-composed (and self-censored) *Letters to Olga.* Havel's eventual success in overcoming his own isolation—he has yet to overcome his suspiciousness about being on the winning side—surely owes something to Gorbachev and *perestroika*. No such victory was won by the Chinese students in Tiananmen Square. But it is nevertheless a tribute to his firmness of vision and fixity of purpose—as if Don Quixote had persuaded all of La Mancha to take a ride on Rosinante.

In this he had powerful opposition, and not only from the regime. Havel's debate with the exiled Czech novelist Milan Kundera was precisely over the capacity of a writer to influence political change through civic action. Kundera's belief that amnesia rules history and that personal risk is therefore foolhardy led him to criticize such petitions as Charter 77 (an appeal for political tolerance and human rights), along with its signatories, as futile and vainglorious. In response, Havel suggests that Kundera's contempt for lost causes reflects a lack of hope. Mysterious and ambiguous in his own writings, Kundera has no understanding of the "mysterious ambiguity of human behavior in totalitarian conditions." It is typical of Havel's generosity that, in refuting Kundera's position, he is capable of expressing admiration for Kundera's prose, even of perceiving some truth in his criticism. There's also some poignance in that mystery and ambiguity are the very qualities some critics find missing from Havel's own plays. But the skepticism Havel praises in Kundera's art he also believes to be clouding his understanding "because it does not allow him to admit that it occasionally makes sense to risk appearing ridiculous and to act bravely."

This quality—a willingness to risk without fear of ridicule—may very well be Havel's guiding impulse. It also explains his affection for hippies and rock musicians and why he called John Lennon (to the irritation of a few American intellectuals) one of the major figures of the century. Havel considers rock-and-roll the expression of a haunted, battered humanity. In a repressive climate it carries the force of a political act. Therefore his spirited support of the Plastic People of the Universe, a rock group arrested and tried by the Husak regime, simply reinforces his defense of besieged artists everywhere from totalitarian attacks "on life itself, on the very essence of human freedom and integrity."

Havel describes his playwriting in much the same terms—

defending what is human against repressive social mechanisms. He openly identifies his work as theatre of the absurd, unlike other writers (Beckett, Ionesco, Genet) who disliked such generic descriptions. But the absurd for Havel is as much a political and philosophical concept as an aesthetic one. He believes, along with the best twentieth-century playwrights, that illusionistic theatre is a sham, that realism is inadequate to describe the obscurity and unpredictability of modern life, that the role of the theatre is not to be positive or instructive, soothing or explanatory, but rather to remind people that "the time is getting late, that the situation is grave." This sounds like a civil defense alarm, and Havel's view of the absurd has much to do with a sense of social crisis, collapsing worlds, language abuse, robotic structures, entropic rule, metaphysical uncertainty—which is to say, with his experience of life in Czechoslovakia. (No wonder he adds that if the theatre of the absurd hadn't existed, he would have been forced to invent it.) Still, Havel's relationship to political theatre is as ambiguous as Chekhov's. The absurd for Havel is simply another form of artistic resistance.

He has a similar sense of his own absurdity, and one of the most endearing things about this book is its self-mocking tone. He expresses real doubts about whether he's worth all the attention he's getting and is unusually honest about assessing his marriage, his talents, and his neuroses, particularly the despondency which followed his release from prison. Completed three years before history endorsed his sense of the absurd by rearranging his destiny, the book finds him already admitting that he is "tired of playing the builder's role, I just want to do what every writer should do, to tell the truth!" As joyous as it is dangerous, truth-telling is recommended for every intellectual because "even the toughest truth expressed publicly . . . suddenly becomes liberating." At all events, it defines the intellectual's essential role—to act as outsider and irritant, "chief doubter of systems, of power and its incantations."

Those systems, powers, and incantations are not just to be found behind what used to be called the Iron Curtain. Havel's sense of crisis is global and embraces Western civilization too— the people of London and New York as well as of Prague and Moscow, not just the workers at the Skoda plant but those at

Gielgud and Olivier

ONCE, in my eagerness to praise Sir Laurence Olivier on the occasion of his death, I unwittingly added to the store of misapprehensions regarding John Gielgud's underappreciated career by saying he nestled in yesterday's theatrical styles. This is my public apology. Gielgud's participation in the plays of Pinter and Bond, as well as his daring contribution to Peter Brook's phallic version of Seneca's *Oedipus*, mark him as a truly intrepid spirit with no fear of modernist directions or avant-garde directors. His own directorial work, while hardly ground-breaking, has generally been underestimated as well. Gielgud's twenty-five-year-old staging of *The Cherry Orchard*—with Trevor Howard as Lopahin—is still a touchstone of Chekhov production, probing more deeply into the play's double-sided humor and sadness than any other English version, including Brook's.

I am, nonetheless, not so willing to retract my opinion that Gielgud lacks Olivier's art of transformation. Gielgud's superb vocal instrument, with its shimmering cello tones, is both his glory and his limitation, being a performance trademark. Gielgud is open to new material but invariably imprints it with his own personal style. And although his vocalizing produces great beauty and emotional power, it usually plants the personality of this actor on the doorstep of whatever role he plays. As Olivier himself rather unchivalrously phrased it in his book *On Acting*, whenever Gielgud was on the verge of making an unusual character choice, he invariably "would dive straight back into the honey."

As a consequence Gielgud normally materializes in contemporary works as a traditional figure—a kind of Edwardian gentleman navigating the shoals of modern life. Sometimes this works well for him; much of the success of the movie *Arthur* was surely the result of juxtaposing Gielgud's formal deportment as an unflappable gentleman's gentleman with Dudley Moore's slurred delivery as a bibulous millionaire. And sometimes this contrast can create wonderful comic shocks, as when, in a priceless moment in the film, Gielgud loftily asks his drunken charge, "Shall I wash your dick?"

On the other hand, his portrayal of Cassius in John Houseman's movie of *Julius Caesar*, while brilliant, was also noteworthy for being totally isolated in style from that of the other actors. It was possible to say, as critics did at the time, that Gielgud was giving a lesson in Shakespearean acting to such inexperienced Americans as Marlon Brando, Edmond O'Brien, and Louis Calhern. But it is also true that Gielgud made no effort whatever to accommodate himself to the casual, naturalistic style of the other actors in the movie. He might have given exactly the same performance on the stage of the Old Vic with a cast of Garrick Club cronies.

This is what I mean by personality acting—the refusal or inability to adapt oneself to the concept, character, circumstance, or style of the occasion. Gielgud is the very best of the personality actors because he doesn't grandstand and because he has an almost religious devotion to the language he speaks. An actor of supreme dignity and intelligence, he never feels compelled to sell his audience on personal charm or idiosyncrasy. Instead he seems to regard himself as an instrument for transmitting great verse and prose, transfigured into passionate sounds through an extraordinary voice box and a genius for poetic interpretation.

Olivier's voice, by contrast, was a rather thin and reedy instrument, capable at times of making stirring sounds but often choppy in accent, occasionally nasal, lacking in timbre. He was a cat who moved more gracefully than he talked, but I think that one of the reasons we revere him is because, dissatisfied with his own equipment, he always pushed himself beyond his native capabilities. Everyone knows the story of how Olivier, preparing to play Othello, trained for months to use the untapped lower registers of his voice, but this was not an isolated stunt. He made similar efforts in every role he acted, whether choosing the heroic yelps of Henry V, the murmurous reflectiveness of Hamlet, or the pinched tenor sniping of Richard III. It was through dissatisfaction with himself that Olivier changed from a Hollywood matinee idol into a great classic actor—rather like the awkward girl who chooses to be a dancer or the stammering teenager who decides to be a public speaker. Gielgud's genius is natural; Olivier's was willed.

"My stage successes," Olivier wrote, "have provided me with the greatest moments outside myself, my film successes the best moments, professionally, within myself." Significantly, he preferred the stage over what he called "that anemic little medium," the movies. Theatre permitted him to transcend his own self—a self in which he always lacked confidence—and enter the self of others. Olivier's celebrated fondness for applying disguise—a hooked nose, false teeth, an eye patch, a shambling walk—marked him as an authentic transforming actor, and there wasn't a character, no matter how repellent, with whom he failed to find some sympathy.

Gielgud is also devoted primarily to the stage, only partly out of choice. His personality is too rich, or perhaps too eccentric, for the realistic medium of film. His greatest successes have rarely been "outside myself," like Olivier's. Makeup is not his forte; he never alters his voice to suit a character; and he very rarely plays villains or character parts unless they suit his personality.

Transforming actors, admittedly, are not usually admired these days, especially if their character work is externally applied. Stanislavsky advised actors to build a character around a core of self, as a guarantee of truthful presentation. The best American character actors—Brando, De Niro, Hoffman—may make major changes in voice or appearance to play a role, but somehow always leave a personal stamp. Brando hoarsened his voice and packed his mouth with wadding in *The Godfather*; De Niro accumulated huge rolls of fat and adopted a broken nose for *Raging Bull*; Hoffman hunched and sagged for *Death of a Salesman*. But their recognition value for the average spectator was never entirely lost, largely because such actors invariably work from a foundation of *personal* truth.

From this coign of vantage, Olivier could be accused, with some justice, of being an external actor, and there is little question that by contrast with the concentrated intensity of the method school, he occasionally appeared showy, stagy, a little on the surface. But considering the range of his roles, critics might conclude that this was a small price to pay for the variety of his characterizations. Few of our method actors have ever wandered far from proletarian and middle-class parts in contemporary American works, while Olivier—committing himself to everything from Sophocles to John Osborne, equally adept in comedies, tragedies, farce, and musicals—played kings and commoners as well as Germans, Irishmen, Frenchmen, Italians, Americans, Jews, and Africans. Not all of these characterizations were equally convincing—like most English actors, he often stumbled over foreign dialect. But he was a complete and universal artist, a walking anthology of great roles, who understood that acting was not just a personal career choice but a method of transmitting an important cultural heritage.

What he always displayed—and what most of our own actors lack—was a consummate love of performing, and his appetite for the stage was communicated in the relish with which he attacked a part. Part of our enjoyment in watching him surely was in watching him enjoy himself. That is why when illness exiled him from the stage he began to ache with nostalgia and regret. "I should be soaring away with my head tilted slightly towards the gods, feeding on the caviar of Shakespeare," he wrote somewhat grandiloquently. "I was made to perform, and it's not easy to be put out to grass, left to feed on memories and friendships." Compare our own actors, feeding not on Shakespeare but on Hollywood lotus blossoms, passionate about every cause but the theatre, when the one condition they are truly empowered to change is the erosion of theatre art and the loss of theatre culture, partly as a result of their own defections for careerist purposes.

I began by trying to draw a contrast between Olivier and Gielgud, but in this regard they share the same values and traditions—a passion for the art they served. That is why we love such actors and why, when they are on it, we love the stage.

[1989]

Memories of Joe Papp

JOE PAPP didn't want the world to know that for years he had been suffering from an incurable cancer. Though the media respected his wishes, everyone in theatre knew he was dying. And when his son succumbed to AIDS last spring at the age of twenty-nine, Joe's intimates knew he couldn't last much longer. A few days before he died, the Jujamcyn organization, in one of those premortem testimonials people were hurriedly trying to give him, made an award to the New York Public Theatre. Some believed Joe would come to pick it up, despite his condition, if only because he had always made a point of accepting awards in person. Joe failed to appear—guests at the event were told he had just broken a collarbone. His organs were failing, his bones were crumbling. He was said to be in incredible pain. The celebratory speeches took on the quality of a memorial service.

Nevertheless, when the news of his death was finally published, it struck many as incredible, inconceivable. If a single quality could be said to characterize Joe Papp (who always seemed ageless) it was vitality, and that word, deriving from the Latin for "strength" and "life," simply can't accommodate the idea of stillness or silence. It seems hardly possible that we will no longer see Joe Papp facing the cameras on the steps of the Public or at some congressional hearing on the state of the arts, or after the opening of one of his shows, praising or denouncing or exhorting in that snappy, scrappy, belligerent, barking voice on the obligations of theatre to society.

I was not a close friend of his. How could I be, as his occasional critic and theatrical competitor? But our feelings for each other whenever we met were warm and cordial, though not without formality. He always called me "Robert," eyeing me with the wariness of a wolf leader checking the rest of the pack. I also think Joe tended to distrust intellectuals, probably because of his populist convictions and lack of formal education. The Brooklyn-born son of Yiddish-speaking working-class parents, he believed theatre was for the young, the poor, and the disadvantaged, and he took it as his mission to transport it to them—sometimes literally, on the backs of mobile touring units reaching black and Latino audiences. Shakespeare in the Park—perhaps his greatest contribution to the theatre—was intended from its inception as a free gift to the public. And although this concept led to a celebrated battle with Parks Commissioner Robert Moses, who didn't want the rabble trampling his Central Park flora, it was central to Papp's democratic belief, derived from audiences at Shakespeare's Globe, that theatre belonged to the people.

Papp's benevolence, however, did not extend to all the people. He had little respect for critics and once threw John Simon out of his theatre. And he had an ill-disguised contempt for the well-heeled middle-aged theatregoer. These feelings were expressed more openly when he took over the Vivian Beaumont at Lincoln Center; later he repeated them as a reason for abandoning it. Ironically, for all his efforts, Papp's audiences continued to be predominantly middle class. So were Bertolt Brecht's, despite similar social convictions. Perhaps Papp came closest to achieving his desired populist mix doing free Shakespeare in the Park. But at the Public he was more likely to attract the faithful theatregoer who used to go to Broadway, unless he did a racial or an ethnic play, when his audiences became more diverse. Like Brecht, however, he never condescended to these audiences or underestimated their capacity to absorb difficult works. Papp, in Chekhov's words, tried "to bring the people up to Gogol, not Gogol down to the people." And among his most effective methods was the way he tried to refresh and reinvigorate Shakespeare production.

One of my earliest reviews, as theatre critic for *The New Republic*, was a 1960 notice of *Taming of the Shrew* in the park, directed by Papp's close associate, Gerald Freedman. The production's boisterous, irreverent, indigenous approach to a familiar classic instantly delivered us from years of enslavement to British models. After a glowing tribute I paid Papp my respects in person, not mentioning that, in my acting days, I had once auditioned before him for the part of Richard III (I experienced the typical actor's chagrin when the role went to an unknown upstart named George C. Scott). At that interview I was again struck by his dynamic personality and darkly handsome appearance. He reminded me of a thirties movie actor, a peppy version of John Garfield, with his compact frame, regular features, and mellow, punchy voice, so redolent of the street. Like many who end up administering theatre, he was initially a performer and later had the opportunity to realize his histrionic talents in public with a rousing cabaret act.

Some years later, as a newly appointed dean, I invited him to teach at the Yale School of Drama. It was 1966 and Papp was down on his luck. Funding for the theatre had hit one of its recurrent dip cycles, and Joe was thinking of closing down operations. I asked him to supervise our student directors and stage a play himself with the professional theatre we were preparing to form. After some reluctance he agreed, a little daunted by Yale, but, like most Jews, instinctually drawn to a pedagogical opportunity. A short time later he acquired the Astor Library on Lafayette Street and initiated the New York Public Theater with productions of *Hair* and *Hamlet*. Despite his new obligations, Papp partially fulfilled his teaching commitments, alternating classes with Gerald Freedman, and before long he had abducted our prize students to become resident directors at the Public—Ted Cornell, Jeff Bleckner, and later A. J. Antoon.

Joe visited New Haven many times in future years, sometimes as an instructor, more often as a scout. He had an affectionate eye for young talent, and many of our graduates (as well as many from our professional company) found their way to the Public, among them such playwrights as Robert Montgomery, Christopher Durang, Albert Inaurato, Keith Reddin, and Harry Kondoleon, and such actors as Meryl Streep, Joe Grifasi, Sigourney Weaver, Izzy Munk, Christine Estabrook, Mark Linn-Baker, Ben Halley, Jr., and William Converse Roberts. The scenic artist Santo Loquasto, along with many Yale-trained scenic, costume, and lighting designers, soon became Papp regulars as well. It is often noted that the list of people who worked with Joe includes just about every gifted theatre artist in America. What a permanent company he could have built with the treasures at his command!

As a matter of fact, Papp regularly announced the formation of such a company—it remained one of his great unfulfilled dreams. Also unfulfilled was his announced plan to build a theatre for playwrights on Broadway, where their work would be carefully produced without interference from timid producers or spoilsport critics. Like most American entrepreneurial empire builders, Joe always had a lot of great ideas up his sleeve. He was in terror of stagnation, and rather than consolidate he always preferred to expand. The Public had five theatres which were almost always filled, and he generally had one or two transfers (*A Chorus Line* being the most celebrated) sitting on Broadway stages. His greatest performances, however, may have been his frequent press conferences where he invariably announced new directions. The one he came closest to realizing—it may yet prove his real legacy—was the Shakespeare Marathon, a plan to produce the entire canon of thirty-seven plays in the space of less than a decade.

Joe took a lot of knocks for this massive undertaking, and the last years of his life were marked by a distinct dip in his reputation. Following the AIDS-related death of his chosen successor, Wilford Leach, he turned to a great variety of directors to help him realize his mission, among them Stuart Vaughan, Gerald Freedman, Liviu Ciulei, James Lapine, Harold Gruskin, Kevin Kline, Steven Berkoff, A. J. Antoon, Joe Dowling, Michael Greif, and JoAnne Akalaitis. Some of these productions were a lot more impressive than the reviews would indicate. But lacking a permanent company of actors or a unifying directorial imagination, they lacked an overall style.

Still, if that was a weakness of the New York Shakespeare Festival, it was also a strength, because it allowed Papp free rein to pick new crops. The theatre was always run according to Joe's personal taste and faith in talent, and so the offerings varied wildly, from the most commercial to the most arcane. Michael Bennett could find a home at the Public for developing *A Chorus Line*, but so could Mabou Mines for developing *The Dead End Kids*, while Papp was able to operate at the same time as the most successful producer on Broadway and as a primary New York facilitator for the avant-garde. No wonder the press began to identify him as the very personification of the American theatre in our time.

Like most paternalistic figures, Joe had family squabbles. The authors of what he called "hunchback" plays—to describe their lack of popular appeal—began to chafe under Papp's proprietary control and sometimes capricious absolutism—first the Public's resident playwright, David Rabe, who left the family in anger, and then Sam Shepard who repudiated the Public Theater production of *True West* after Papp fired the director and took over himself. In the most painful of these quarrels, Papp broke off with his long-term managing director and closest friend, Bernard Gersten, in a dispute over whether to produce Michael Bennett's *Ballroom*. When Papp rejected the musical for the Public, Gersten took it to Broadway, and Papp announced he would never speak to him again. Gersten often attempted to repair the breach, once paying a visit to Joe's cabaret performance in the Village where Papp refused to acknowledge his presence in the audience or open his dressing room door. It was not until years later, when Papp was near death and Gersten was helping to nurse him, that the two estranged friends managed to renew their old bonds.

Joe wasn't too happy with me either over an article I wrote called "News Theatre" which criticized what I saw as his growing impulse to make headlines as well as art. I questioned the cult of personality that had made Papp the biggest star in his theatre while speculating on the later consequences of his glorification by the media. He was especially rankled by a quote from Daniel Boorstin on the subject of the celebrity hero: "The newspapers make him, and they unmake him—not by murder but by suffocation and starvation." Joe replied in an angry letter: "The artistic product is my news. The attempt to broaden the audience for new plays is my news. Finding and producing new writers is my news. Introducing and developing new directors, designers, and actors is my news. Raising funds for all of these efforts is my news." I now believe that despite a tendency, identified more with commercial enterprise than with nonprofit activity, to imprint his own personality on his theatre, Joe eventually managed to avoid the traps of celebrity and stick to his declared purpose, "to create a meaningful theatre for popular audiences." But I also believe that, as Boorstin prophesied, the media abandoned him in the last years of his life, which were characterized, if not by "suffocation and starvation," then by an indifferent and even hostile climate for his work.

Before his death Papp made news again by turning down a

substantial NEA grant rather than sign the new obscenity clause. But aside from praise for that courageous gesture, he was the subject of considerable opprobrium and scorn. The Shakespeare Marathon was, for the most part, attacked by the daily press; most of the Public offerings were dismissed; and he was criticized for naming the controversial avant-garde director JoAnne Akalaitis as his successor rather than someone more in the mainstream. Although Papp was rumored to have harbored second thoughts about that appointment, it was just one more proof of his unpredictability and of the way he loved to pull the noses of the critical fraternity.

Testimonials to Papp began to accumulate before he died, even from those who had savaged him most. Inevitably *A Chorus Line,* which he regarded as an annuity for doing more important work, was singled out as his greatest achievement. As one of Joe's occasional critics, who nevertheless always loved and respected him, I recognize how hard it is to pay appropriate homage to one who meant so much to so many—audiences of every class and color, people of every age, artists of every persuasion. The American theatre has suffered many indignities and humiliations in the past ten years, but none more demoralizing than the loss of Joe Papp.

[1991]

The Clarence Thomas–
Anita Hill Hearings:
Caricatures in Search of an Author

A LARGE cast of leading and supporting actors was recently assembled for the top-rated, and sometimes X-rated, miniseries produced by the Judiciary Committee in the Senate Caucus Room. But the various characters involved in this three-day epic could never quite make up their minds whether they were enacting a work by Shakespeare, Pirandello, or Gogol. Were the charges of sexual harassment leveled by Professor Anita Hill against Judge Clarence Thomas a nontraditional variant of the conflict in *Measure for Measure*, where an innocent woman labors to receive justice from the reputedly spotless hypocrite who, misusing his authority, attempted to seduce her? Were we witnessing another version of *Right You Are (If You Think You Are)*, in which, after private lives have been painfully invaded by benighted commissioners, the heroine proves to have no fixed identity other than what people believe her to be? Or were we being treated to a rollicking revival of *The Inspector General*, Gogol's farce about self-serving impostors and corrupt officials, each accusing the others of his or her own failings?

Any of those playwrights could have provided infinitely deeper insight into the nature of character than was offered by the members of the motive-hunting committee. What the hearings lacked most was a creative imagination that could have gathered the accumulating ambiguities and conflicting testimonies into a compelling and coherent action. Senator Alan Simpson of Wyoming, who prides himself on his literary background, was alone in recognizing the relevance of dramatic art to what was occurring in the hearing room. Not only was he learned enough to correct Chairman Joseph Biden's misattribution to Shakespeare of the phrase "Heaven has no rage like love to hatred turned / Nor hell a fury like a woman scorned" (noting it was coined by Congreve). He also grabbed the opportunity to recite in full a famous passage from *Othello* ("Good name in man and woman, dear my Lord, / Is the immediate jewel of their souls") in defense of Clarence Thomas's tarnished reputation.

What Simpson failed to inform an audience clearly stunned by his erudition was that this eloquent justification of personal integrity is uttered not by Othello, not by Cassio, not by Desdemona—all of whom are libeled in the course of the play—but rather by the dissimulating villain Iago, who is stonewalling. Judge Thomas, vigorously nodding in agreement after characterizing the hearings in his own literary fashion as a Kafkaesque "high tech lynching for uppity blacks," offered no protest or correction. He was too busy enacting the racially oppressed innocent. Indeed, the wholehearted defense of his character by all the Republican committee members was a heartwarming endorsement less of his virtue than of his acting ability.

For Thomas clearly walked away with the performance honors. Professor Hill, her hands folded primly on her dress, gave a subdued reading of her text with virtually no highs and lows, as she coolly itemized Thomas's references to his sexual prowess, the alien matter atop his Coke can, and his favorite porno star Long Dong Silver (why wasn't *he* called as a witness?). But Judge Thomas, alternately raging and shaking like a wounded animal baying at the moon, at times seemed almost hurt enough to withdraw his name from nomination: "No job is worth what I've been through—no job. No horror in my life has been so debilitating. . . . I will not provide the rope for my own lynching." (Compare Iago in Senator Simpson's favorite play, Act III, scene iii: "Take mine office . . . O monstrous world! Take note, take note, O world, / To be direct and honest is not safe").

Thomas's defense was possibly influenced as well by Richard Pryor's advice about what to do when your wife finds you in bed with another woman: Deny it at all costs ("Who do you believe—me or your lying eyes?"). Certainly his judicious posture at the witness table—index finger on cheek, middle finger on lower lip, trunk erect—was in high contrast to the horny office Lothario depicted by Professor Hill. So was the testimony of his two female employees, J. C. Alvarez and Phyllis Berry, who played to the class resentments and soap-opera ethos of the television audience by declaring that Professor Hill was "aloof" and "holier than thou," and that she had a secret passion for Judge Thomas. Most fetching of all was white-haired Charles Kothe, former dean of Oral Roberts Law School, who defended Thomas by saying he delivered eloquent prayer orations, apparently unaware that just one day earlier the police had picked up the spellbinding preacher Jimmy Swaggart in a car containing a prostitute and pornographic magazines. All of this delicious theatre may account for the astonishing reversal in audience sympathy that developed after Thomas's testimony. For despite his admission that he had failed to watch the performance of his costar in a crucial episode of the series, despite the corroborating testimony of highly credible witnesses supporting Professor Hill's story, despite the evidence of her polygraph test, the polls made it clear that most spectators were more persuaded by Thomas's tearful-defiant histrionics than by the methodlike understatement of his accuser.

Or perhaps they were simply distracted by the really horrendous acting of the supporting cast. Senator Biden, who originally inspired the drama by failing to investigate Professor Hill's initial charges, couldn't even manage a coherent line of dialogue, so eager was he to appear fair, impartial, and, above all, equally sensitive to racism and sexism. Consider a typical passage where he is questioning the Judge: "You emphasized here today early— and this is, again—we're all trying to find out what it could be, what could be your motivation, if in fact what you say is true and what she says is true, how this happened.... I do not have the transcript from this morning, and please correct me if I'm wrong, but that you said you had a special obligation, as a consequence of his referral.... Did that special relationship—obligation, wrong word—obligation, did that impact on your relationship, professional or otherwise, with Anita Hill?" (This babble is the obviously clumsy improvisation of an amateur actor, but it might also be interpreted as a subtle attempt to emulate the artful meandering of a David Mamet character.)

Or take the performance of Senator Strom Thurmond, who rarely emerged from narcolepsy in the entire three days of testimony unless to correct Biden's blunder that he hailed from

North rather than South Carolina, or to comment on the sprightliness of his aged colleagues (his own reverence for youth was signified tonsorially by his dyed black hair). Long revered as the *éminence grise* of bigotry in the Senate, this stubborn advocate of segregation was being forced to play one of the most difficult roles of his life, that of a man who revels in the idea of sending an African-American to the Supreme Court. But the condition of rubicund mummification in which he sat throughout the course of the proceedings may have been a symptom of the Brabantio complex—paralysis at the sight of a black man seated next to a white wife. As for our noted Shakespearean scholar, Senator Simpson—hunched, owlish, his glasses perched low on his nose, his long fingers ruffling documents—he often seemed to have been auditioning for Lionel Barrymore's role as the miserly banker in *It's a Wonderful Life*.

Simpson had two rivals in his bid to be the Mr. Nasty Badman of this drama. That natty embodiment of Mormon disapproval, Orrin Hatch of Utah, a slab of enameled glass stuck into a tab collar and pinstripe shirt, was usually so upright, or uptight, with rage you thought he was going to shatter. Determined to display his delicate sense of priorities, he railed against leaking staff members, special interest groups, "slick lawyers," the Soviet Union, and any other contemptible forms of life he could think of, at the same time proudly flourishing his research into previous references to the same porno star in an Oklahoma court case and (lest he be outdone by the erudite Senator Simpson) previous allusions to pubic hair in *The Exorcist*. Senator Hatch seemed to be persuaded of Clarence Thomas's innocence not so much by any internal evidence as by the fact that if he had ever used the "sick" dirty words alleged to have been spoken to Anita Hill, the Judge would have been consigned to a psychopathic ward. Obviously Hatch has not spent much time in the Senate cloakroom.

Hatch had considerable competition in character assassination from craggy Senator Arlen Specter of Pennsylvania, a plodding actor playing a remorseless small-town prosecutor, whose comparisons of minute differences in testimony, though worthy of a Talmudic scholar, led him to conclude, entirely without evidence, that Professor Hill was guilty of "flat-out perjury." It was this charge that finally vitalized the previously lethargic Edward Kennedy to utter cries of "Shame" both in the Caucus Room and later on the Senate floor. This brought those inevitable references to the bridge at Chappaquiddick and his own checkered sexual history, making it obvious why he had spent so much of the hearings silently slumped in his chair. But Kennedy's reticence prevented him from playing an unfilled role in this drama, that of advocate for a woman whose character was being persistently blackened because she had brought an unpleasant message. Among the other Democrats impotent to block the defamation and slander that greeted Professor Hill, Howell Heflin was too befuddled, Howard Metzenbaum too feeble, Dennis DeConcini too coopted, and Herb Kohl (making repeated references to Hill and Thomas as "Africans," despite panicked gestures from his staff) too dim-witted. The Duke never managed to expose Angelo and exonerate Isabella. The real Inspector General stayed home. Mr. Smith never went to Washington.

Ultimately the theme of this drama, for all the concern with Judge Thomas's office conduct toward Anita Hill, was not sexism or racism, and not even competence, despite his questionable qualifications for the job. It was veracity. There may be a statute of limitations on sexual harassment, but even the slightest possibility that a Supreme Court judge has lied to protect his nomination, and is therefore morally unfit for office, suggests that our country has even worse theatre to come. The characters performing in this tragicomic event may have lacked an author. But Senator Simpson is correct in saying that Shakespeare still provides the most incisive key to its meaning—not Iago's manipulation of the truth to hide his motives, but Lear's anguished perception of the way the world is run by figures of authority.

> Through tattered gowns small vices do appear;
> Riches and furred gowns hide all. Plate sin with gold,
> And the strong lance of justice hurtless breaks;
> Arm it in rags, a pygmy's straw does pierce it.

Through the cynical choice of an administration uninterested in the future of this nation beyond 1992, and with the help of a

Harold Clurman and the Group

WHY do Harold Clurman and the Group Theatre continue to exercise such a magnetic hold on our hopes and dreams—the Group as a kind of theatrical Camelot with Clurman in the unlikely role of Arthur Pendragon? It's a bizarre analogy, considering that Clurman looked more like a Russian boyar than a medieval knight, despite his flamboyant way of dressing, and that the screaming quarrels of the cantankerous Group actors were such a far cry from the chivalric tourneys associated with Arthurian legend. Yet there was a powerful idealism always at work in this legendary thirties organization, and it was Clurman who articulated its standards of artistic aspiration.

Harold was that rare thing in the American theatre—a creative artist with a philosophical passion. The various productions he staged for the Group, and later for the commercial theatre, were of very high quality, but it is as an intellectual inspiration that he is now largely remembered. This is a paradox because Clurman had little respect for intellectuals or academics. But despite his oft-expressed belief that the essence of theatre lay in music, flash, and voluptuous actresses, he never ceased to demand that the American stage transcend its impure commercial roots. There is an inexorable pull in our society, reflected most coarsely in our theatre, to plunge into an inviting mainstream and be washed by the currents of money, celebrity, glamour, and, above all, acceptance. Like the rest of us, the Group Theatre was not impervious to those pulls, for all its idealism, and even Clurman, for all his single-mindedness, was never altogether successful in maintaining an alternative institution free of commercial values. He was a sworn enemy of the competitive spirit that drives our country, and he had nothing but scorn for what he called the "self-preservation and self-aggrandizement" of most theatre folk. The Group was based on the ideal of the collective, or cooperative interdependence, which of course is the animating force behind all great theatre. And this social ideal, no matter how feeble it is in practice, has somehow remained a dream of almost all of us in the performing arts. Still, as Clurman often noted, it was an ideal that went against the American grain, which is fundamentally individualistic. "For a group to live a healthy life and mature to a full consummation of its potentiality," he wrote in *The Fervent Years*, "it must be sustained by other groups—not only of moneyed men or civic support, but by equally conscious groups in the press, in the audience, and generally in large and comparatively stable segments of society. When this fails to happen, regardless of its spirit or capacities, it will wither."

He was writing the obituary of his own theatre, giving the reasons why it collapsed. This splendid, ambitious institution, though it embodied so much hope, never attracted the kind of fiscal and journalistic group support it needed to survive. When the prevailing culture won't join you, it is a huge temptation to join the prevailing culture. And along with all the external causes of the premature death of the Group, there were internal ones as well, primarily the defection of many of its most gifted artists to Hollywood.

The obvious difference between commercial theatre and alternatives like the Group is that—*at least in theory*—the one is motivated by profits and the other by art. When money is the primary goal of any theatrical enterprise, all decisions fall into lockstep— the writing, the casting, the design, the choice of theatre, the length of the run. Appropriate actors are supplanted by inappropriate stars, plays are rewritten for greater audience appeal, people are fired on the basis of premature judgments, and so forth. This was the system that the Group set out to reform; yet in some sad way, and not unlike today's nonprofit theatre, it was slowly drawn into the very conditions it had set out to change.

It was not the purpose of the Group just to put on shows but rather to build a permanent theatre, one which would develop both its own artists and its own audience in order, in Clurman's words, "to grow with the years and make a contribution to our social-cultural life in the manner of certain State theatres abroad." Without dependable financial support, however, the Group was forced to operate continually on the hit-or-miss system that characterizes Broadway, measuring the run of its plays by box office receipts and critical reception. To rehearse a play for eight or nine weeks and then to close it after eight performances was the cause of Clurman's and the company's most dispirited moments—especially when the aborted works were among those the Group believed in most, including two or three by Odets.

The Group, therefore, was still mired in the commercial system when all its instincts lay elsewhere. It was responsible for producing some wonderful new American plays, but it never staged a classic, not even Chekhov, despite its long postponed plan to do *The Three Sisters* in a new version by Odets. As Clurman explained, "A first-class production of a classic can hardly be financed in New York without the support of a star name." Remember that when you wonder why Lee Strasberg mixed together all those ill-equipped Studio-trained Hollywood stars for his smorgasbord *Three Sisters* thirty years later. And remember it when you wonder why the septuagenarian Tony Randall felt compelled to play the youthful Khlestakov in the National Actors Theatre production of *The Inspector General.* Clurman wrote: "The basic defect in our activity was that while we tried to maintain a true policy artistically, we proceeded economically on a show business basis. Our means and our ends were in fundamental contradiction."

For all these contradictions, the thing that has proved great and lasting about the Group was its idea. Clurman defined the terms on which a serious American theatre would henceforth be approached and the standards by which it would henceforth be criticized. For despite its own loudly articulated ideals, the nonprofit resident theatre movement in this country—in many ways a legacy of the Group—has suffered the same kind of deterioration in values, and for many of the same reasons. Lacking those other moneyed and critical groups that might support a collective effort, these theatres also have often been forced to proceed on a show business basis. Or as the Shubert Organization's Gerry Schoenfeld puts it, "There's no profit like nonprofit." Clurman was always clear-eyed about the Group's compromises. I'm not sure our current system of theatres is quite so self-critical. And lacking enough strong voices to remind us of how we betray our own values, we often fall victim to a kind of delusory self-exoneration.

Still, the Ideal continues to draw us upward and onward, like

Lionel Trilling: Memories of an Intellectual Father

ONCE upon a time, young people had intellectual heroes. Mine was (and still is) Lionel Trilling. I had been reading Trilling's essays with tremors of excitement whenever they appeared in *Partisan Review*. After he collected them in book form as *The Liberal Imagination*, I was—to use one of his favorite words—*enchanted*. The year that seminal work was published (1950), I had the good fortune to be a graduate student at Columbia, completing a master's degree in dramatic literature. I hastened to enroll in every course Trilling gave, and later, when going for my doctorate, was admitted into the legendary Trilling-Barzun seminar.

In the first course I took from him, a massive class in nineteenth-century romantic literature, I was one of two or three hundred anonymous students, but I imagined Trilling was speaking directly to me. His lecturing style was not particularly dynamic. He spoke softly, even a little haltingly, as if in fear of framing a sentence that would not stand the test of time. The real classroom star of the English department then was Marjorie Nicholson, whose course in eighteenth-century literature was delivered without notes but with every syntactical nuance in place (one knew exactly which sentences were separated by periods, which by semicolons). By contrast, Trilling always seemed a little uncomfortable on the podium, slightly hunched, bemused, ironic, applying body English to his vocal inflections and verbal English to his speaking style. Lecturing was not his native gift.

Still, he mesmerized me, and I eagerly anticipated that hour on Tuesday, Thursday, and Saturday mornings when he would walk through the door, lay his books carefully on the table, and begin to speak. What was it? Those haunted eyes, darkly ringed, that aquiline nose, that shock of white hair? The retiring, unfailingly courteous manner? The hope that he might break off into an intimate reflection, a sudden revelation of his personal life? Anyhow, I was enthralled by the man, and my hand ached from scribbling crabbed notes in bulging notebooks, recording his insights into Wordsworth or Keats or Coleridge (he was then auditioning the essays that would later appear in *The Opposing Self*). The romantic poets were of no great interest to me at the time. I was chasing after Shakespeare and Jonson, in hot pursuit of Ibsen and Chekhov. But I was also chasing Trilling, an entirely hypnotic man, at a stage in life when intellectual issues have an emotional power amounting almost to a passion.

I imagined Trilling was my father; the passion I felt for him was filial. He actually looked like my father, another gentle Jew with deep-set eyes and snow-white hair. My own father, however, had barely completed fourth grade, and while he tolerated my scholarly ambitions he couldn't understand them. He was disappointed that I hadn't joined him in business; he thought literature a profitless indulgence. When I would ask for money to buy a book, he'd give me a puzzled look and say, "What do you need it for? You already got a book." Trilling had all the tender virtues of my warmhearted Dad plus the one thing my father couldn't share with me, a concern for things of the mind. I adopted him without his consent and competed fiercely for his affection with my siblings among his favored students.

The arena was the Trilling-Barzun doctoral seminar in literature, which I had determined to join despite my interest in drama. Jacques Barzun was on leave for the first semester; Trilling interviewed me alone. He was not happy about my theatrical interests. Drama for him was what Sir Philip Sidney called a poor stepsister of the arts, not a serious literary pursuit. Was he thinking about the inferior dramatic efforts of his romantic poets—Keats, Shelley, Byron? No, it was the dramatic genre as a whole. How about Shakespeare and Molière, Sophocles and Racine? Better on the page, he said. We had a serious disagreement, but he took me in anyway. Only later did I learn that in his flaming youth Trilling had been deeply attracted to the theatre and had even published an early (uncollected) essay on O'Neill.

Up to this time I had written scads of uncompleted material—novels, plays, short stories, poems, essays. I couldn't finish anything. I hated my own writing. Often I didn't get past the first page. In the seminar—a group of ten or eleven Trilling disciples—we were each required to submit an essay on a topic of our choice, to be read (more accurately annihilated) by the entire class. Mine was on Joyce's *Ulysses*, a piece I had labored over for weeks and, to my surprise, actually finished. To my greater surprise, it was warmly received by my teacher and my fellow students, and the awkward young man who until then had been hesitant even to open his mouth in such heavyweight company became overnight a member of the Trilling elect.

In the second semester of the seminar, when Barzun joined Trilling at the top of the long table, I submitted an essay on *Don Giovanni* called "The Hero as Seducer." It took the fanciful position that Don Juan had a position in Christian hagiography similar to that of Eros and Aphrodite in Greek mythology—that he embodied the spirit of seduction in a culture that did not recognize nonmarital sex. Barzun trashed the essay; Trilling sat back bemused. His comments were mostly editorial, directed toward my style. After class he asked to see me in his office in Hamilton Hall and, instead of criticizing my essay further, suggested that I call his friend, Robert Warshow, and do a book review for *Commentary*. I was flushed with pride and excitement. Warshow sent me a collection of *Saturday Evening Post* stories, and I wrote a sociological analysis proving how most of the authors included were writing secretly about adoption. Was I thinking of my own relationship to Trilling? Following the usual editorial agonies (at that time, in 1953, the magazine was more concerned with tormenting contributors over their style than liberals and radicals over their politics), my piece was accepted for publication, later appearing not as a review but as a featured article. I was in the *Reader's Guide to Periodical Literature*! I was immortal! I could have died the next day without regret. I was not to publish in *Commentary* again for four more years, despite five or six interim efforts, all rejected after endless revisions. But Trilling had determined me in a career as a critic. His help and example had resolved my life.

In later years I went my own way, studying, teaching, and writing about dramatic literature, and performing in plays, while most of Trilling's other disciples joined him in his areas of interest: nineteenth-century literature, American literature, modern British literature. The filial bond I felt at Columbia was never broken, but I suspect he continued to find my interests somewhat frivolous. Our relationship remained cordial though not very personal, even when I began teaching in the same department. In an essay called "The Madison Avenue Villain," published in *Partisan Review* in 1960, I had the temerity to criticize Trilling for his involvement with the Reader's Subscription—a commercial book club which I pompously believed was compromising his critical integrity. He never responded, and for a time relations between us cooled.

I was not following the path of his other adopted sons— Norman Podhoretz, Steve Marcus, Norman Mailer, Jason Epstein, et al.—and he was never able to reconcile himself to my obsession with the theatre. I was grieved by this. Couldn't he see that my criticism was an effort to bring his literary and human values to bear on the themes of dramatic works? Couldn't he understand that a disciple was not obliged to labor in the same vineyard? Couldn't he realize that everything I wrote about the theatre was an attempt to pay tribute to my intellectual father? Somehow I think he did. In succeeding years he was always gracious in his comments about the books I wrote, and, after I married, my wife and I were often invited to join him and Diana in their Claremont Avenue apartment for good meals and conversation. Norma's interest in their son, Jim, made the Trillings beam, for he was the apple of their eye.

When I went to Yale in 1966 our communications for a while were desultory. I think I pained my teacher with my early opposition to the Vietnam War. The Columbia he loved was blowing up before his eyes after a sequence of occupations and police busts. But when I began to share his doubts about the violent tendencies of the more radical young, and published my misgivings in a series of articles, he expressed his gratitude and support. He was being attacked by radicals, including his former disciple Podhoretz (now chief editor of *Commentary*), as a mandarin reactionary. A few years later he was being attacked by conservatives, again including Podhoretz (now a reactionary himself) as an unfashionable liberal. Like many men of the middle, Trilling was being squeezed in the vise of an ideological age, and the humane values which informed his writing and his life were being treated as the relics of a prehistoric time.

When we next met in 1972—it was on shipboard sailing for England—he had physically altered. I was taking a year's leave of absence from the tumult at Yale to act as theatre critic for the *Observer*, Lionel and Diana were spending the year in Oxford. I was shocked by his appearance. His eyes had sunk more deeply into his skull; his body was frail; his hands played around the steamer blanket on his deck chair. But his mind was as clear, as alert as ever, and the book he published that year, *Sincerity and Authenticity*, proved to be one of his deepest cultural probes. Norma and I saw the Trillings frequently that year, either in Oxford or in London, at dinner in each other's homes with Betsy and Ronald Dworkin, Mary and Richard Ellmann, and Jonathan Miller. It was reassuring to watch him grow stronger and more vigorous, basking in the admiration of his peers. We talked a lot about the past and about the strange fate of his brand of liberalism in contemporary America. We went to four-star restaurants in London before going to the opera; we reaffirmed and strengthened an old bond.

Norma and I helped persuade the Trillings to spend a summer month on Martha's Vineyard in 1973 or 1974 (shortly before he died). Vietnam and the sixties, all those fierce confrontations and painful divisions, were over. People were eager to make peace with one another and reestablish community. We gave a dinner at our house on Lambert's Cove in an effort to create a rapprochement between the Trillings and Lillian Hellman, old friends whose friendship had been soured by politics. Norma prepared a fine meal and the conversation over food was jolly. Then Lionel or Diana said something that incensed Lillian. Although it was too innocuous to remember, she roundly denounced it (using a favorite phrase) as "the most conservative thing I ever heard." Lillian called a taxi immediately and flounced out of the house.

Years after he died, Lillian assailed Lionel in *Scoundrel Time* for what she alleged to be his inadequate response to McCarthyism. It was a cruel imputation against a man of very complicated views, and it deeply wounded his widow. By that time, however, Trilling had become fair game for many political and literary headhunters. It was not an age for complication, and for a while his reputation was in eclipse. Cultural criticism had become almost entirely obscured by the new semiotic theories then (and now) in vogue, and the elegant, discriminating essays of Trilling were no longer being read. The notion at the very root of Trilling's humanistic school that there was some relationship between the life of the mind and life itself had fallen into shadow. Graduate students were no longer joining English departments to examine social, political, and artistic issues but rather to engage in arcane theorizing.

It is their loss. Trilling never touched a subject without placing us in our age. Even his parenthetical insights, when writing of Freud or Sherwood Anderson or the meaning of a literary idea, had the nature of epiphanies. Trilling's style, not to mention his personal manner, seemed to some excessively cultivated. Never to me. He taught us to write as if we were speaking, and, in his case, his writing was a true extension of his personality. I suppose it is possible to say that he had submerged his essential self under an English manner, that he owed more to Matthew Arnold than to his Anglo-Jewish antecedents. And it is true that, compared with redskins like Philip Rahv, Irving Howe, or Lionel Abel, he looked like a man who had not kept touch with his immigrant roots. Yet who has the right to choose a man's persona for him? Trilling penetrated more deeply into the subjects he touched than any American critic before or since (his only rival is Edmund Wilson), and a less ideological time will some day again regard with awe and astonishment the exemplary qualities of his mind.

In 1975 I collected some of the fugitive pieces I had been writing in a book called *The Culture Watch*; it was dedicated to "My teacher Lionel Trilling." The essays reflected my continuing effort to treat dramatic literature as a human and intellectual expression, an approach I had learned at the feet of my revered teacher and intellectual father. I wanted, belatedly, to acknowledge my debt to him, and to express my support at a time when he was temporarily in eclipse. After I sent off an early copy of the book, Diana called to say how much Lionel appreciated the acknowledgment. He would have written himself, but he was in the hospital with a serious complaint which she wouldn't name. It was pancreatic cancer. Two months later this gracious man was gone.

[1987]

Postscript

MY BOOK ends with a tribute to Lionel Trilling that might seem inappropriate considering his lifelong indifference to the stage. But I deliberately placed this essay at the conclusion. It seemed to complete a circle. My continuing quarrel with the simplistic politics of the American theatre resembles in kind (not, of course, in subtlety) Trilling's dispute with the liberal intellectual politics of his time. My teacher's arguments stemmed from a deep sympathy with basic liberal values, and so do mine, though my level of exasperation is admittedly lower. Trilling subscribed to the "hard" liberalism of Arnold and Freud, as contrasted with the "soft" liberalism of Vernon Parrington and Erich Fromm. This soft liberalism, with its roots in guilt and its stalks in sentiment, turned many of his contemporaries into fellow travelers of Stalinism, just as it has turned many of mine into fellow travelers of Political Correctness. But I learned from Lionel Trilling that one could embrace liberal goals without taking mindless shortcuts to achieve them.

My intellectual position has occasionally alienated me from my colleagues in the theatre, just as my theatrical associations have distanced me from my intellectual friends. But if I can boast of a single consistent purpose, it is to merge these two disparate worlds, to help facilitate an American theatre worthy of respect. I am rarely happier than when I see people of sensibility responding to penetrating plays; I long for a society in which great drama is an essential part of everyday life. Sometimes the effort seems a little quixotic, especially when one considers the deterioration of the not-for-profit theatre in our bad economic times. But when one looks at the quality of people still working on the stage, against all odds, one's heart is lightened and the goal seems less distant.

Index

Abel, Lionel, 260
Abkarian, Simon, 157, 158
Abrams, Floyd, 36
Absurd, theatre of the, 233
Actors Equity, 22
Adler, Luther, 98
Aeschylus: *Agamemnon*, 155–156;
    Eumenides, 10, 154, 157, 158;
    Libation Bearers, 154, 156; *Oresteia*,
    10, 154–155, 195
Aesthetic correctness, 173
Affirmative action, 23, 213
African-American theatre, 5, 14–15,
    23, 136–138, 139
African-Americans, 22, 47, 48, 66,
    68, 168, 209–212, 245–250
Agamemnon (Aeschylus), 155–156
Ahlstedt, Börje, 83, 186, 187
AIDS: *Angels in America*, 40,
    175–181, 182–185; *Baltimore
    Waltz*, 136, 138; *Destiny of Me*, 160;
    homosexual artists, 37; *Lips Together,
    Teeth Apart*, 107; Mapplethorpe,
    35; Papp, 239, 242; related dramas,
    15, 159; and Theatre of Guilt, 14;
    and Tony Awards, 145; and Yuppie
    Realism, 106
Akalaitis, JoAnne, 5, 22, 56, 57, 102,
    104, 105, 129, 132, 133, 170–174,
    180, 181, 242, 244
Albee, Edward: *Three Tall Women*,
    204–208; *Tiny Alice*, 87; *Zoo Story*,
    207
Alceus, 191
Aldwych (theatre), 169
Alexander, Jane, 162, 163
All for Love (Dryden), 168, 200
All My Sons (Miller), 12, 15
Allen, Woody, 42
Alley Theatre (Houston), 148, 163
Almeida Theatre, 168, 199
Altman, Robert, 96
Alvarez, J. C., 246–247
American Conservatory Theatre, 172
American Repertory Theatre, 22, 60,
    109
American Symphony Orchestra
    League, 67

American Theatre (magazine), 3
Anderson, Bibi, 187
Anderson, Jean, 78
Anderson, Laurie, 134–136, 138, 149
Anderson, Maxwell, 93
Anderson, Sherwood, 260
Andrews, Raymond, 149
Andy Warhol's Factory, 43
Angels in America (Kushner), 15, 40,
    159, 172, 175–181, 182–185, 186,
    193, 195
Animal Crackers (film), 108
Anti-Semitism, 30, 64, 213, 223
Antitheatre, 52
Antoon, A. J., 241, 242
Armstrong, Louis, 140, 141
Arnold, Matthew, 260
Art on Trial (Hess), 39
Arthur (film), 235
Artist's Space, 35
Arts, war on, 26–40, 173
As Is, 15, 159
As You Like It (Shakespeare), 228
Asian-Americans, 22, 168, 210–211
Assassins (Sondheim/Weidman), 95–96
Aston, Lucy, 78
Astor Library, 241
Atkinson, Brooks, 55
Atrides (Mnouchkine), 153–158
Audience participation, 45, 46
Auletta, Robert, 163
Austen, Jane, 69
"Avant-Garde Performance and the
    Effervescent Body," 41
Avari, Erick, 133
Awake and Sing (Odets), 12
Aylward, John, 198

Back to Methuselah (Shaw), 195
Baitz, Jon Robin, 14; *Film Society*,
    88; *Substance of Fire*, 87–90
Baker, Dylan, 94
Baker, Jordan, 207
Baldomero, Brian R., 117
Baldwin, Alec, 144
Baldwin, James, 47
Ballroom (Bennett), 243
Baltimore Waltz (Vogel), 15, 136, 159

A NOTE ON THE AUTHOR

Robert Brustein is the founder and artistic director of the
American Repertory Theatre at Harvard University, where
he is also professor of English. He is theatre critic for *The
New Republic* and the author of a number of distinguished
books on theatre and drama. Mr. Brustein is the former
dean of the Yale School of Drama and the founder and
director of the Yale Repertory Theatre. He has twice been
awarded the George Jean Nathan Award for dramatic
criticism, in 1962 and 1987, and has also received the
George Polk Memorial Award for outstanding criticism.

ELEPHANT PAPERBACKS

Literature and Letters
Stephen Vincent Benét, *John Brown's Body*, EL10
Isaiah Berlin, *The Hedgehog and the Fox*, EL21
Robert Brustein, *Dumbocracy in America*, EL421
Anthony Burgess, *Shakespeare*, EL27
Philip Callow, *Son and Lover: The Young D. H. Lawrence*, EL14
James Gould Cozzens, *Castaway*, EL6
James Gould Cozzens, *Men and Brethren*, EL3
Clarence Darrow, *Verdicts Out of Court*, EL2
Floyd Dell, *Intellectual Vagabondage*, EL13
Theodore Dreiser, *Best Short Stories*, EL1
Joseph Epstein, *Ambition*, EL7
André Gide, *Madeleine*, EL8
Gerald Graff, *Literature Against Itself*, EL35
John Gross, *The Rise and Fall of the Man of Letters*, EL18
Irving Howe, *William Faulkner*, EL15
Aldous Huxley, *After Many a Summer Dies the Swan*, EL20
Aldous Huxley, *Ape and Essence*, EL19
Aldous Huxley, *Collected Short Stories*, EL17
Sinclair Lewis, *Selected Short Stories*, EL9
William L. O'Neill, ed., *Echoes of Revolt: The Masses,
     1911–1917*, EL5
Ramón J. Sender, *Seven Red Sundays*, EL11
Peter Shaw, *Recovering American Literature*, EL34
Wilfrid Sheed, *Office Politics*, EL4
Tess Slesinger, *On Being Told That Her Second Husband Has
     Taken His First Lover, and Other Stories*, EL12
B. Traven, *The Bridge in the Jungle*, EL28
B. Traven, *The Carreta*, EL25
B. Traven, *The Cotton-Pickers*, EL32
B. Traven, *General from the Jungle*, EL33
B. Traven, *Government*, EL23
B. Traven, *March to the Montería*, EL26
B. Traven, *The Night Visitor and Other Stories*, EL24
B. Traven, *The Rebellion of the Hanged*, EL29
Anthony Trollope, *Trollope the Traveller*, EL31
Rex Warner, *The Aerodrome*, EL22
Thomas Wolfe, *The Hills Beyond*, EL16

Theatre and Drama
Robert Brustein, *Dumbocracy in America*, EL421
Robert Brustein, *Reimagining American Theatre*, EL410
Robert Brustein, *The Theatre of Revolt*, EL407
Irina and Igor Levin, *Working on the Play and the Role*, EL411
Plays for Performance:
     Aristophanes, *Lysistrata*, EL405
     Pierre Augustin de Beaumarchais, *The Marriage of Figaro*,
          EL418
     Anton Chekhov, *The Cherry Orchard*, EL420
     Anton Chekhov, *The Seagull*, EL407
     Georges Feydeau, *Paradise Hotel*, EL403
     Henrik Ibsen, *Ghosts*, EL401
     Henrik Ibsen, *Hedda Gabler*, EL413
     Henrik Ibsen, *The Master Builder*, EL417
     Henrik Ibsen, *When We Dead Awaken*, EL408
     Heinrich von Kleist, *The Prince of Homburg*, EL402
     Christopher Marlowe, *Doctor Faustus*, EL404
     The Mysteries: Creation, EL412
     The Mysteries: The Passion, EL414
     Sophocles, *Electra*, EL415
     August Strindberg, *The Father*, EL406